SIMPLY TINA

TINA TURNER Photographs by **PAUL COX**

CONCEPT & DESIGN FABRICE COUILLEROT
FOREWORD MARTYN WARE
TEXT DARYL EASLEA

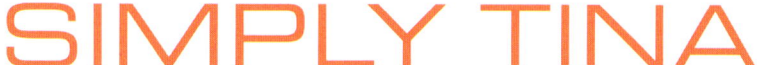

OMNIBUS PRESS
London / New York / Paris / Sydney / Copenhagen / Berlin / Madrid / Tokyo

Cover, internal design and creative direction by Fabrice Couillerot
All pictures © Paul Cox / www.paulcoxphotos.co.uk
Text by Daryl Easlea, except foreword © Martyn Ware and introduction © Paul Cox
Picture research by the author
Photogravure by Nathalie Cicurel @ Poisson Rouge, Paris

Paul Cox thanks
My thanks to Tina for being such a great subject. Fabrice Couillerot's enthusiasm, creativity and time dedicated to this book has meant our original idea has now been accomplished. Thanks to Roger Davies, Bernard Doherty and also to my family for their support.

Fabrice Couillerot thanks
I love working with Paul because he is such a talented, one-of-a-kind and humble photographer – just look at his photos and you'll understand. Our collaboration has been very organic, natural and creative over the years. He is also a wonderful person, as is his wife Helen, who has been a major help in all our ventures. My dearest thanks to you both.
Martyn Ware for generously writing such a heartfelt foreword.
Daryl Easlea for skilfully crafting the stories behind the pictures.
Nathalie Cicurel at Poisson Rouge for making all the photographs in the book shine their brightest, Solfegue Dobaria and Milo Cuffini.
David Barraclough for being such a lovely and professional person to work with, as well as the rest of the team at Omnibus: Claire Browne, Greg Morton, Giulia Senesi and David Stock. Etienne Foucher, Chris Tinker, Ernest and Firmin, Corin Johnson and Christian Voges.

Tina has been a significant part of my life since the moment I first heard her astounding presence fuzzily crackling over my transistor radio performing 'River Deep Mountain High', dominating the awe-inspiring Phil Spector Wall of Sound production. I grew up in a household of two older sisters whose record collection consisted mainly of American soul and Motown recordings, and as soon as they bought 'River Deep', it became my go-to 7-inch. Look up the word 'evocative', and it should mention this monolith of narrative operatic drama. Tina seemed to be speaking directly to me and sharing her fictional life story, including this child. She introduced her technicolour world of poverty, love, desire and most of all the delicate nuance of human emotion.

Fast forward to 1981. Glenn Gregory, Ian Marsh and I were flying to Los Angeles for the first time to meet a demigod. I had nearly finished the first British Electric Foundation album, but for the final track, at the last moment James Brown had backed out of recording 'Ball Of Confusion', The Temptations' hit protest song. We were on a mission to convince Tina to record with us in London, and we were very, very nervous and excited. We needn't have worried – she was as gracious and down to earth as you could possibly imagine, putting us at ease with English tea and biscuits. She agreed, travelled to London, nailed the vocal first take and was in and out of the studio in an hour! The ultimate professional. But what struck me most was that she approached the performance almost as an acting challenge; her interpretation of the lyric was as studied and performative as any Hollywood actor would approach a lead role.

She was also humble, often talking about her teenage fan-girling of Otis Redding, Sam Cooke and later David Bowie, Mick Jagger and Rod Stewart. Of course, our recording of 'Let's Stay Together' became so iconic that even the Reverend Al Green himself gave it his seal of approval.

Tina's performance training both live and in the studio was incredible – despite the trials and tribulations of her relationship with Ike, she was a professional and, more to the point, *characterful* interpreter of lyrical meaning. It is no coincidence that her immense legions of fans see her as a superstar who appeared to sympathise with their own lives. Her journey was their journey. Her emotions were their emotions. This is an extremely rare quality, to be an avatar for their life's experiences.

And boy, could she dance – her joyous spirit bursting through! Always stylish, and always in her own style. In addition to all her many talents, she even co-wrote the legendary 'Nutbush City Limits'.

As her post-Ike independence and confidence grew, she nurtured her own talent, took risks and became an accomplished film actress. She lit up the screen with her incandescent presence, particularly in *Mad Max Beyond Thunderdome*, where she performed with unexpected assurance and gravitas. Tina's Buddhist beliefs gave her an inner strength, which flowed effortlessly into all areas of her multifaceted career. In her later years, she supervised the writing of *Tina* the musical, and several biopics, carefully nurturing her future legacy as an inspiration to many people across the world and for all time.

This book beautifully embodies Tina in all her glory, her fragility, her life-force, her humour, her joy and sometimes her pain… her entire life journey is here.

I miss her, you miss her, we will all miss her for ever – but at least we have these precious memories…

There will never be another Tina.

Martyn Ware
London, July 2023

To the memory of Tina Turner

A few years ago, I was asked to contribute a selection of my photographs to *Tina: That's My Life*, which was published to coincide with her eightieth birthday. I was delighted to be a part of the book as I'd always enjoyed photographing Tina and the project led me to do a deep dive back into my archive. It was at that point I realised I had a huge range of images – enough for my own photo book of her.

My first encounter with Tina was at her legendary appearance on *The Tube* in 1983. Her performance brought the house down and even delayed the Channel 4 news. It was also the start of a 20 year working relationship between Tina, myself and Roger Davies.

Simply Tina contains a mixture of some of my favourite shots of Tina and many unseen images. Over the years I've covered many of her music videos and photographed her on location, live and in the studio. At the beginning, I would make use of quieter moments to encourage her to step away from the video and into some mini-sessions.

Looking through my archive I have many fond memories of long days on location in the UK and overseas. Tina and Roger liked that I could work quickly, under pressure and unobtrusively to get results they were happy with.

Photographing Tina was always fun and incredibly rewarding. She was a true, down-to-earth superstar, whose radiance shone through my lens.

My last photo shoot with Tina was in her beautiful French garden in 2004. Wearing high heels as she walked down some steps, she lost her balance and tumbled forward. I thought that might mean the end of the photo shoot, but like a true professional she did a graceful forward roll on to the lawn and managed to stand up, still in her high heels, making light of the situation with a joke. Typically Tina!

My sincere thanks to Fabrice Couillerot for his drive and enthusiasm in collating and designing this book. I couldn't have done it without him.

Paul Cox
London, July 2023

1983

THE TUBE
with Heaven 17 and Annie Lennox

Paul Cox was asked by EMI to photograph Tina Turner's appearance on *The Tube*, Channel 4's live music magazine show. It was an important performance as it was to showcase 'Let's Stay Together', Tina's first single for four years, produced by Greg Walsh and UK synth guru Martyn Ware (Human League / Heaven 17 / BEF). At the time, it was one of many jobs for Paul in his busy schedule. 'I knew of Tina,' he says, 'Everybody was just blown away with her full-on power. She threw everything into it.' It was the start of a working relationship between Tina and Paul that was to last over two decades.

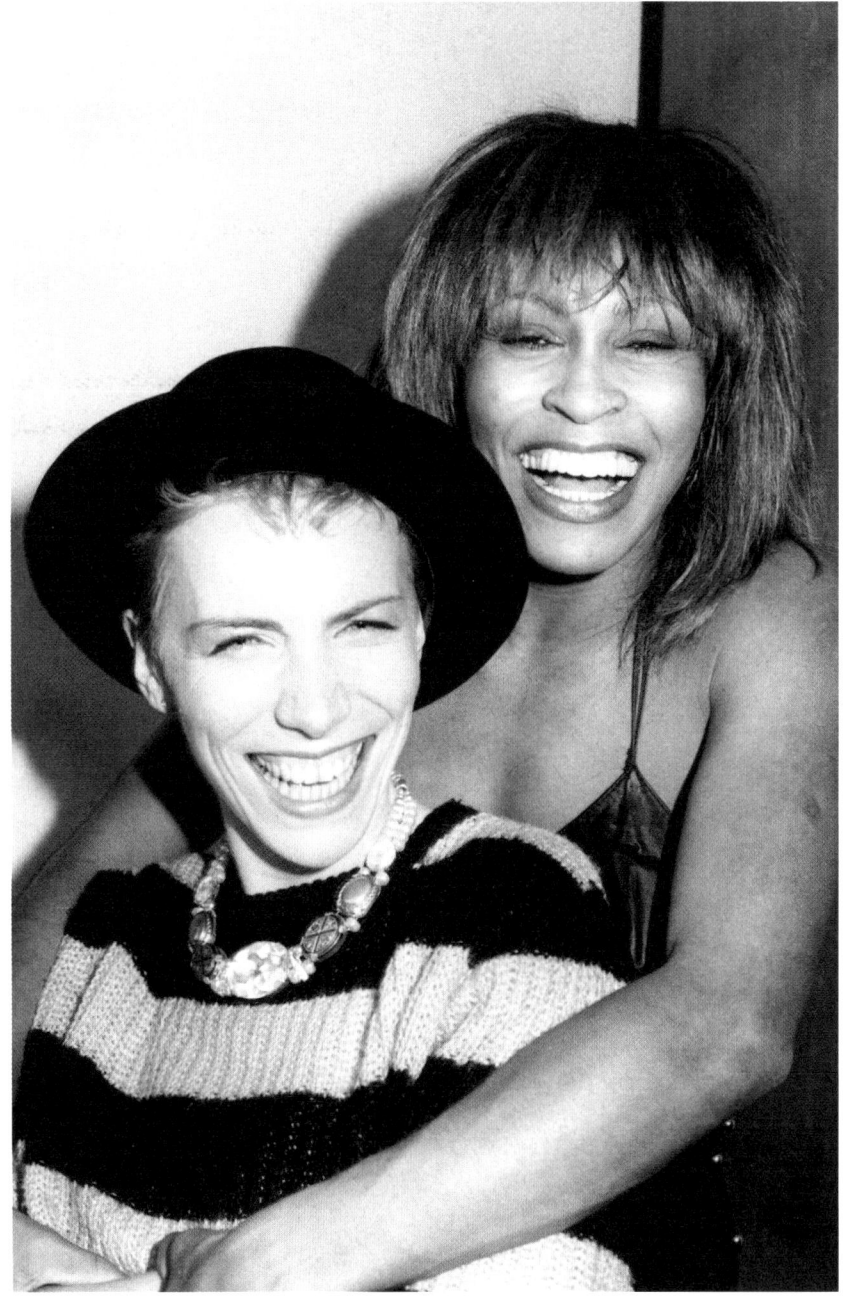

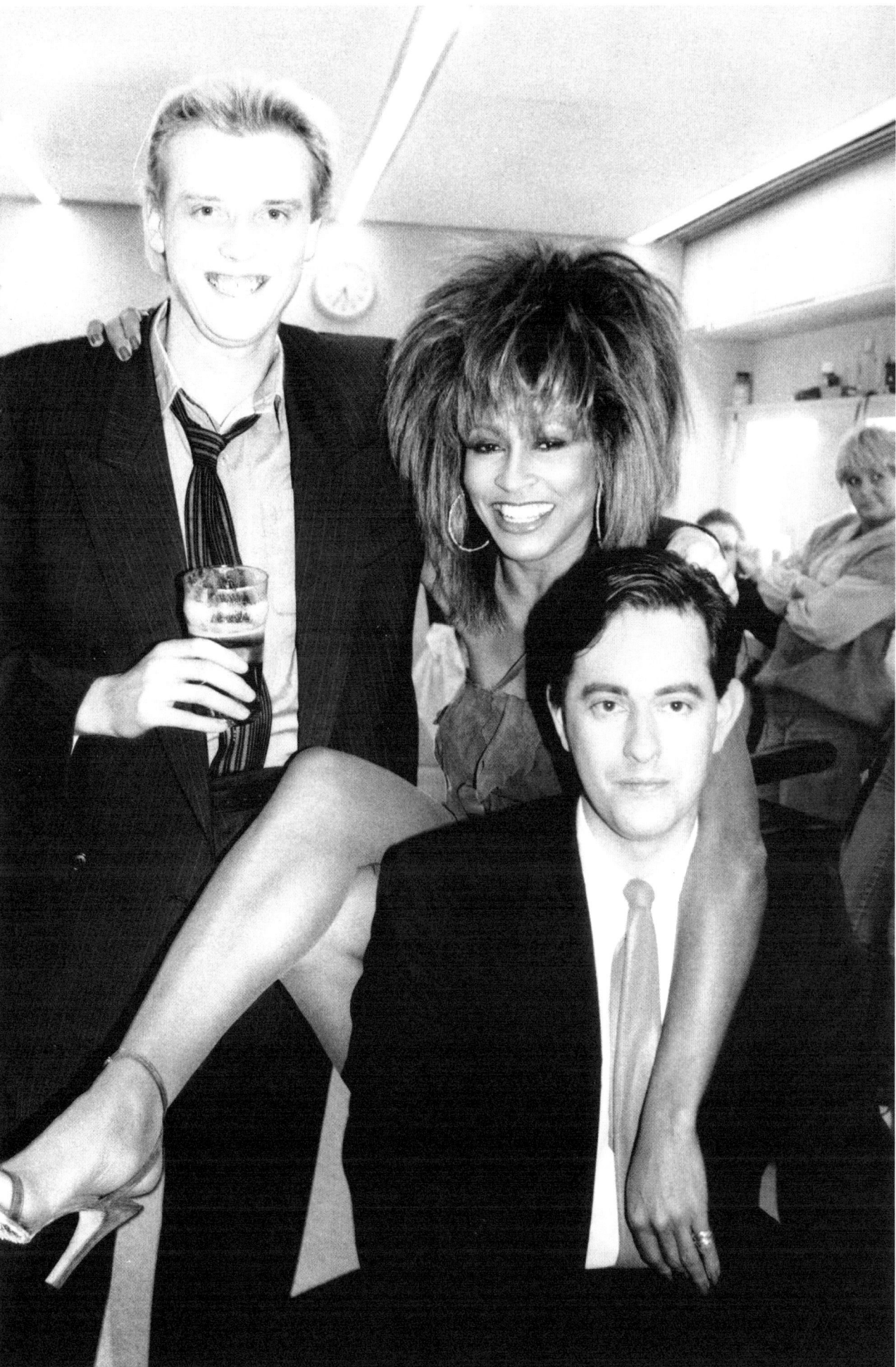

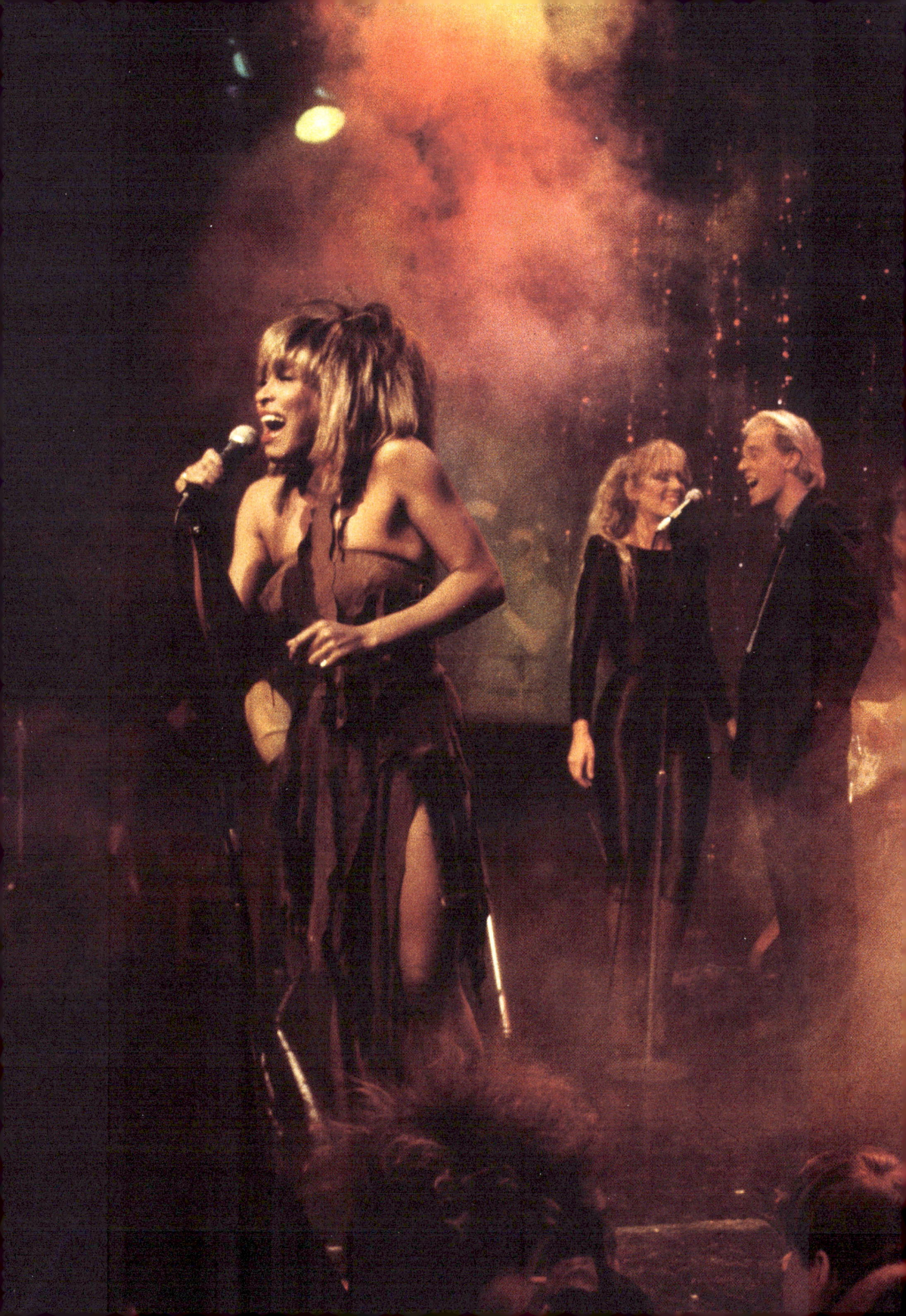

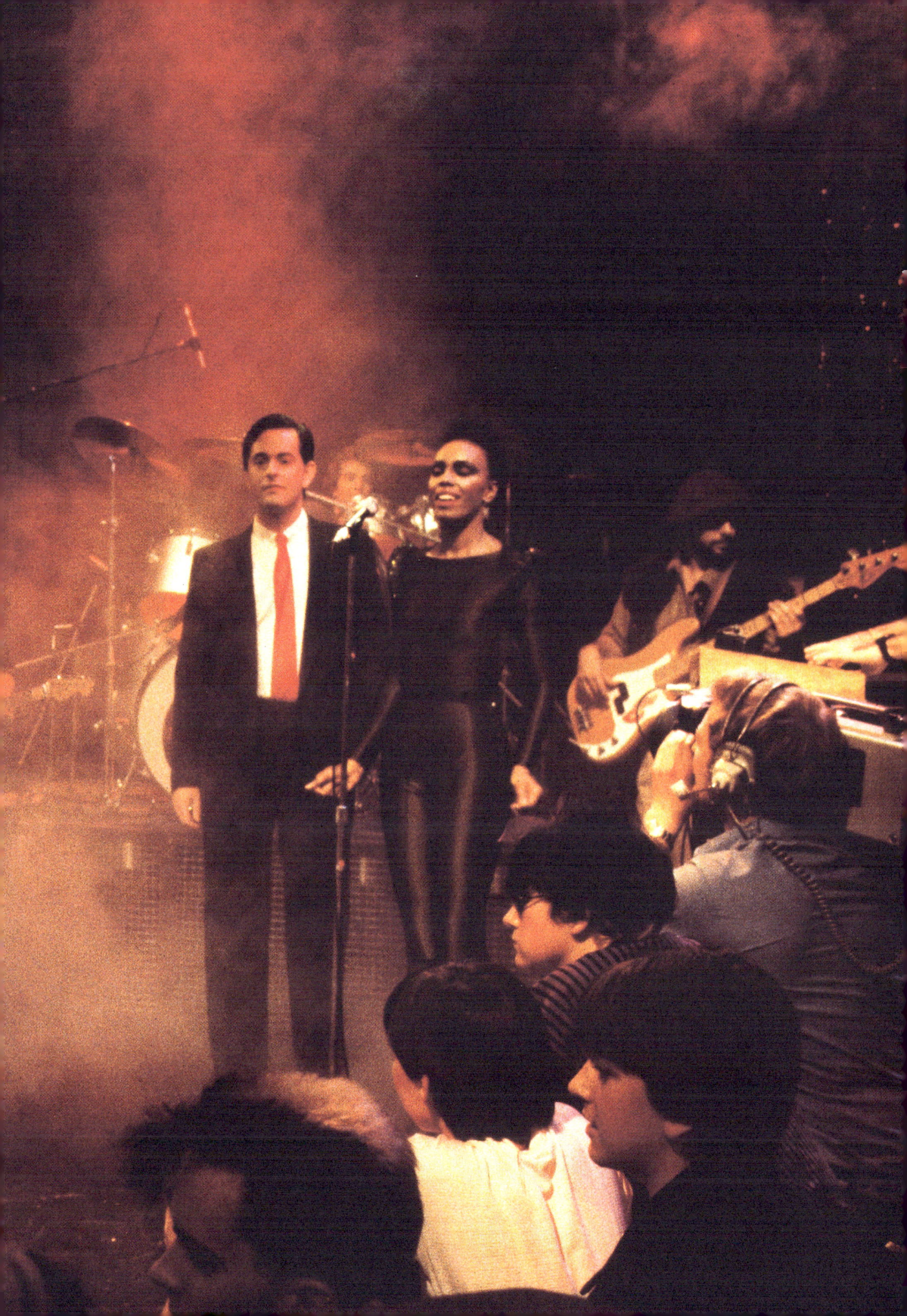

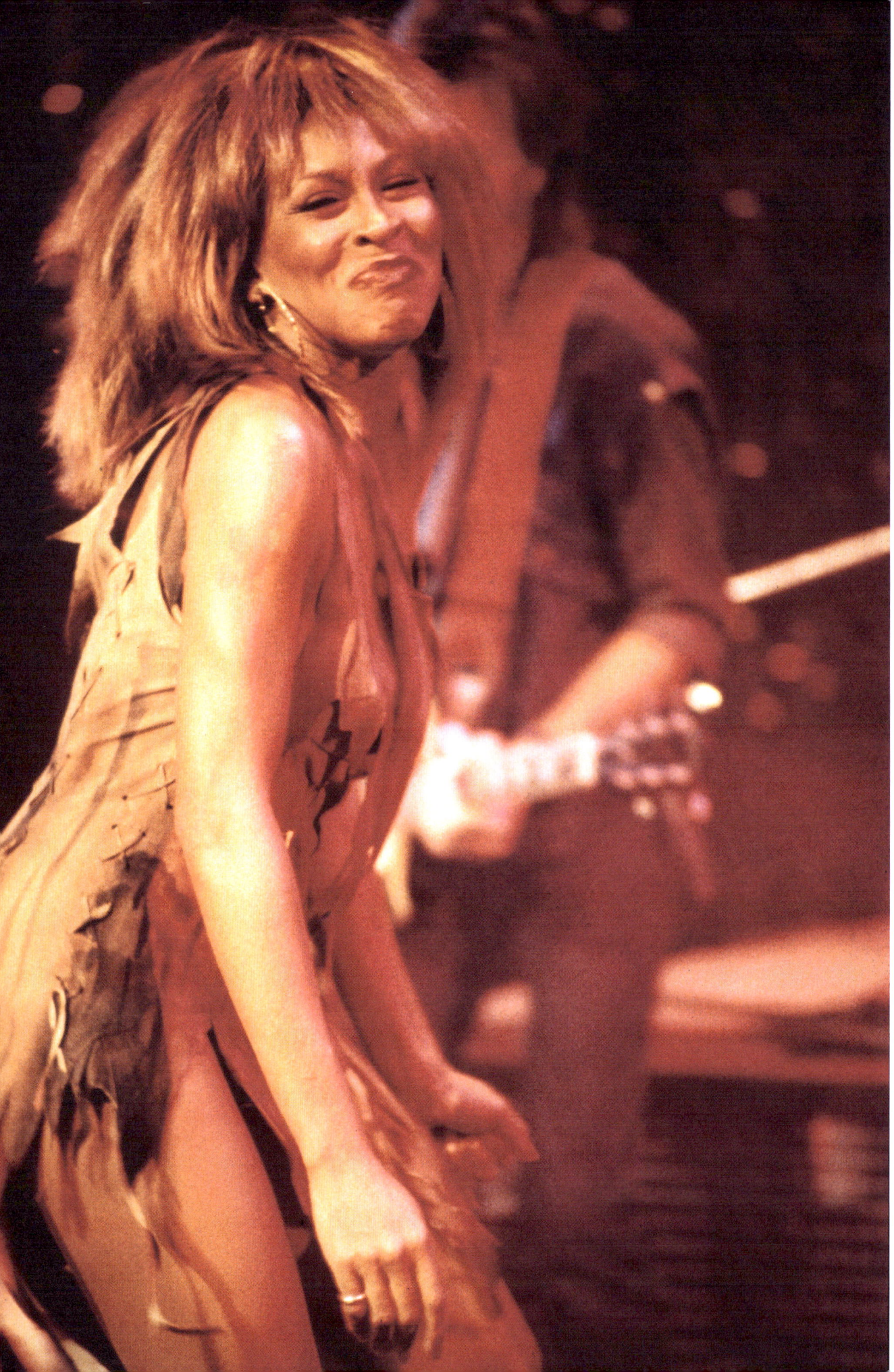

1983

THE VENUE, VICTORIA, LONDON

With 'Let's Stay Together' in the Top 10, Tina played a gig at The Venue, the Virgin Records-owned concert hall on London's Victoria Street. Paul was there with his camera. 'Sometimes it happens like that, if you've done a good job, the record company will send you on to the next thing. I was asked to cover it because I'd commented that I thought she was really good.' After a set that fully embraced her past, contained her new single and contemporary covers of 'Let's Pretend We're Married' by Prince and 'Cat People (Putting Out Fire)' by David Bowie, Tina was presented with a disc recognising sales of over 250,000 copies of 'Let's Stay Together'.

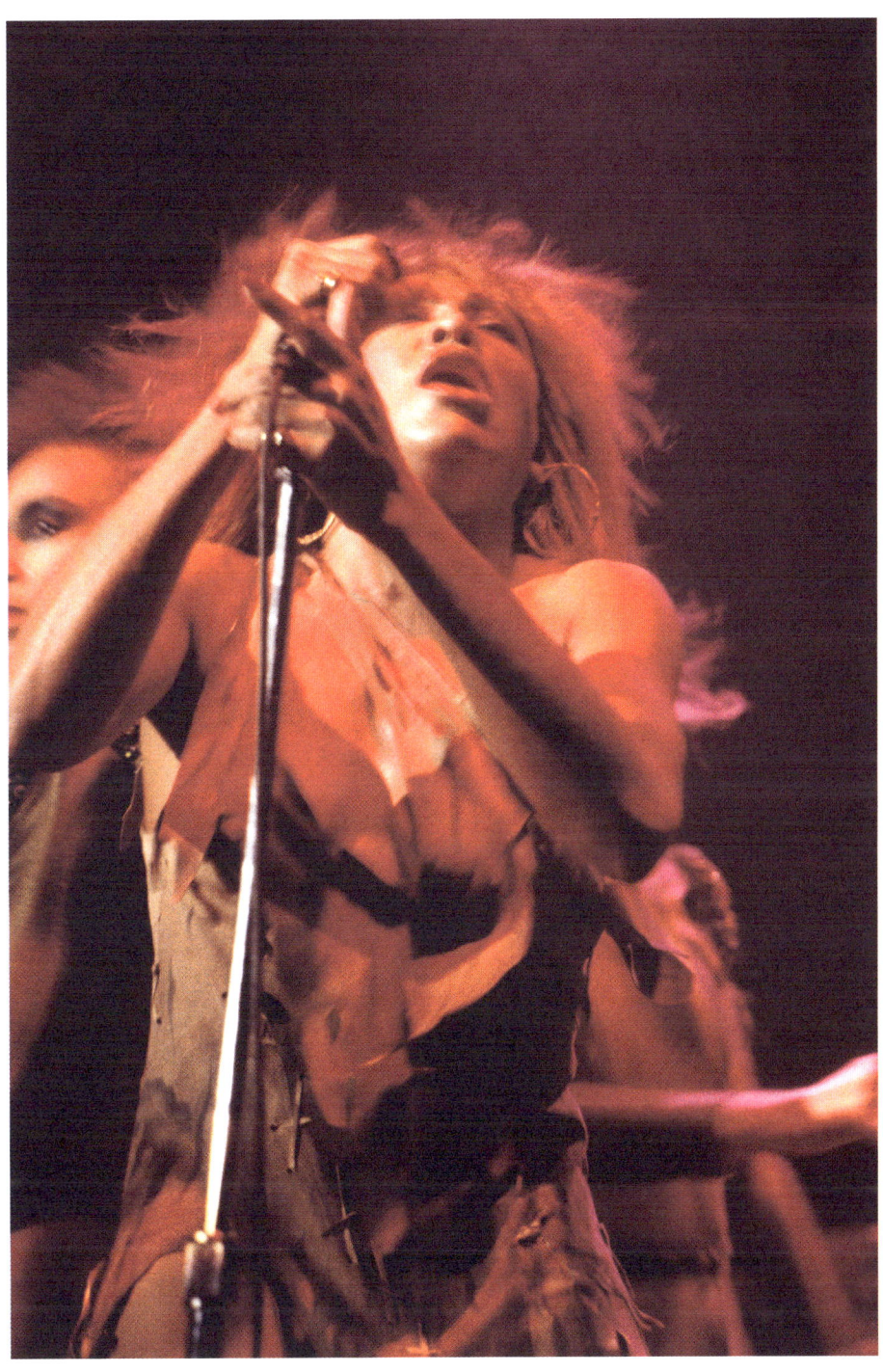

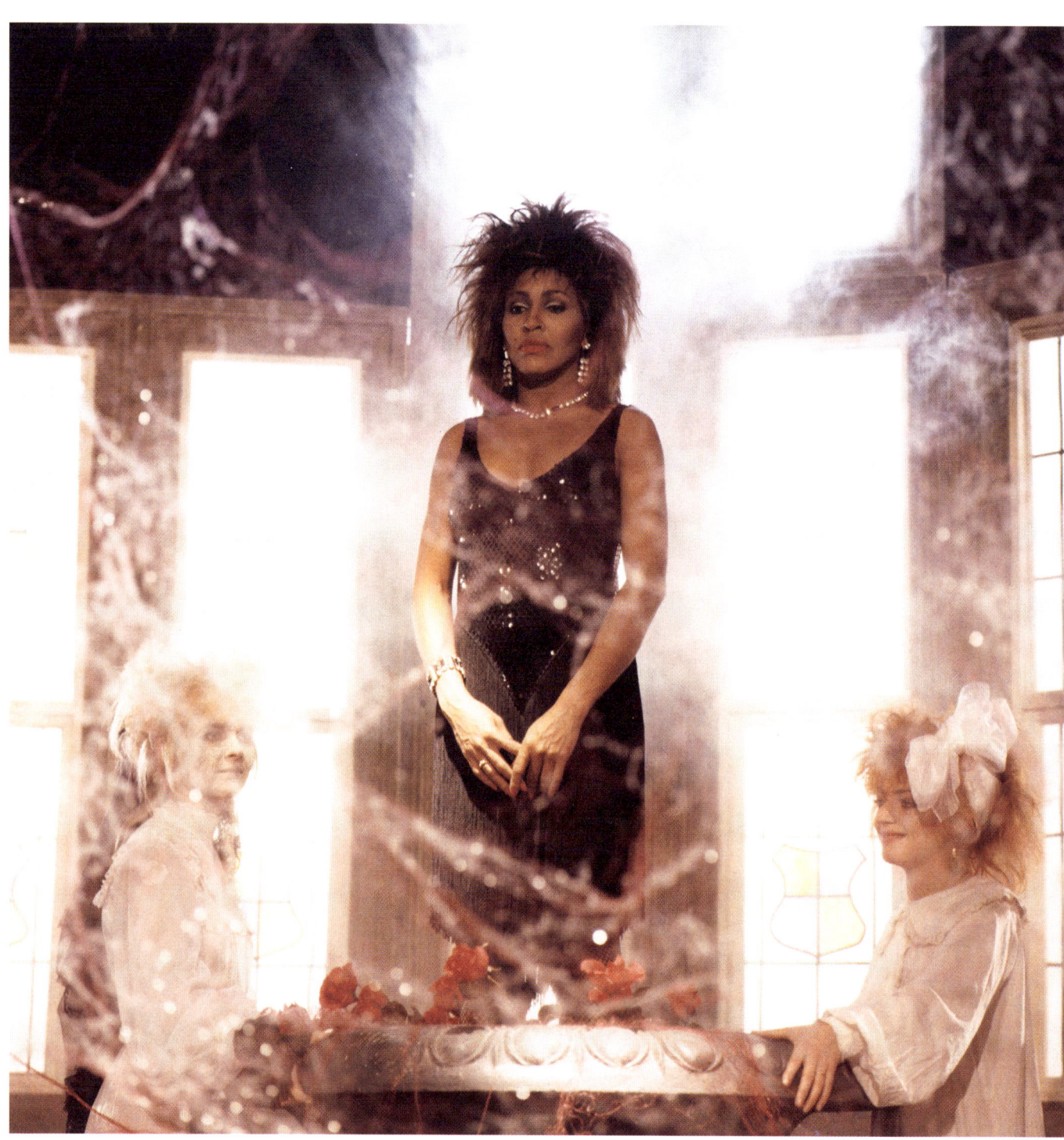

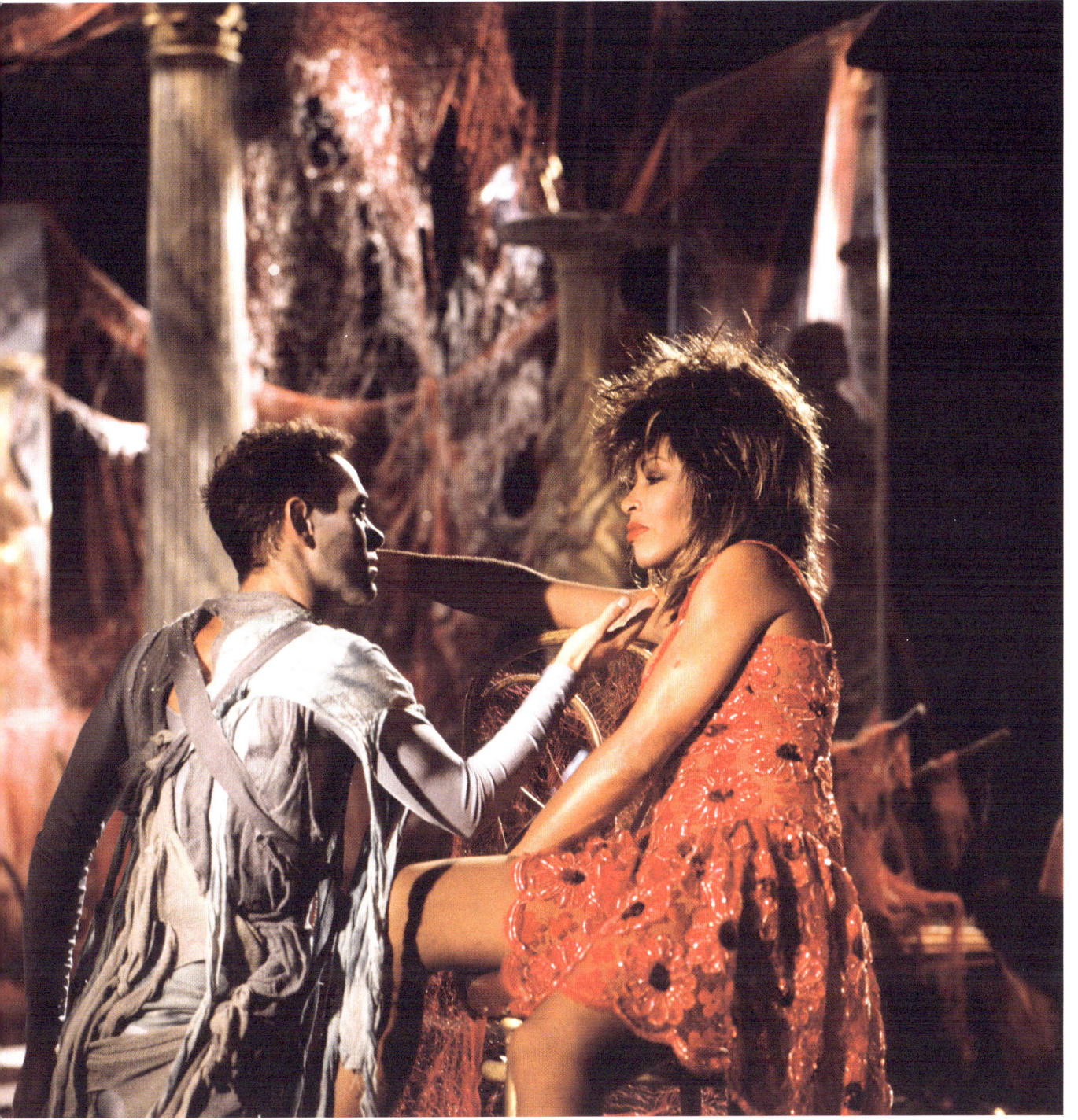

1984

LONDON'S RIVOLI BALLROOM
'PRIVATE DANCER' **video shoot**

Tina had become a proper superstar in the year since Paul last shot her with the release of the *Private Dancer* album in May 1984, and its third single, 'What's Love Got To Do With It', reaching the US number one that September. Paul would visit the sets of her videos to take promotional pictures, starting with this, the 'Private Dancer' single shoot, at the Rivoli in Southeast London. Tina looked regal amid the peak eighties' cobwebs and hairbows of Brian Grant's iconic video. 'Tina liked being directed,' Paul says. 'They were extravaganzas, mini films – complete with Arlene Phillips' choreography. It was a wholly different way of seeing Tina.'

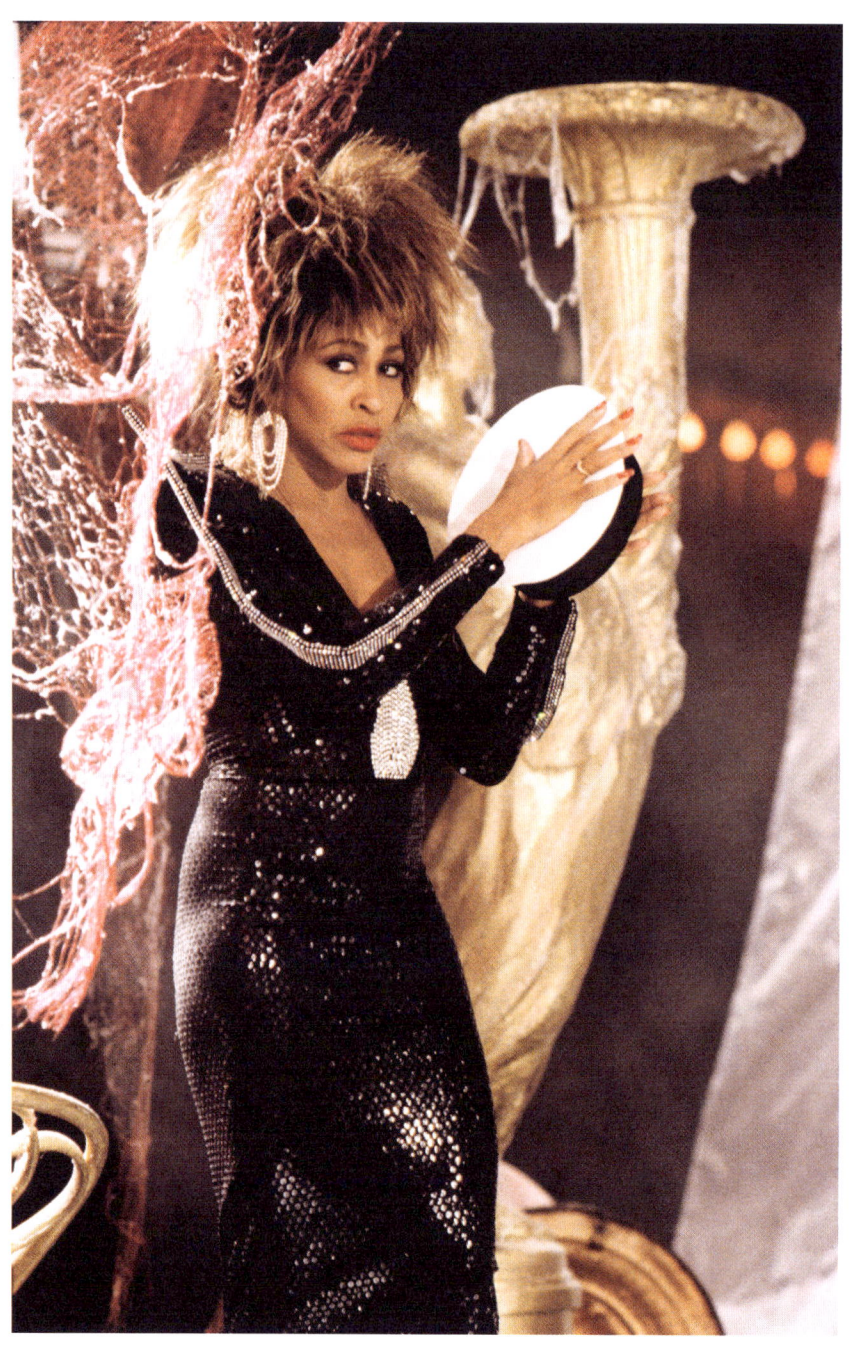

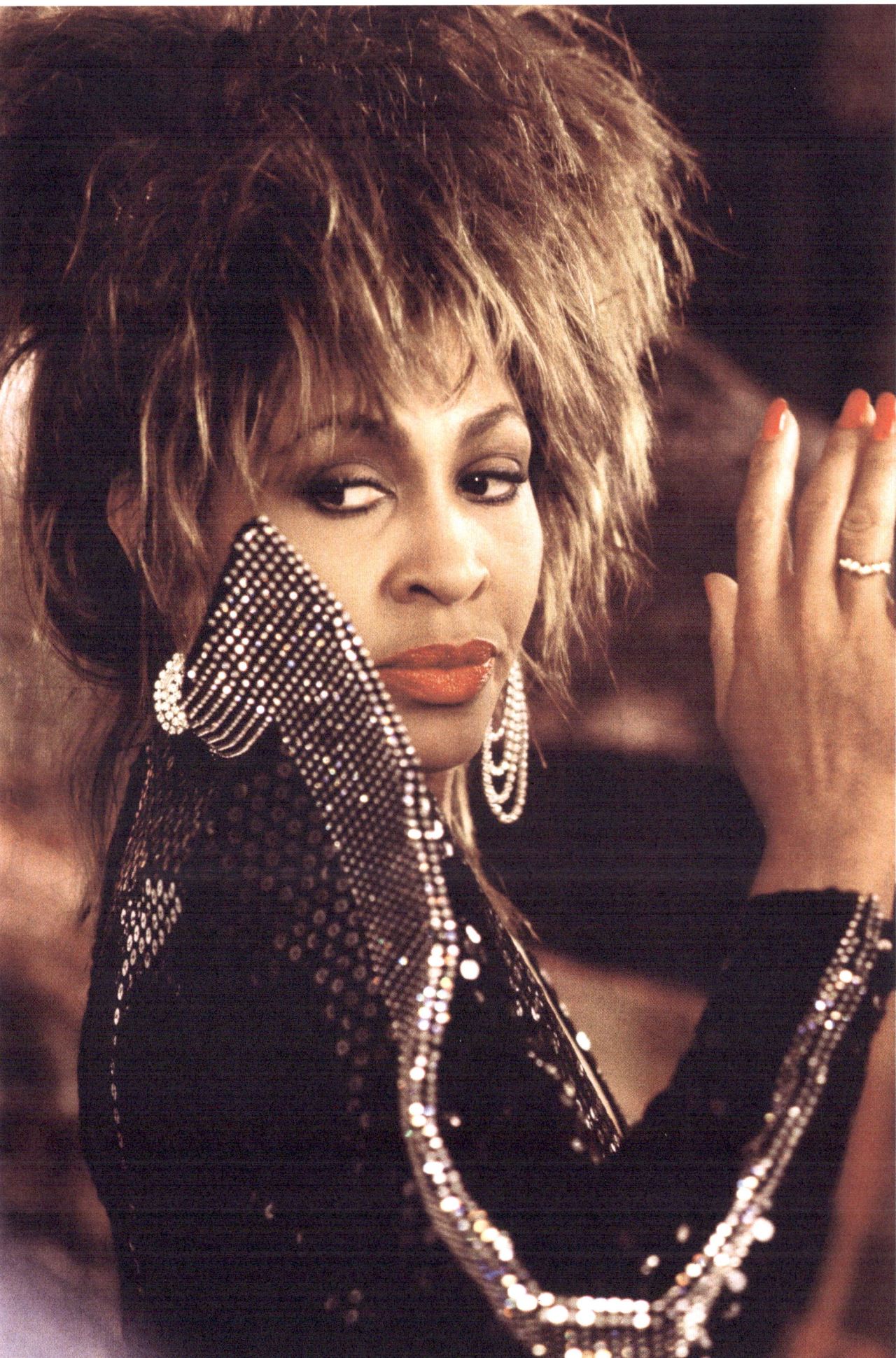

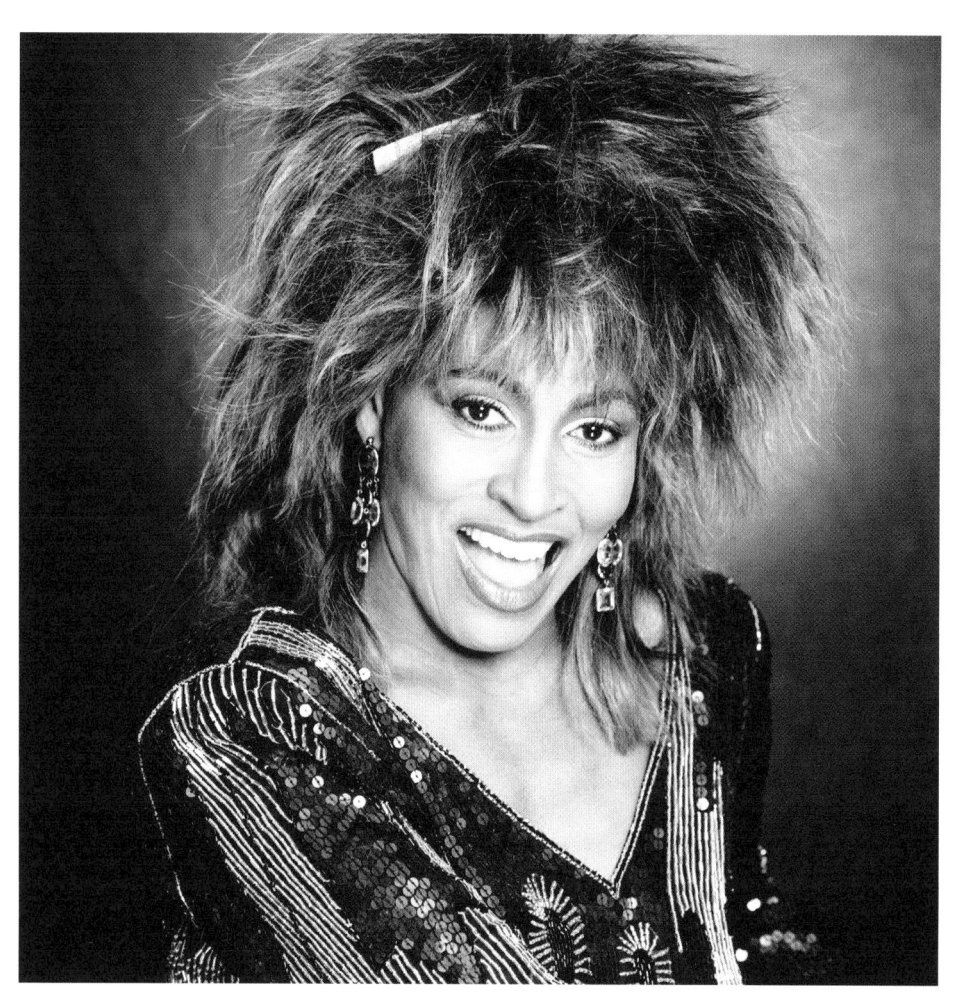

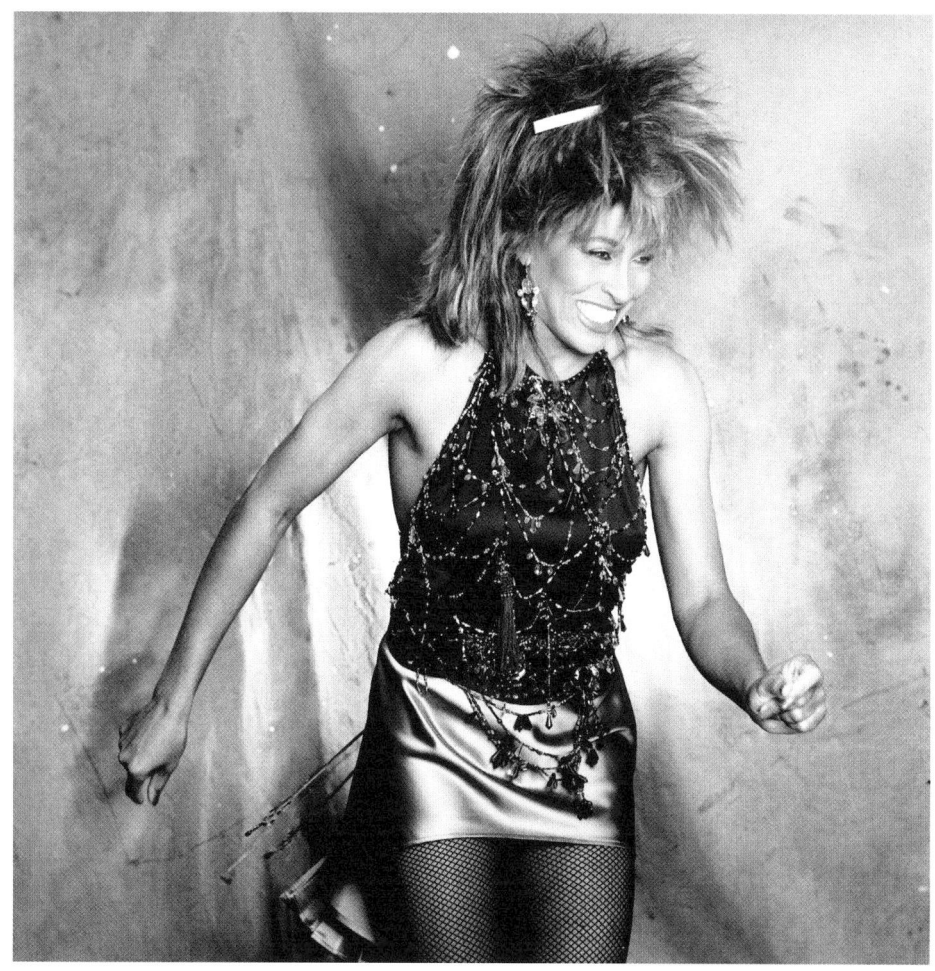

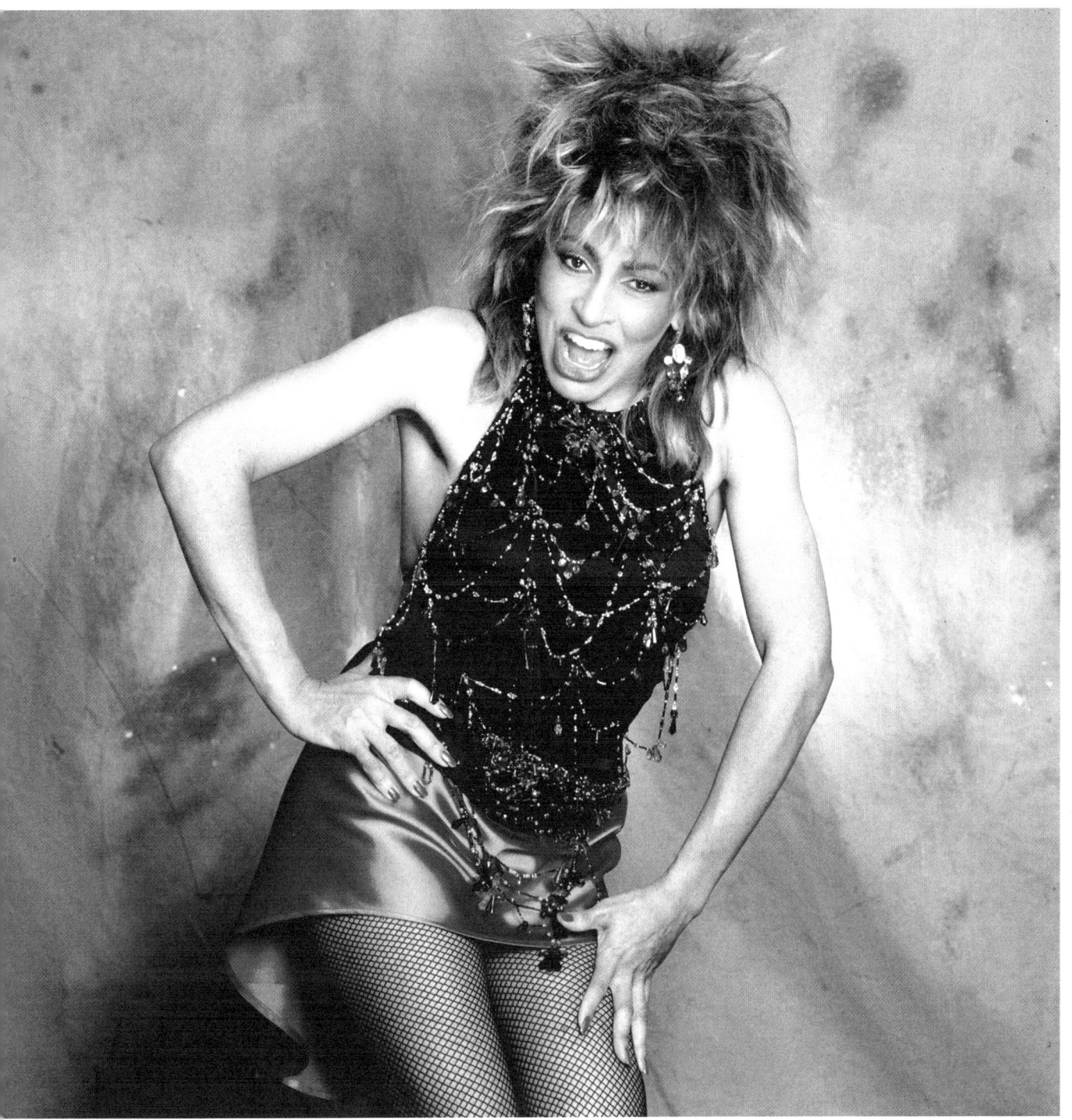

1985
HAMMERSMITH ODEON

Tina did a promotional shoot at Hammersmith Odeon in early 1985, when she was rehearsing there for her Private Dancer World Tour that began in Helsinki that February. 'This was when I started to get to know Tina's manager, Roger Davies,' Paul says. 'He would give me a *whole five minutes* with her! That canvas backdrop was quickly thrown up in the dressing room.' Then came some performance shots. 'It was a nightmare to get decent pictures of her, because she moved so fast,' Paul laughs. 'She was like a hurricane once she got going. Most of her stuff was very high voltage.'

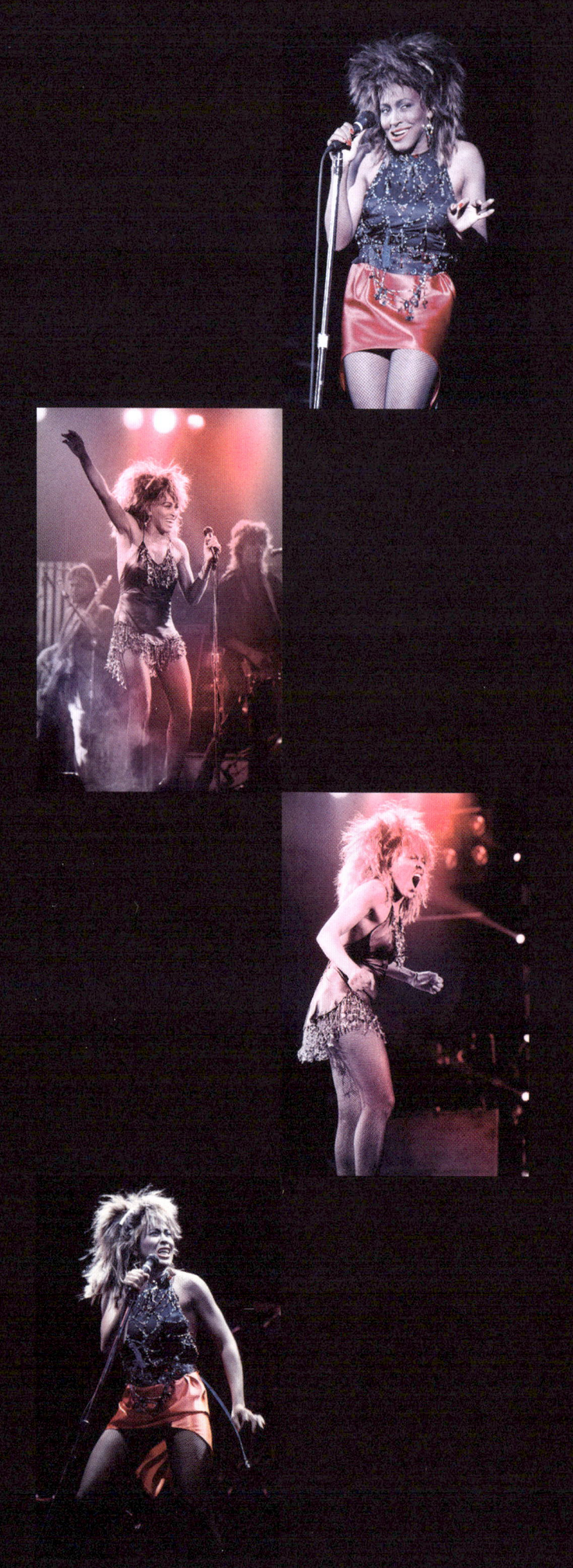

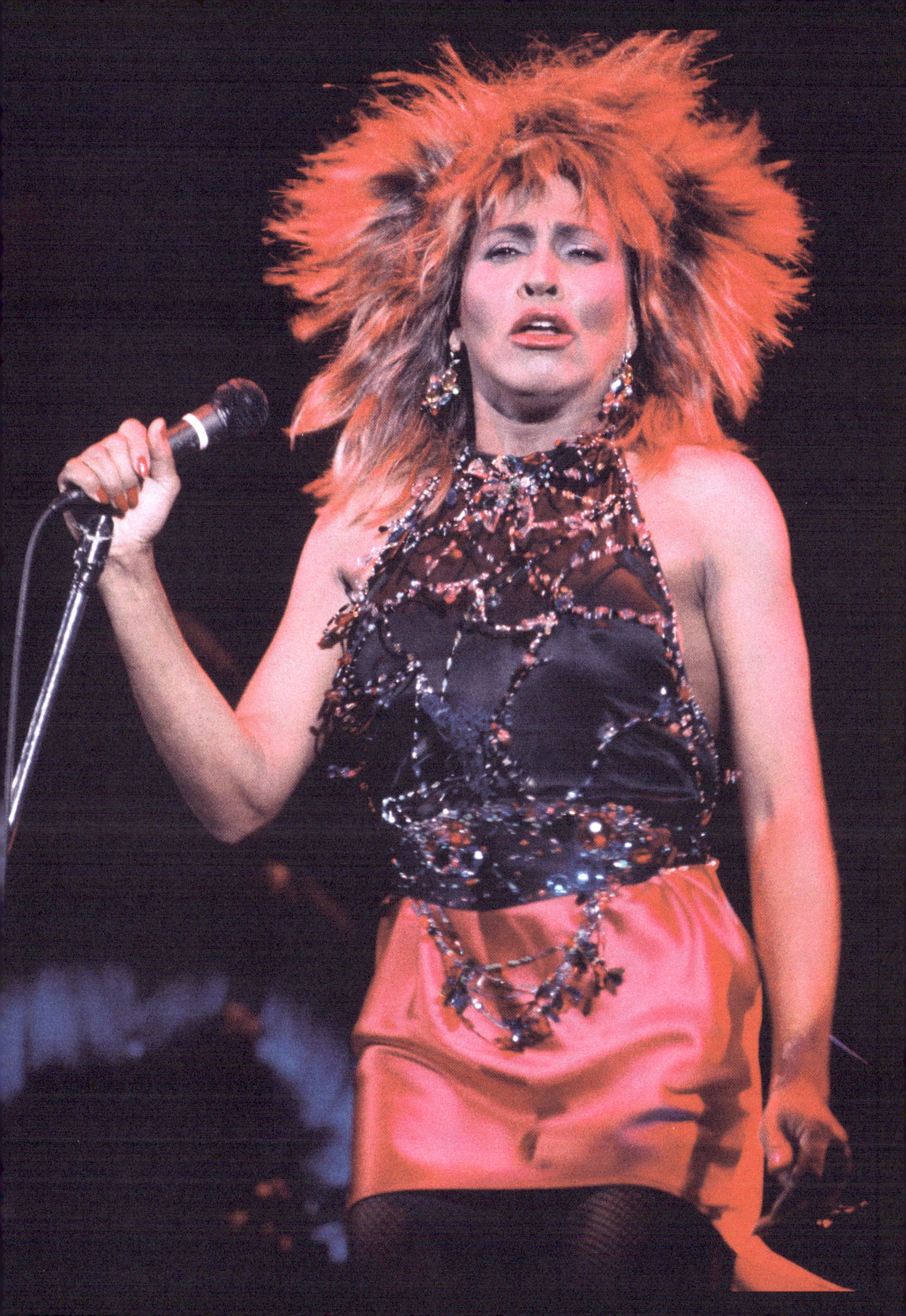

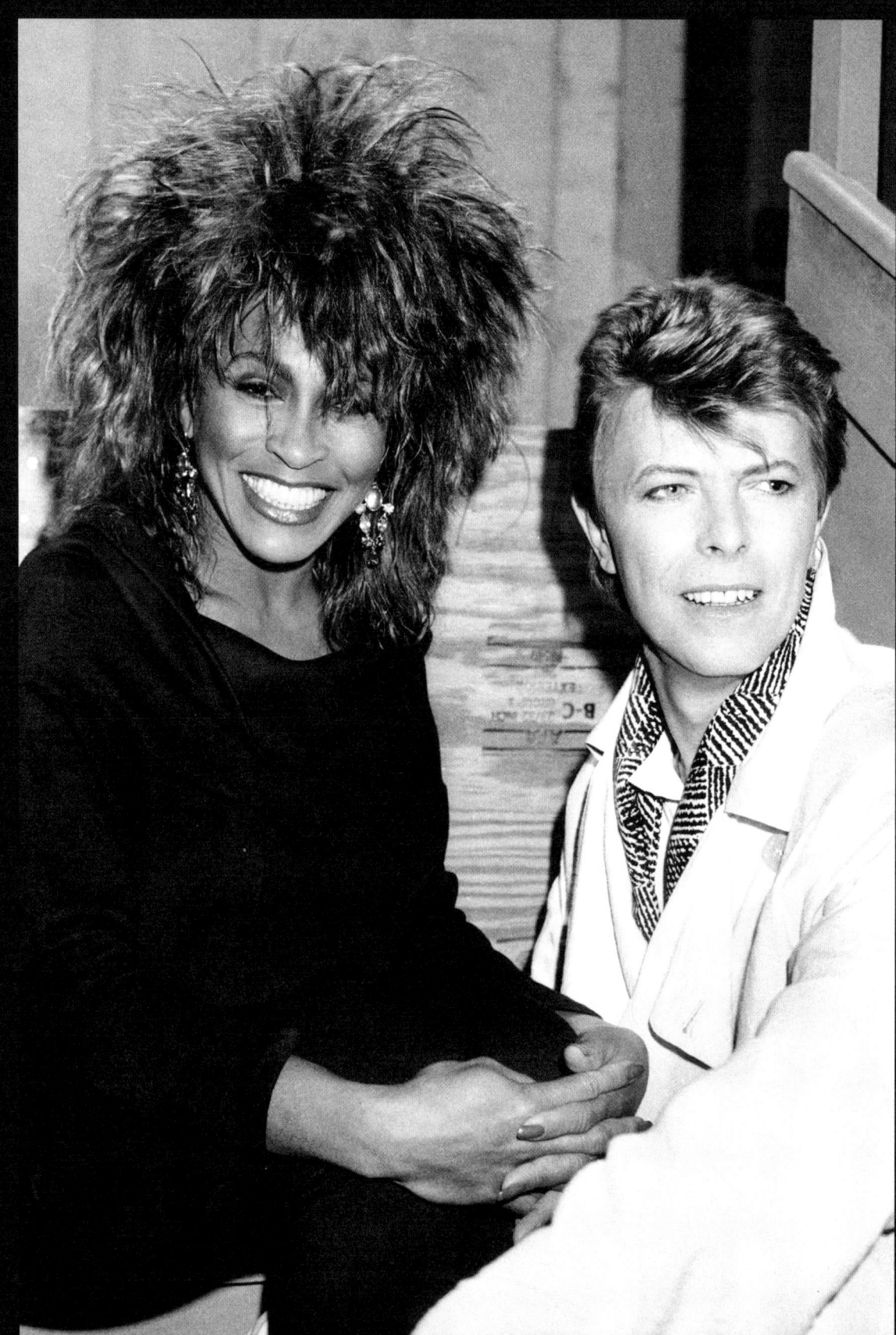

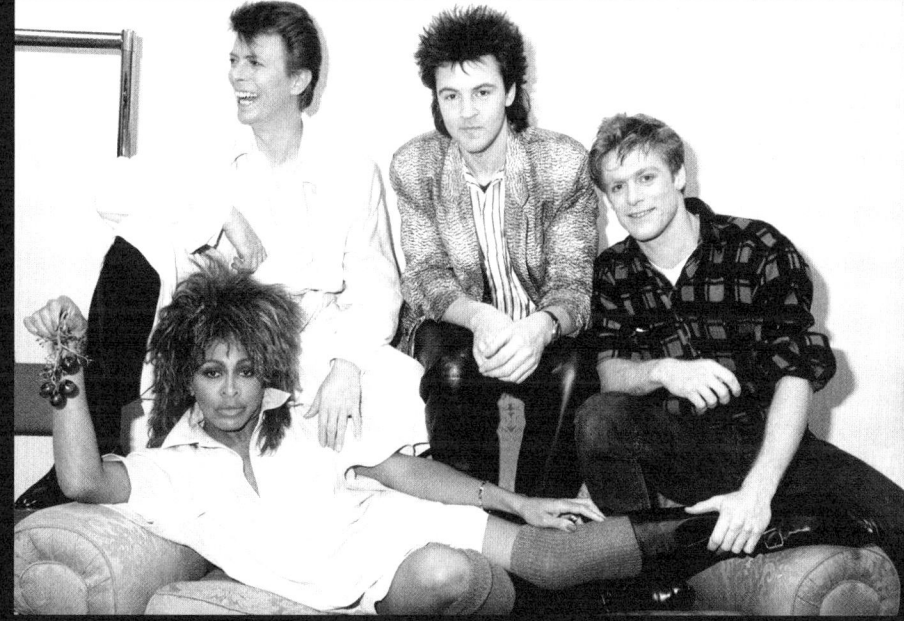

1985

AT THE NATIONAL EXHIBITION CENTRE IN BIRMINGHAM
'TONIGHT' with David Bowie

When Tina's Private Dancer Tour reached Birmingham, both nights were filmed by David Mallett for a long-form video. Paul was on hand to photograph them, including Tina's performance of 'It's Only Love' with Bryan Adams, and her remarkable duet of 'Tonight' with David Bowie. Bowie had been instrumental in getting Tina her deal with Capitol Records in 1983, and their chemistry was intimate and electric. 'They were just nice with each other,' Paul remembers. 'Very close. It was one of those situations, no pressure whatsoever, it's gotta happen NOW! Two seconds, a roll of film. Snap! Snap! Snap!'

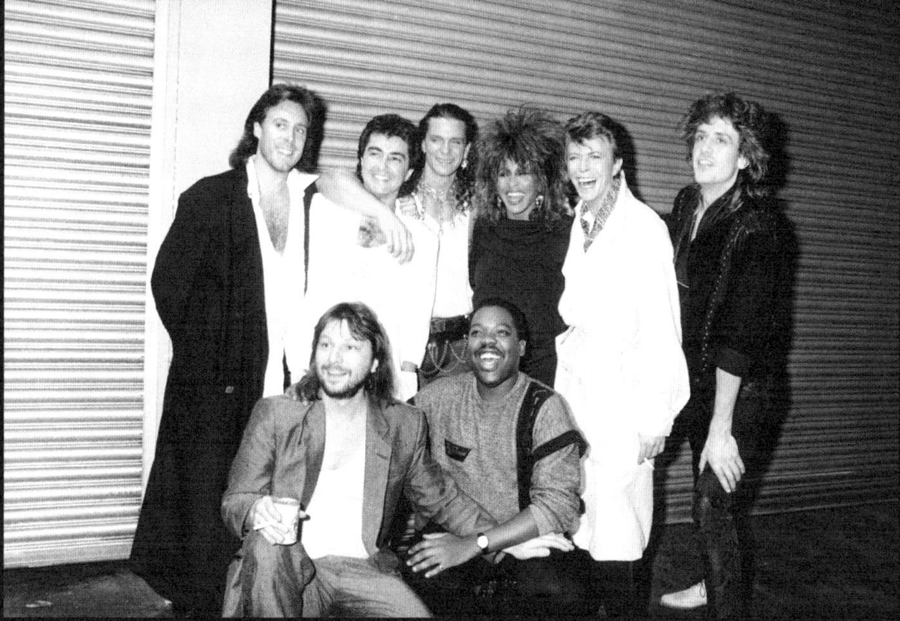

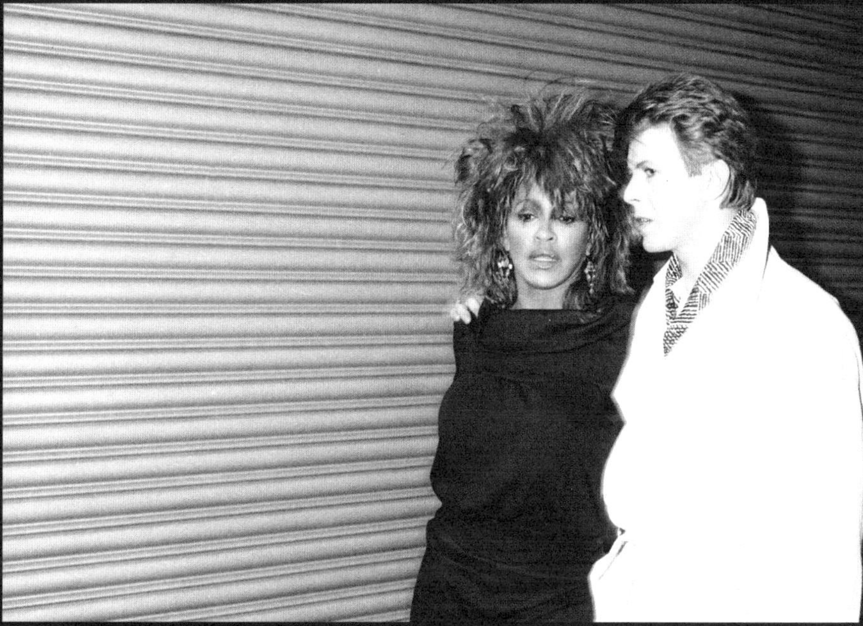

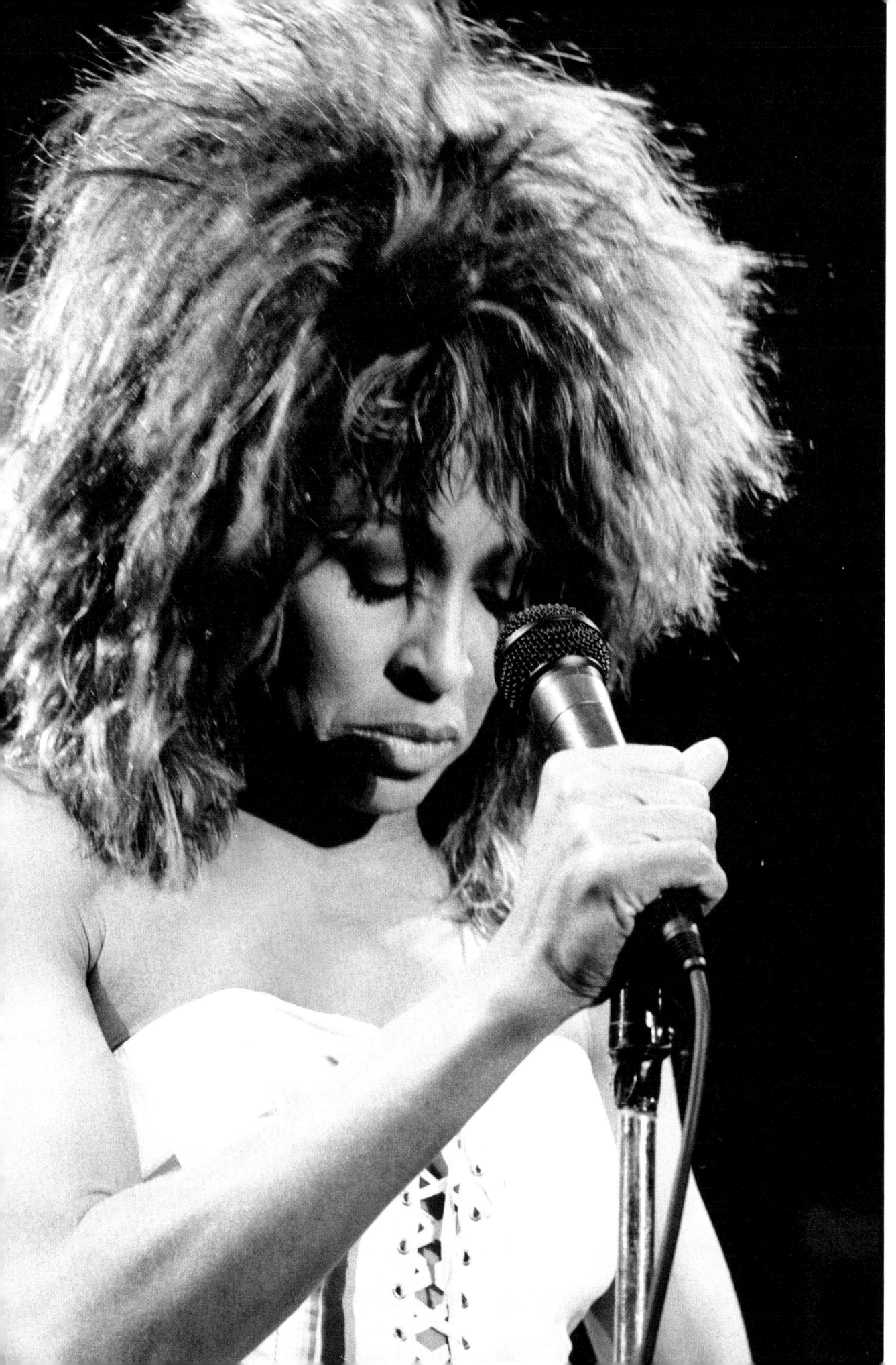

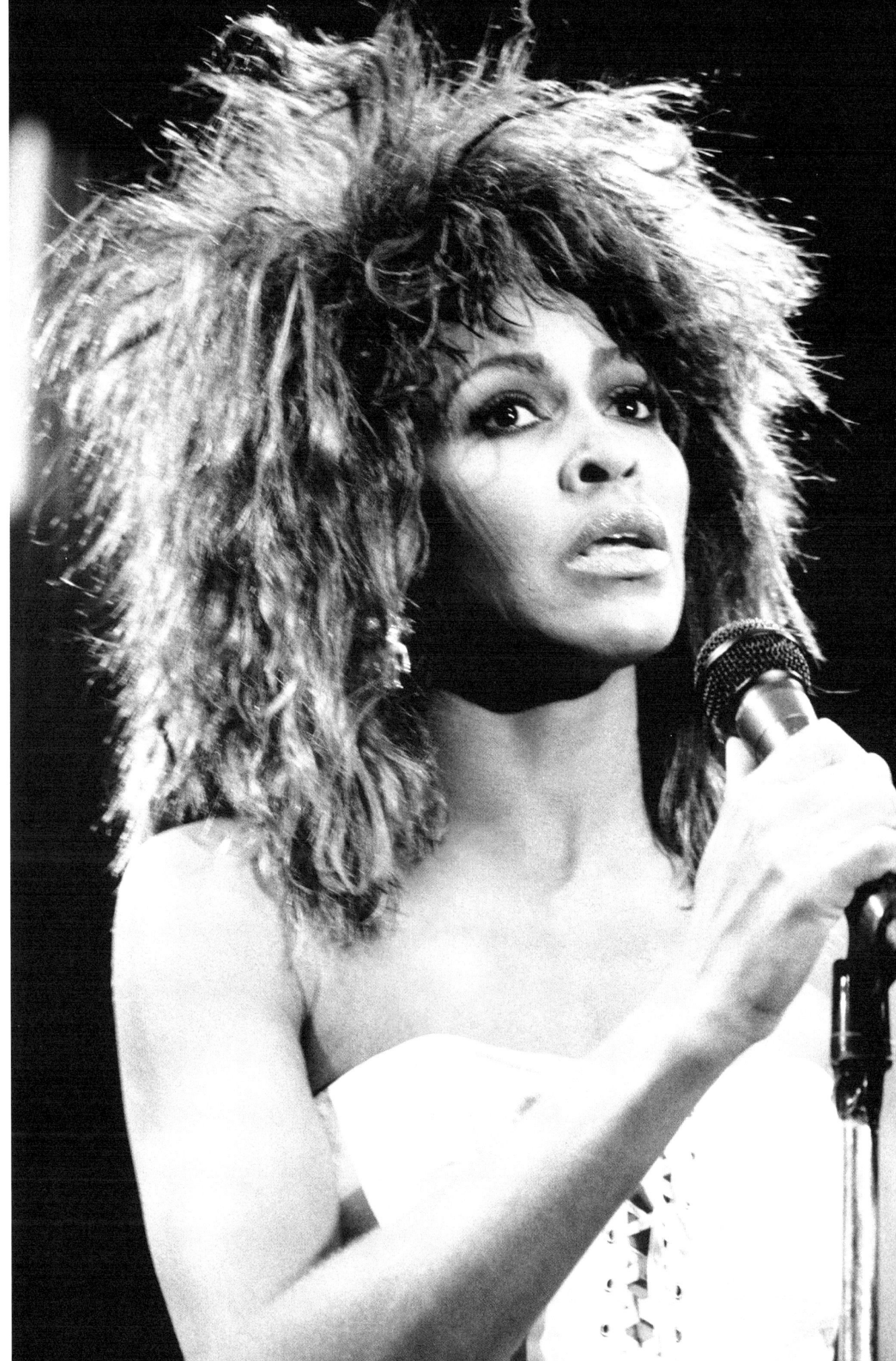

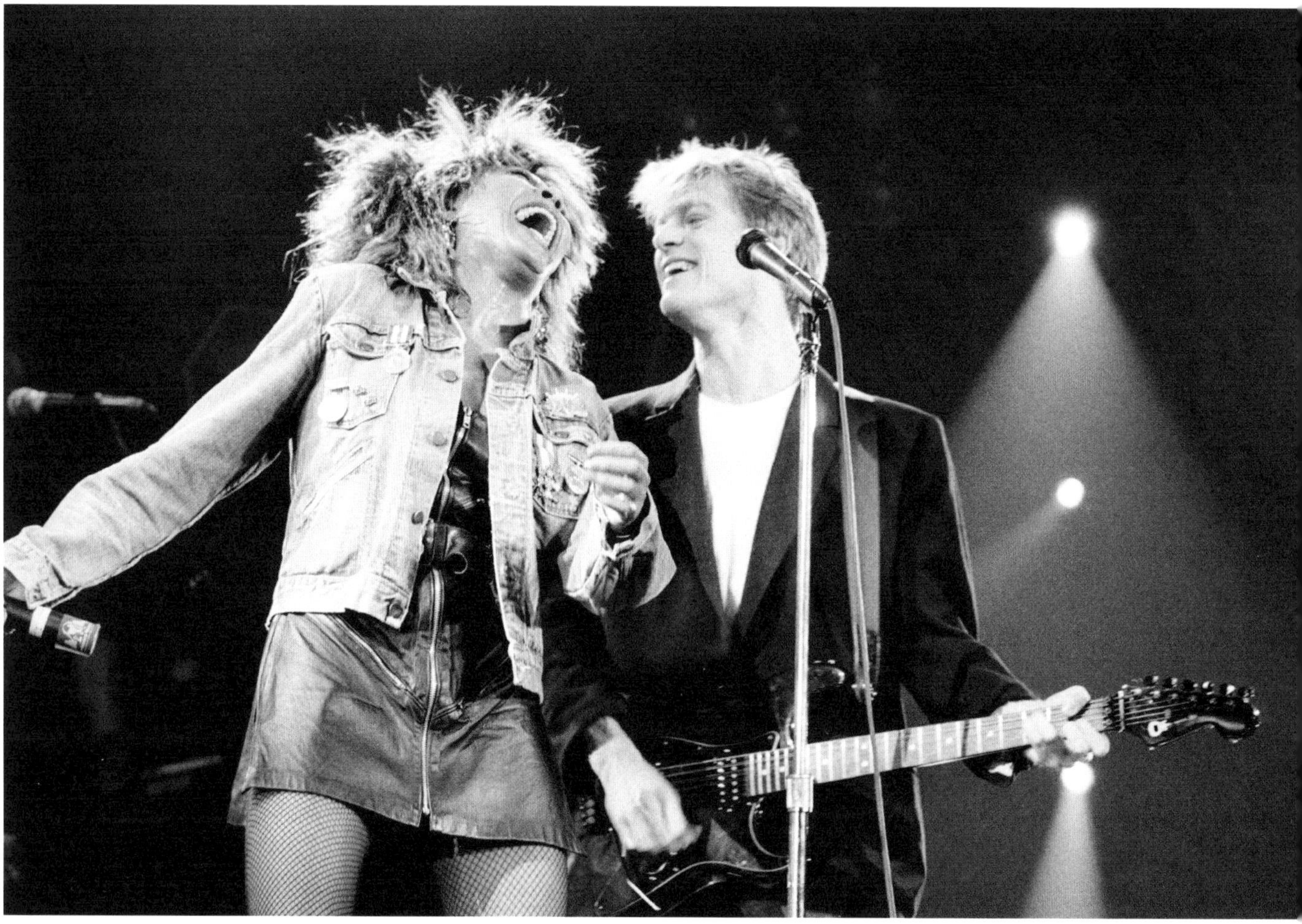

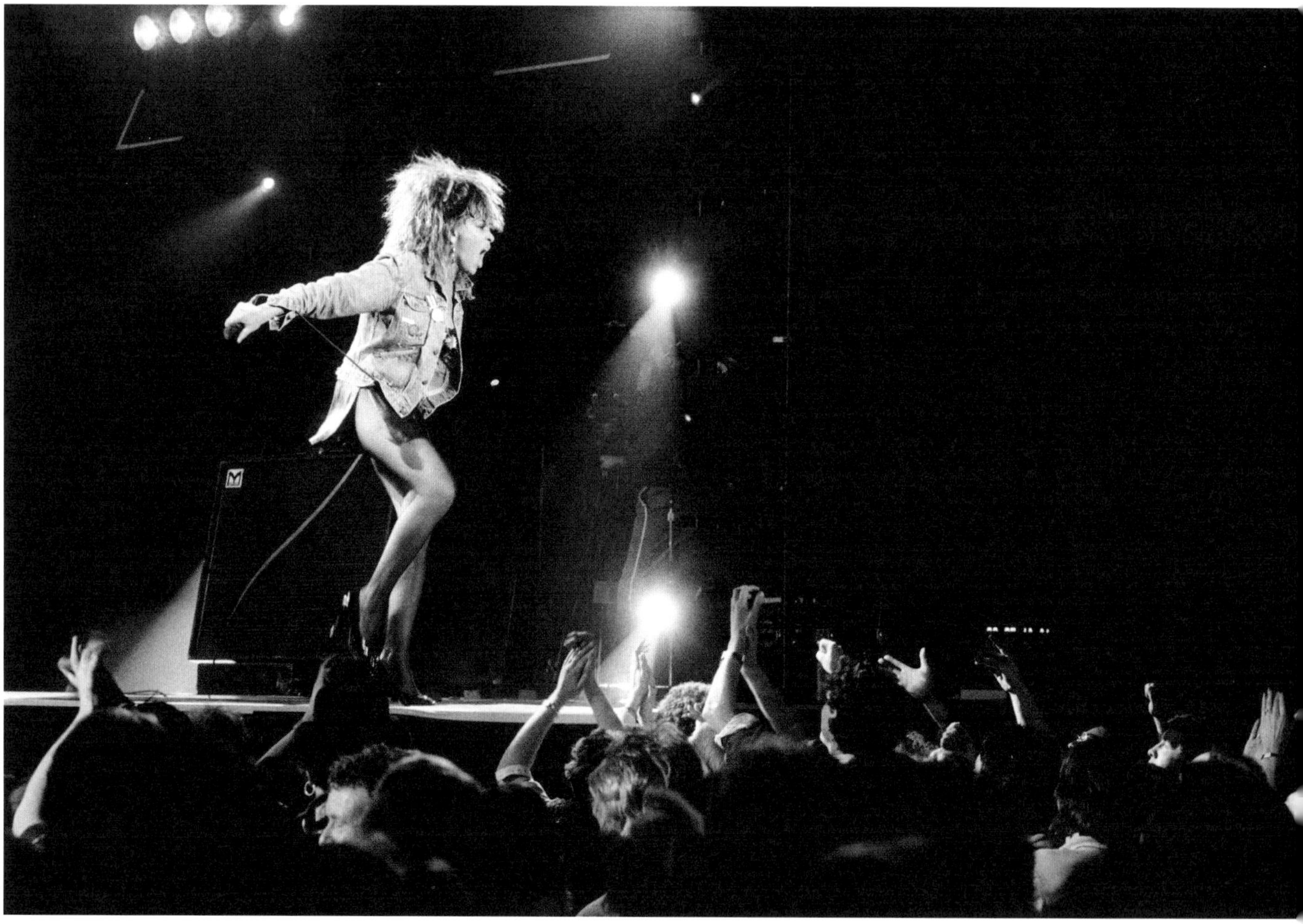

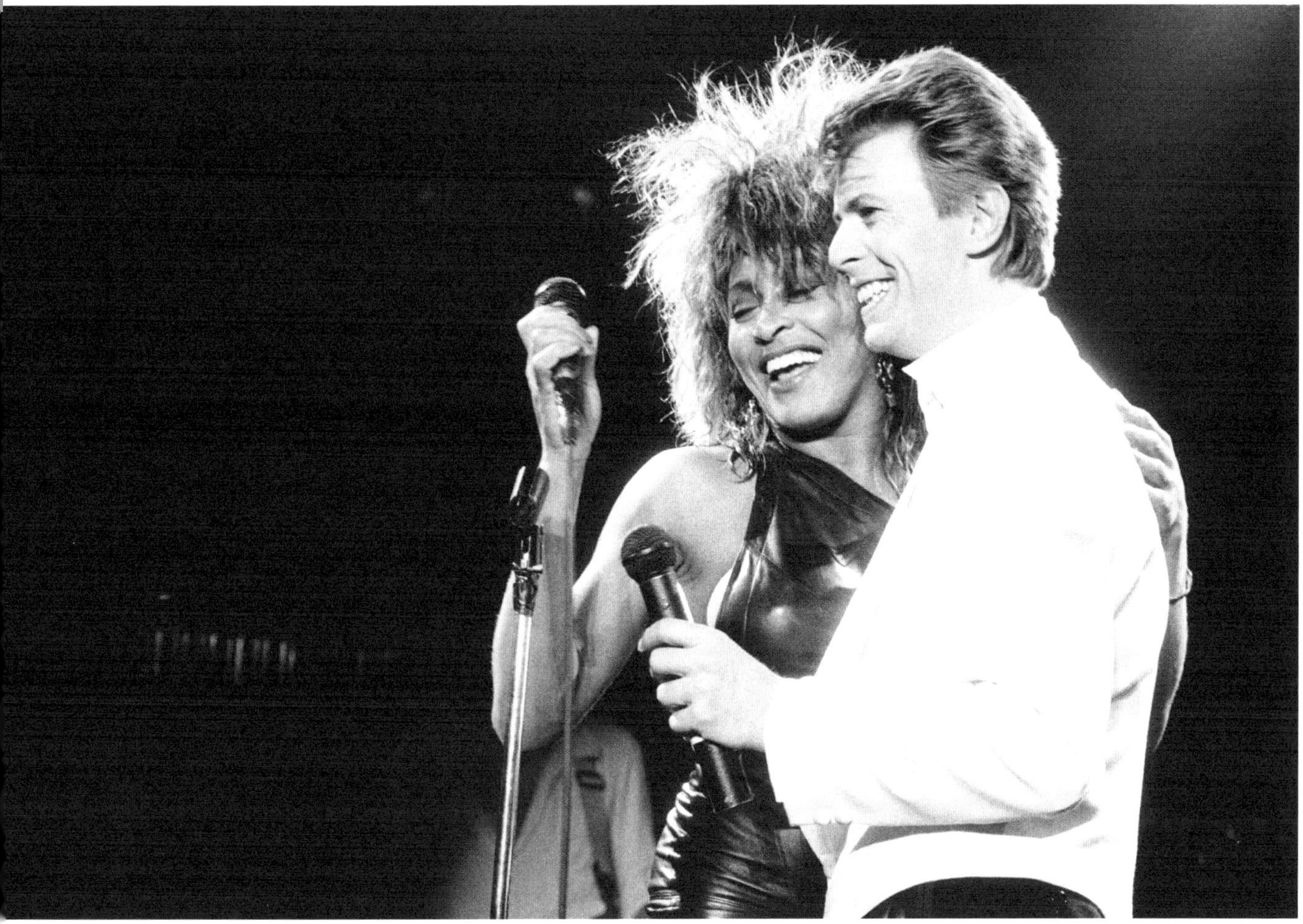

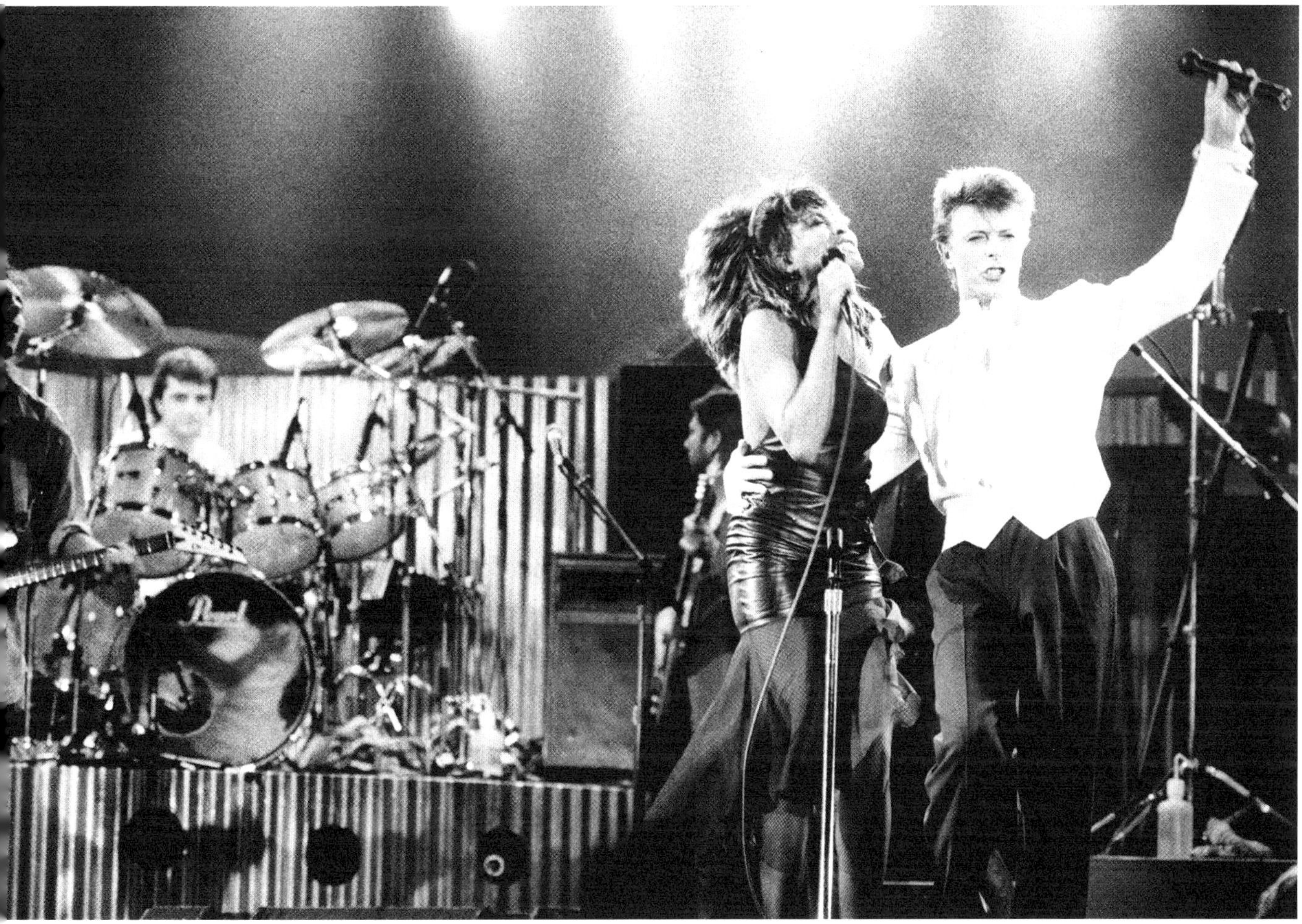
Pearl

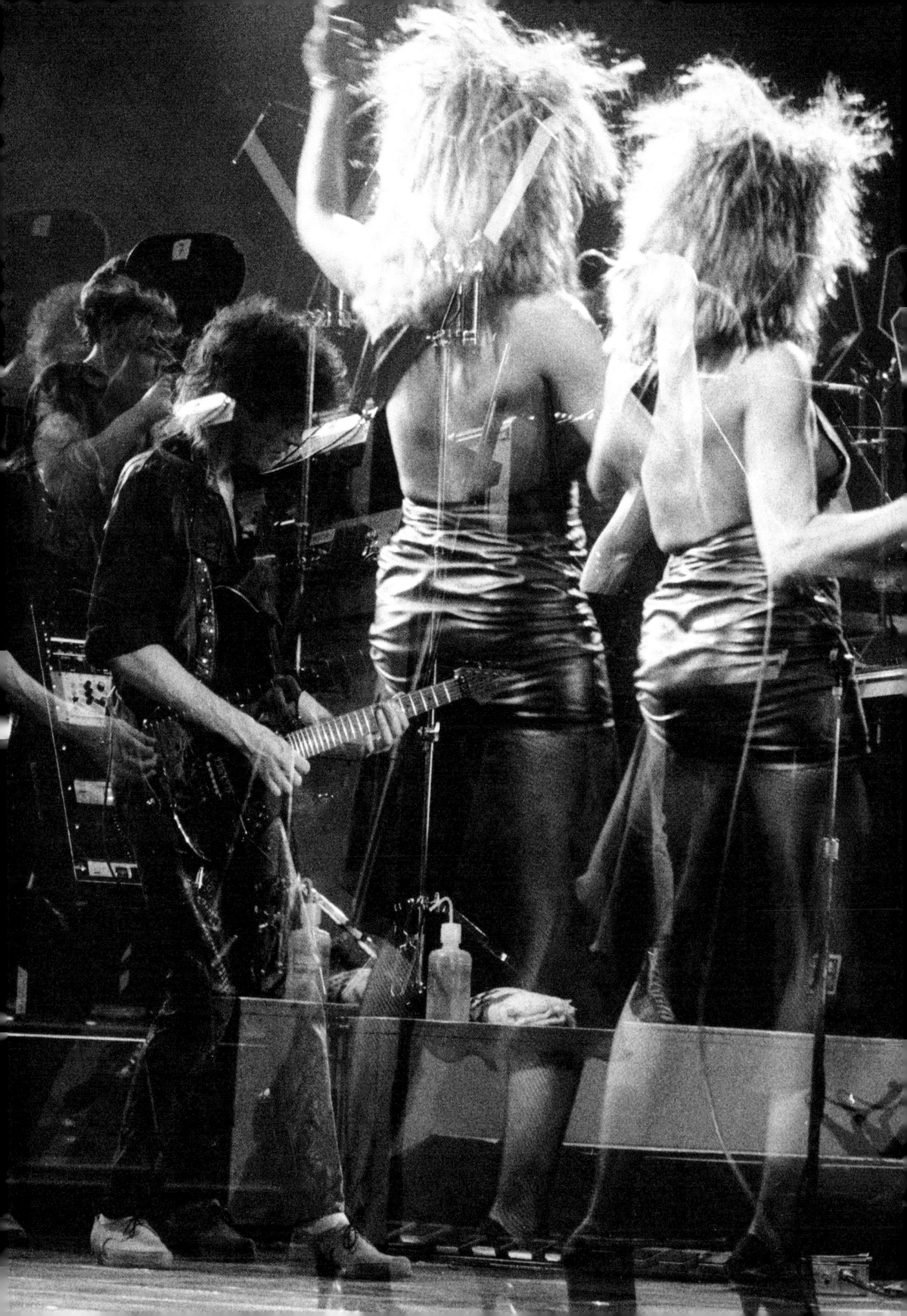

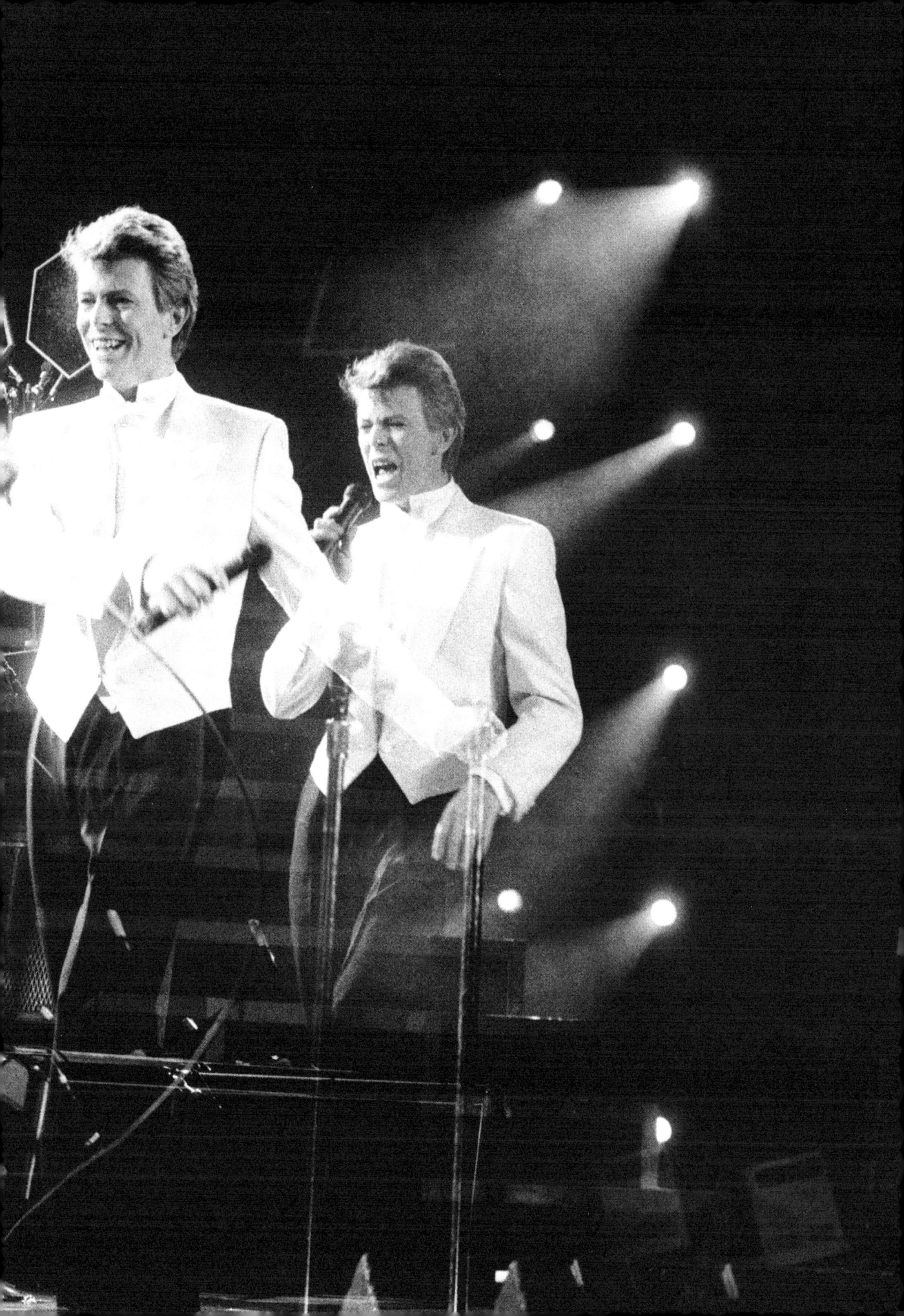

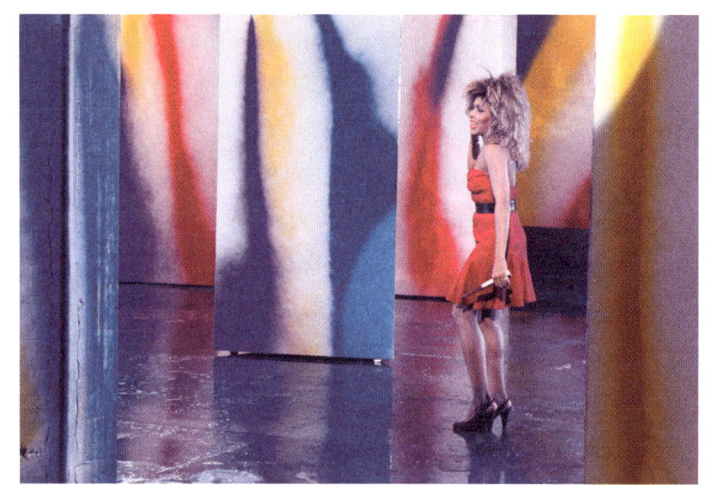

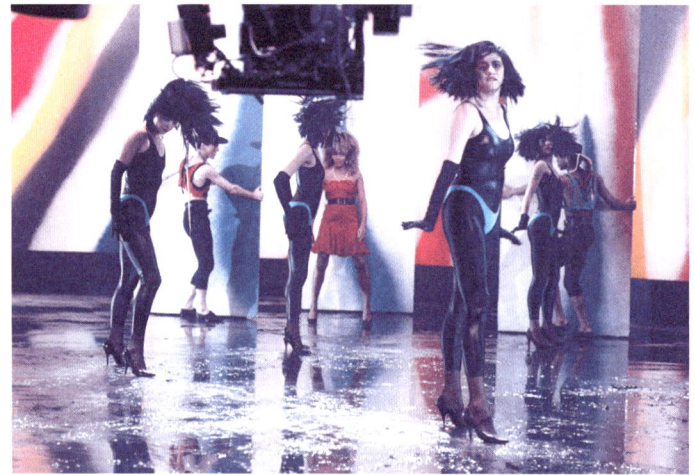

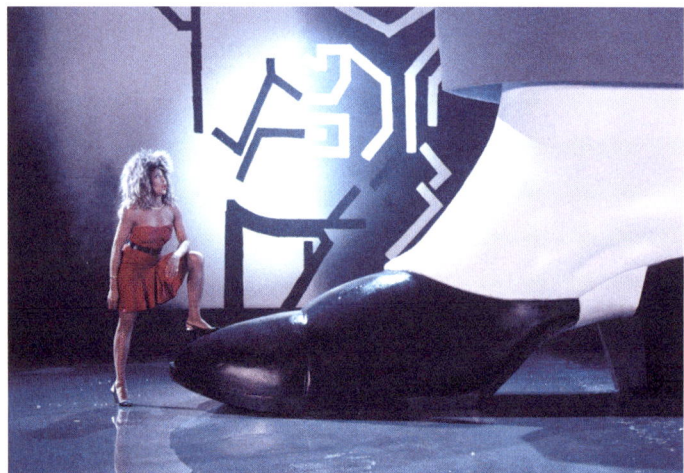

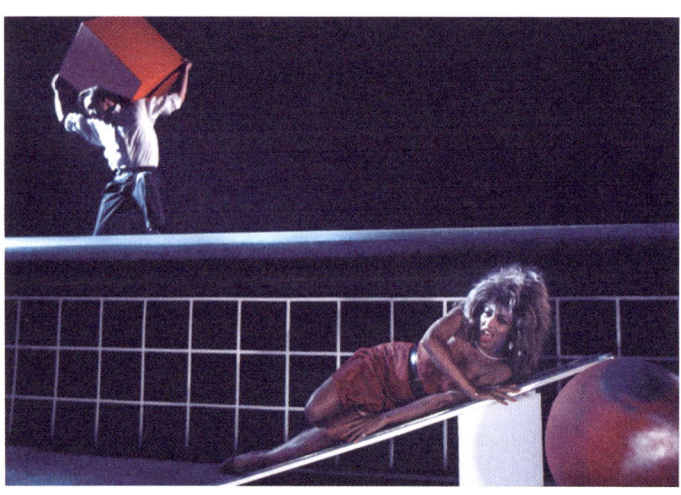

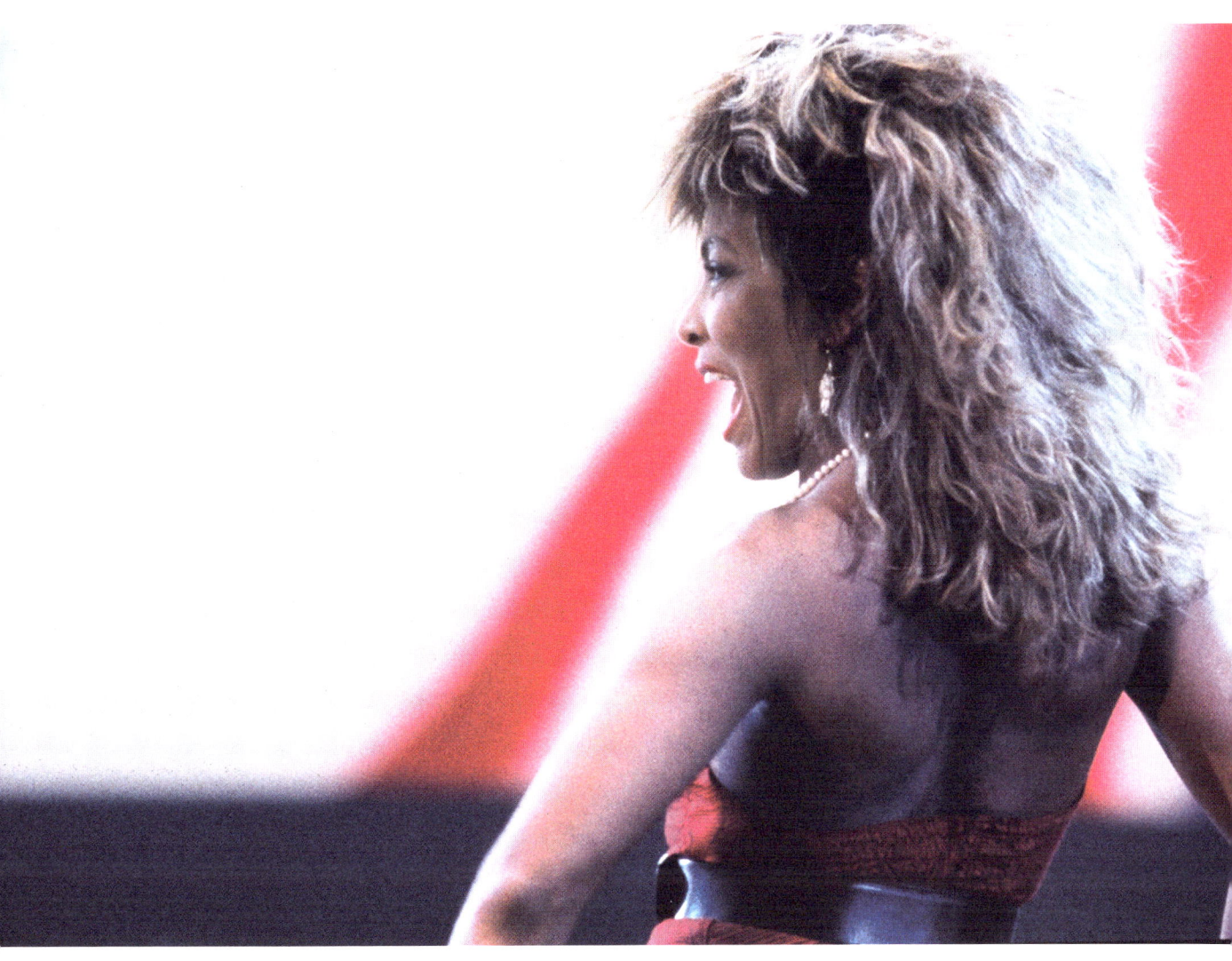

1986
'TYPICAL MALE' video shoot

In 1986, Tina released *Break Every Rule*, her follow-up album to *Private Dancer*. Its lead single, 'Typical Male' – partially thanks to the music video being directed by Brian Grant – reached number two in the US. Tina was perfect for the promotional videos during the MTV boom: a performer since the fifties, she danced her way lightly through the scenarios presented to her straight from the storyboards of the hottest directors. 'It was all the craziness of the big shoot,' Paul says. 'I'd have to take photographs quickly because I didn't want anybody else in the shot. I asked her to do the one where she's strutting across the floor. I love that.'

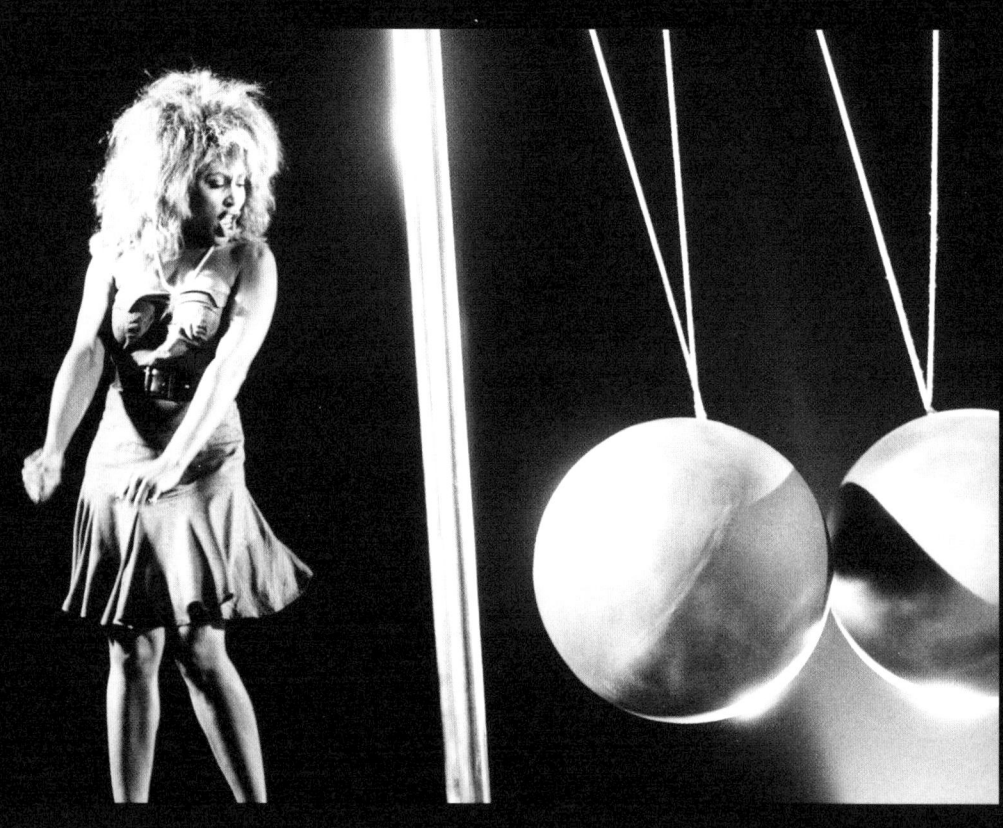

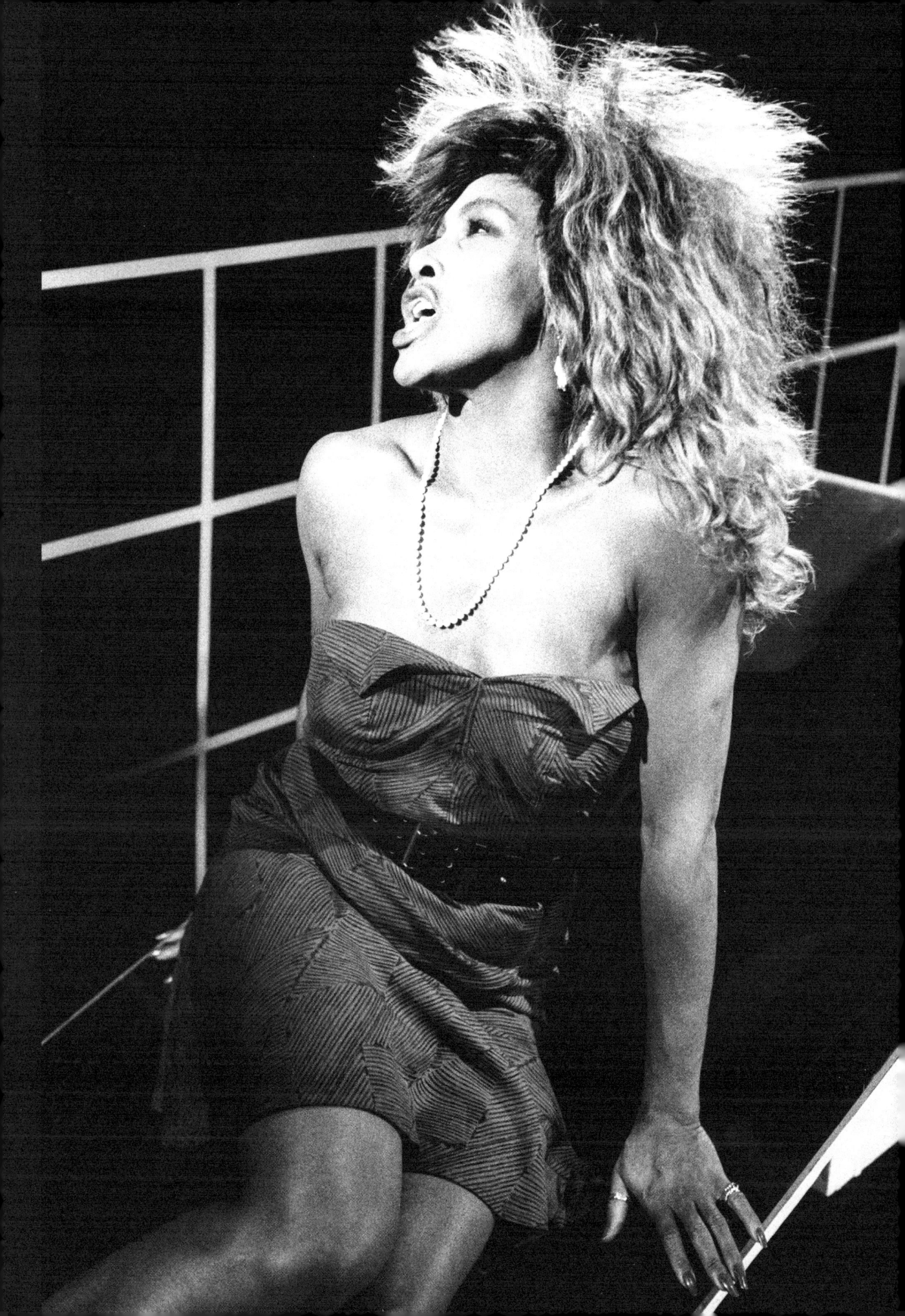

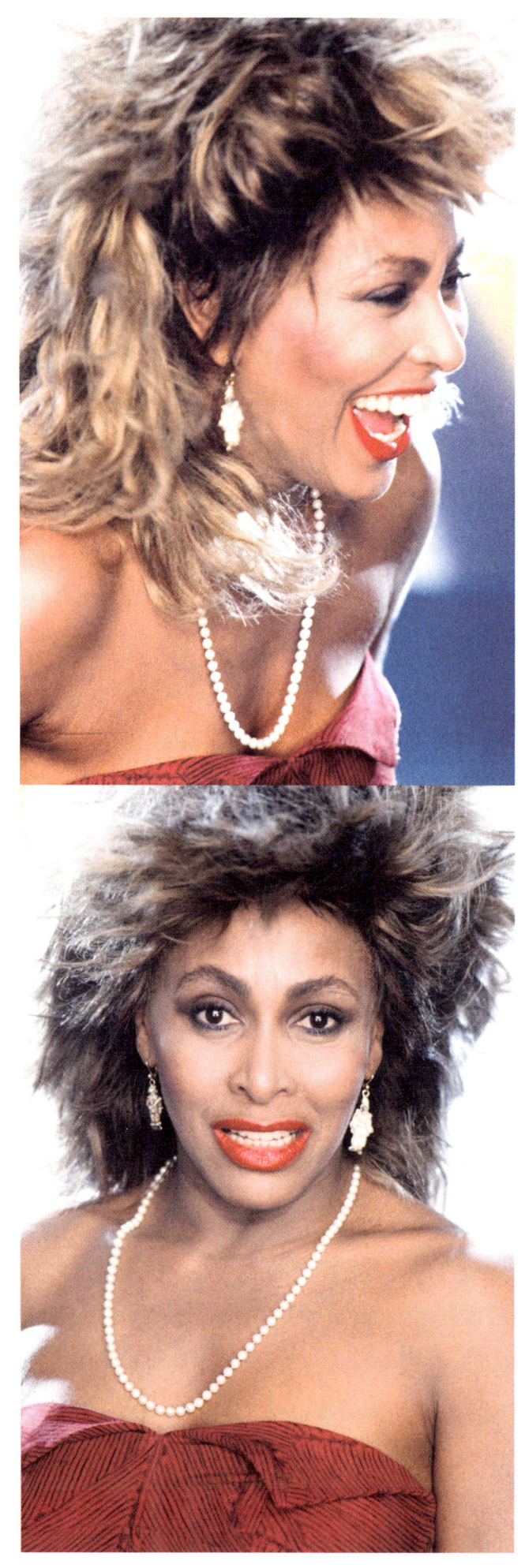

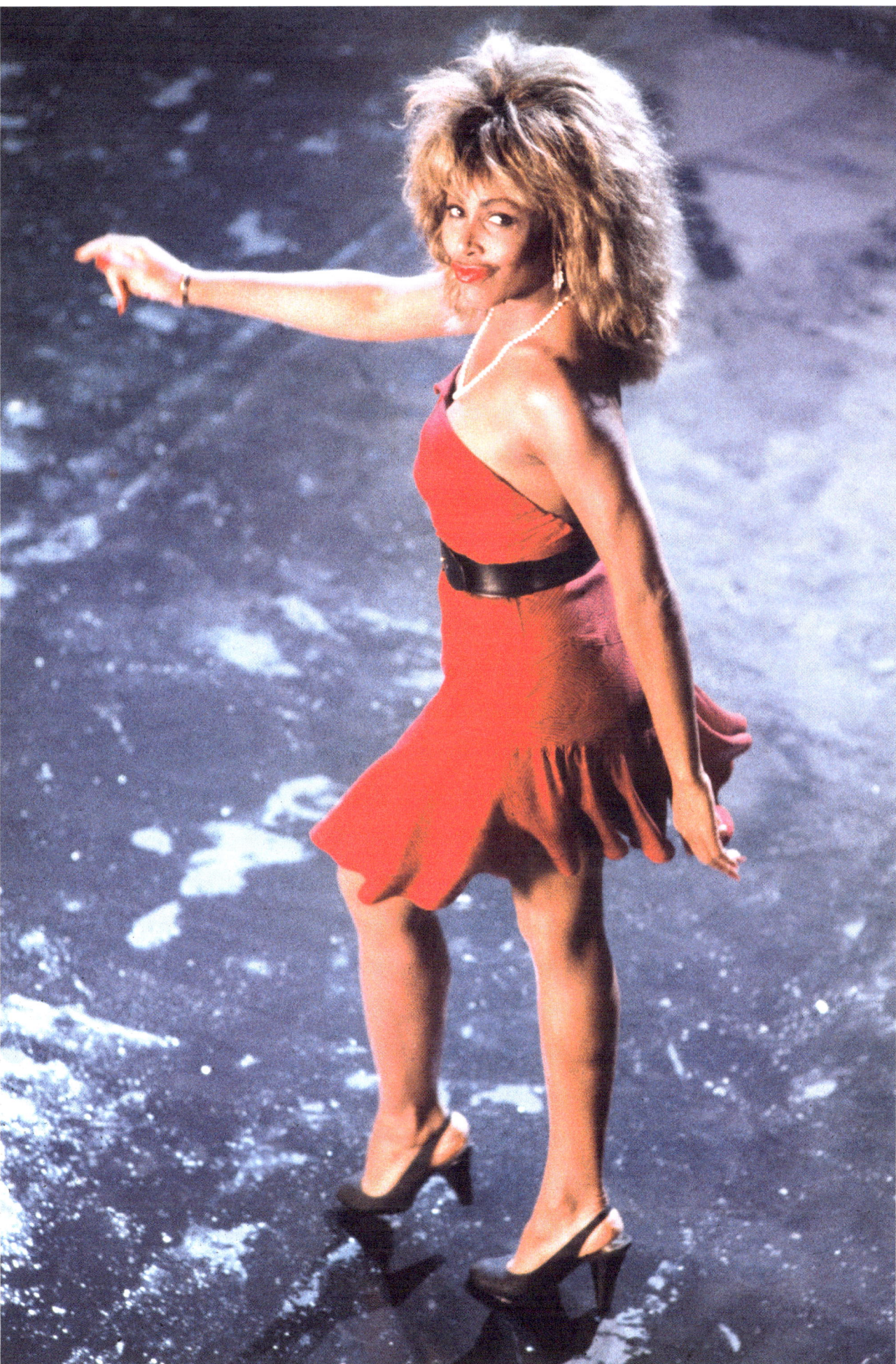

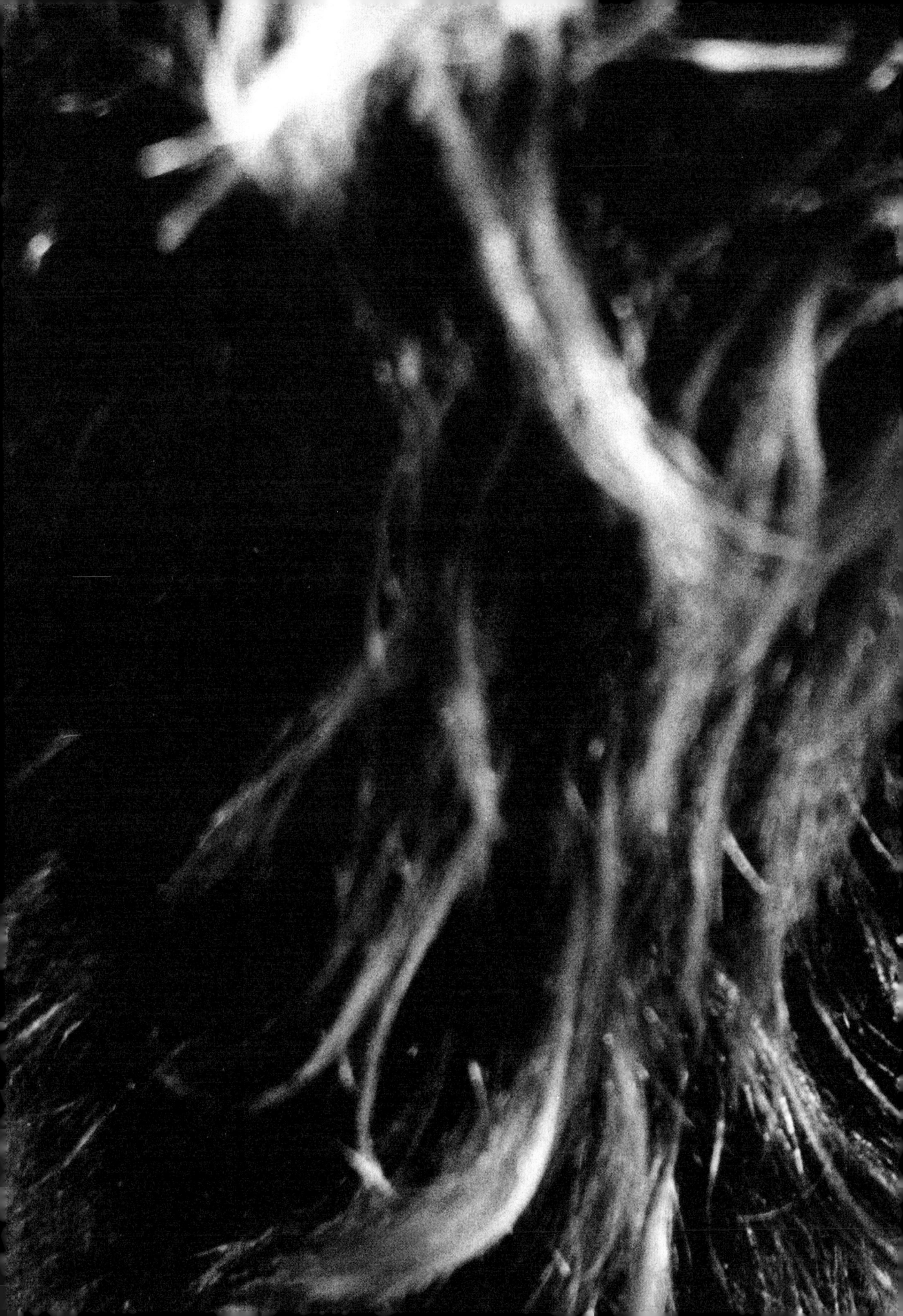

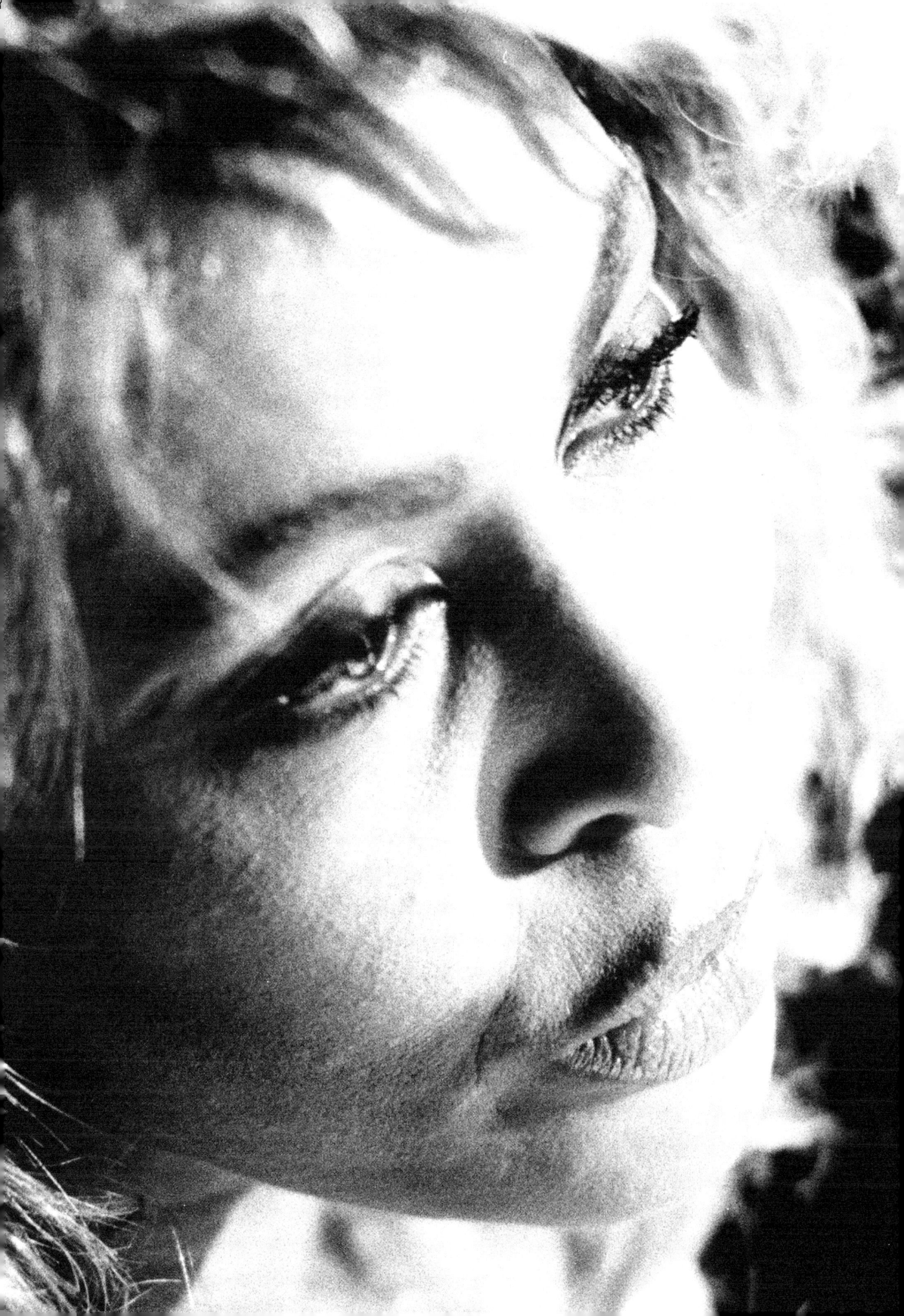

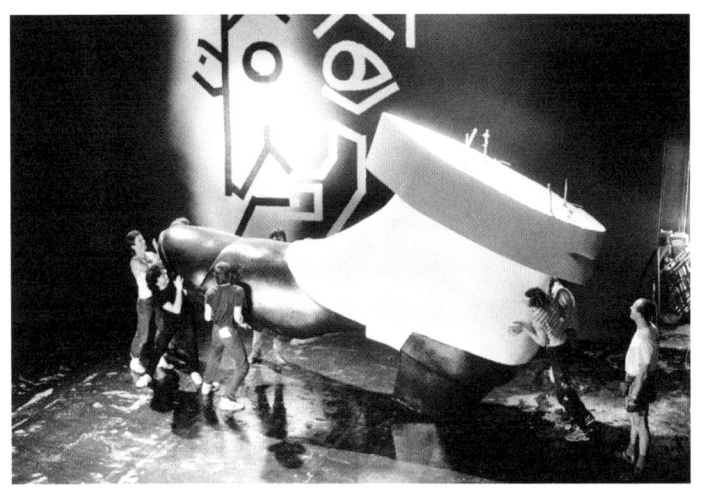

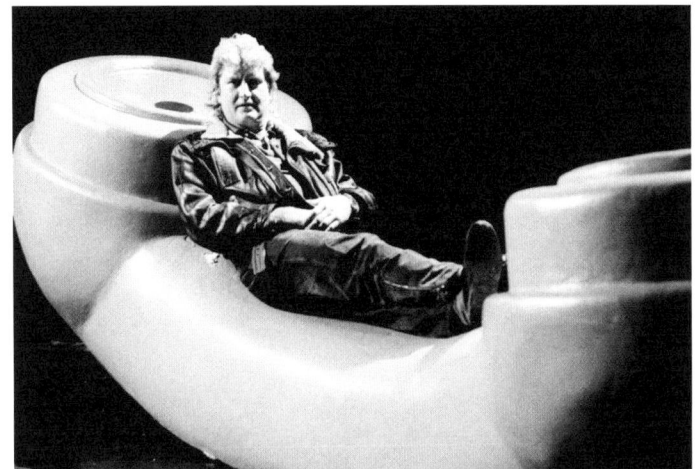

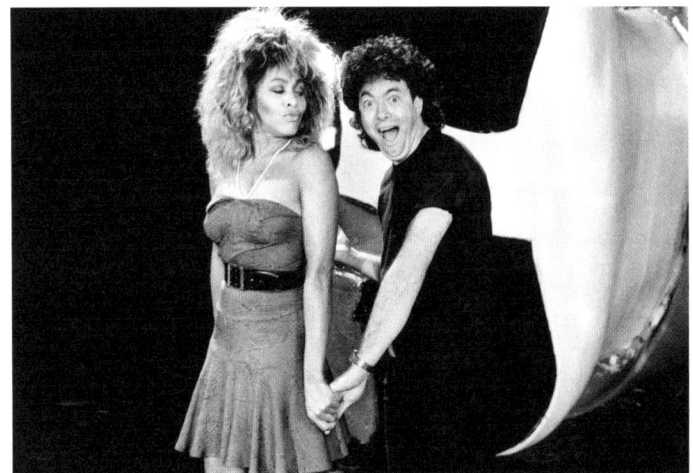

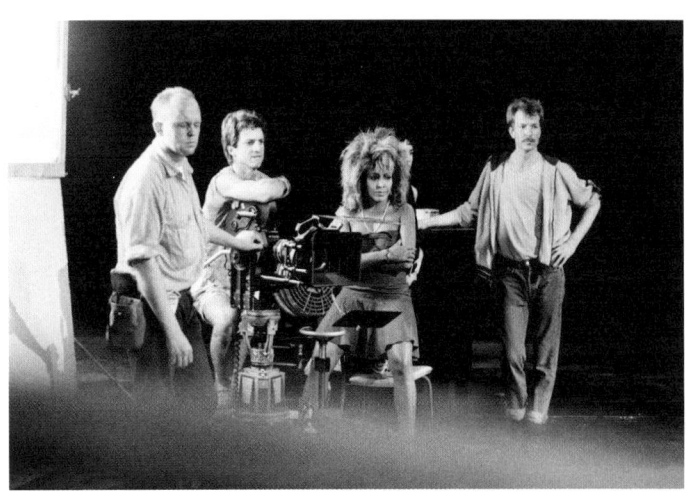

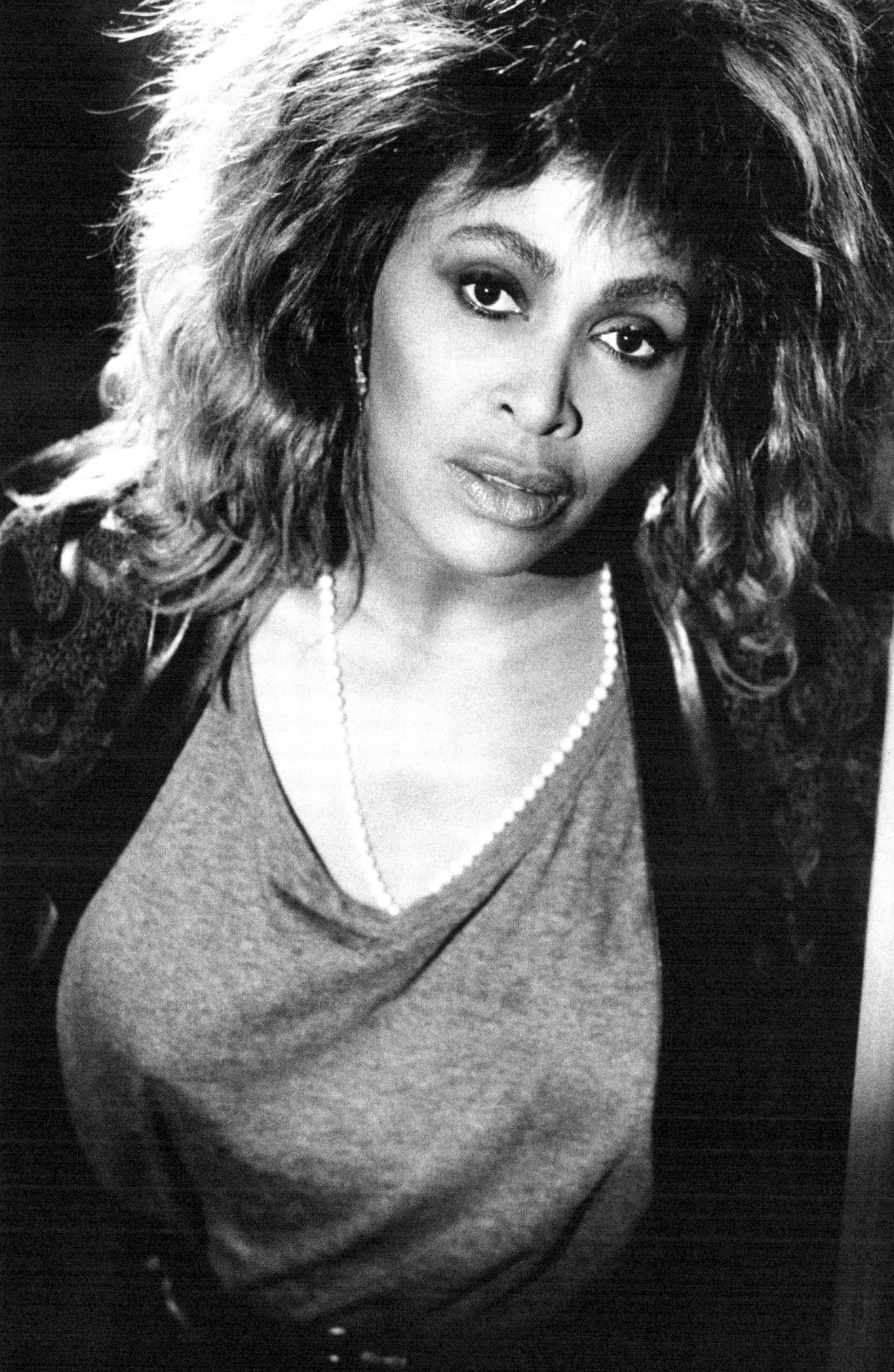

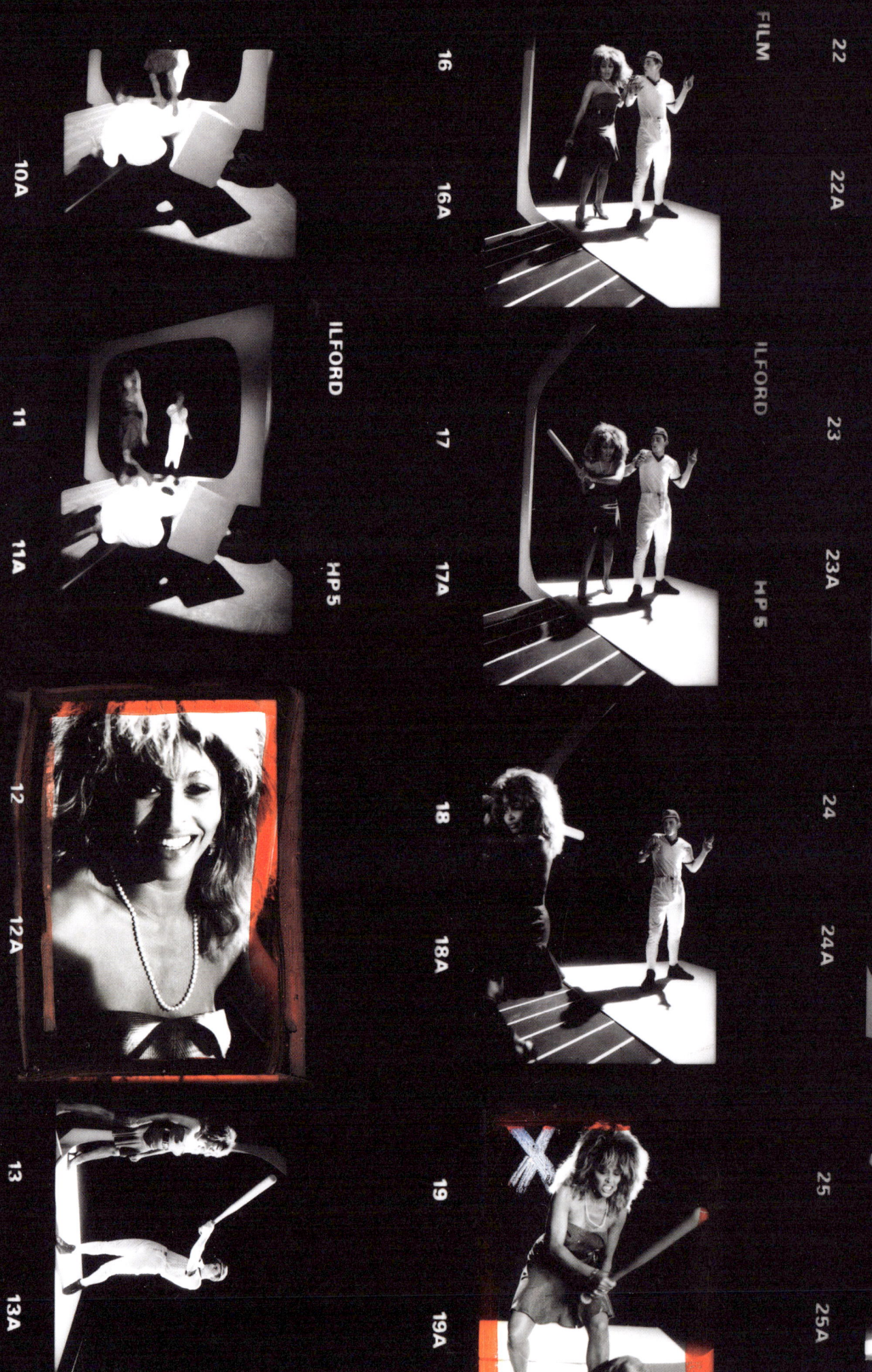

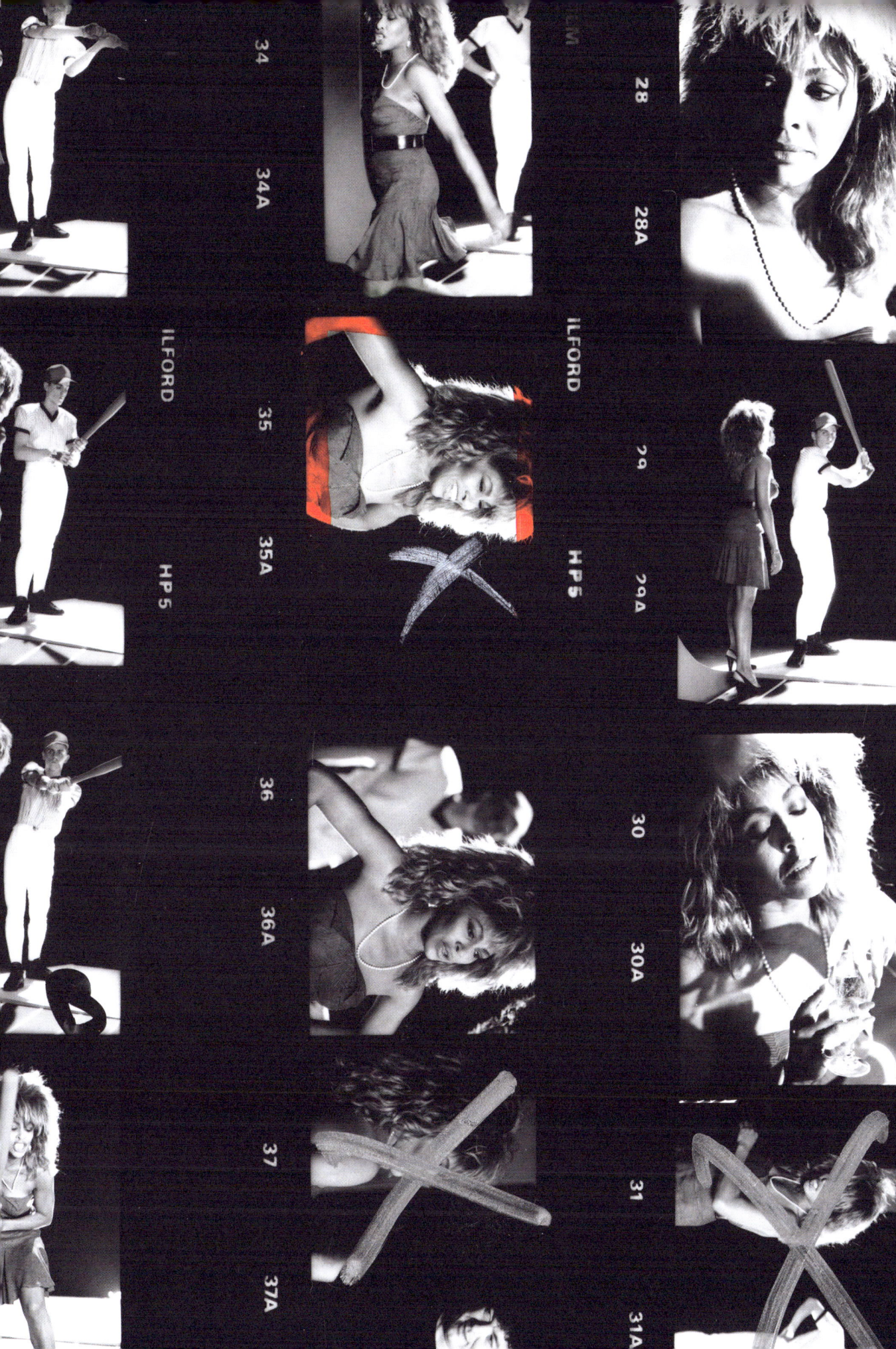

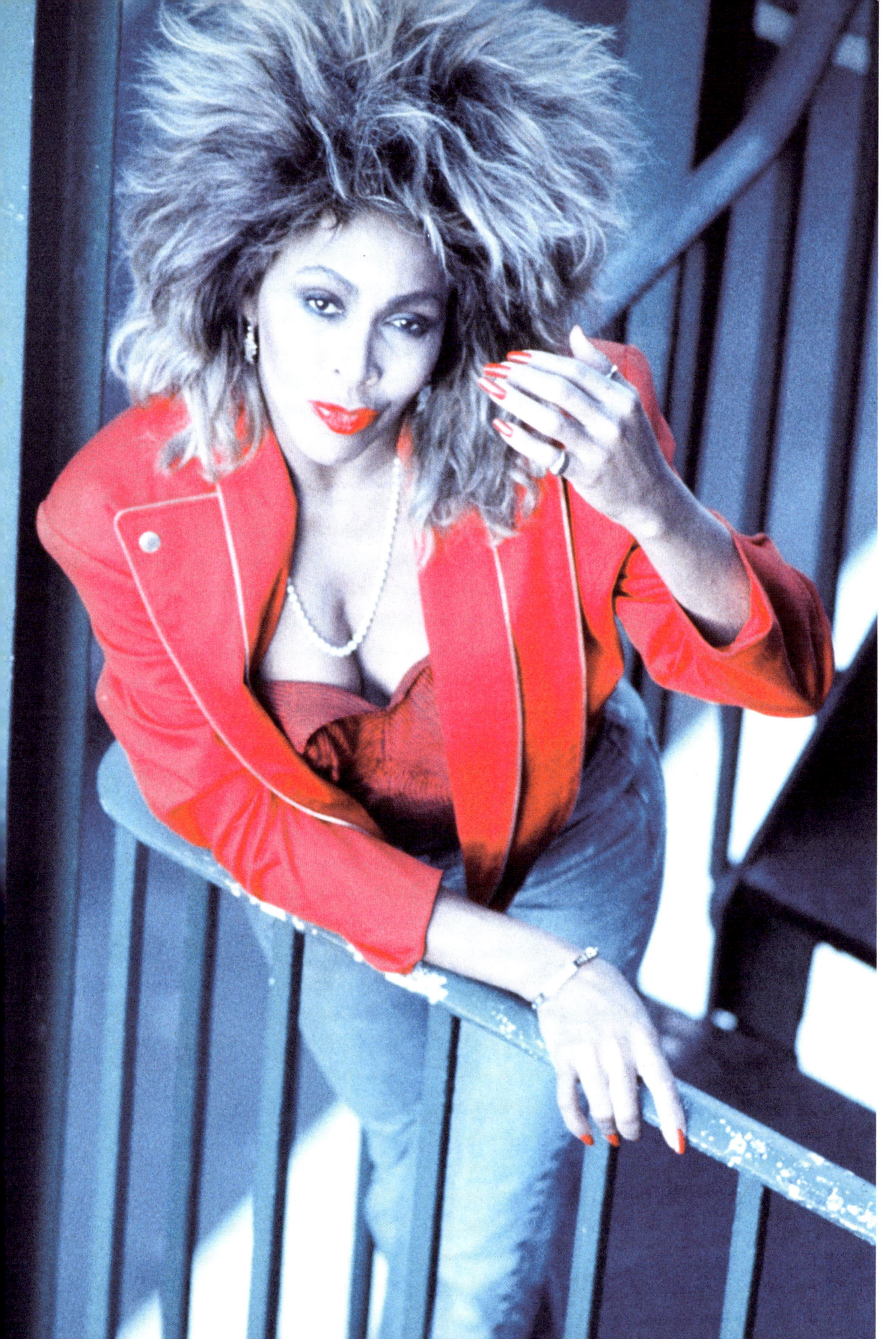

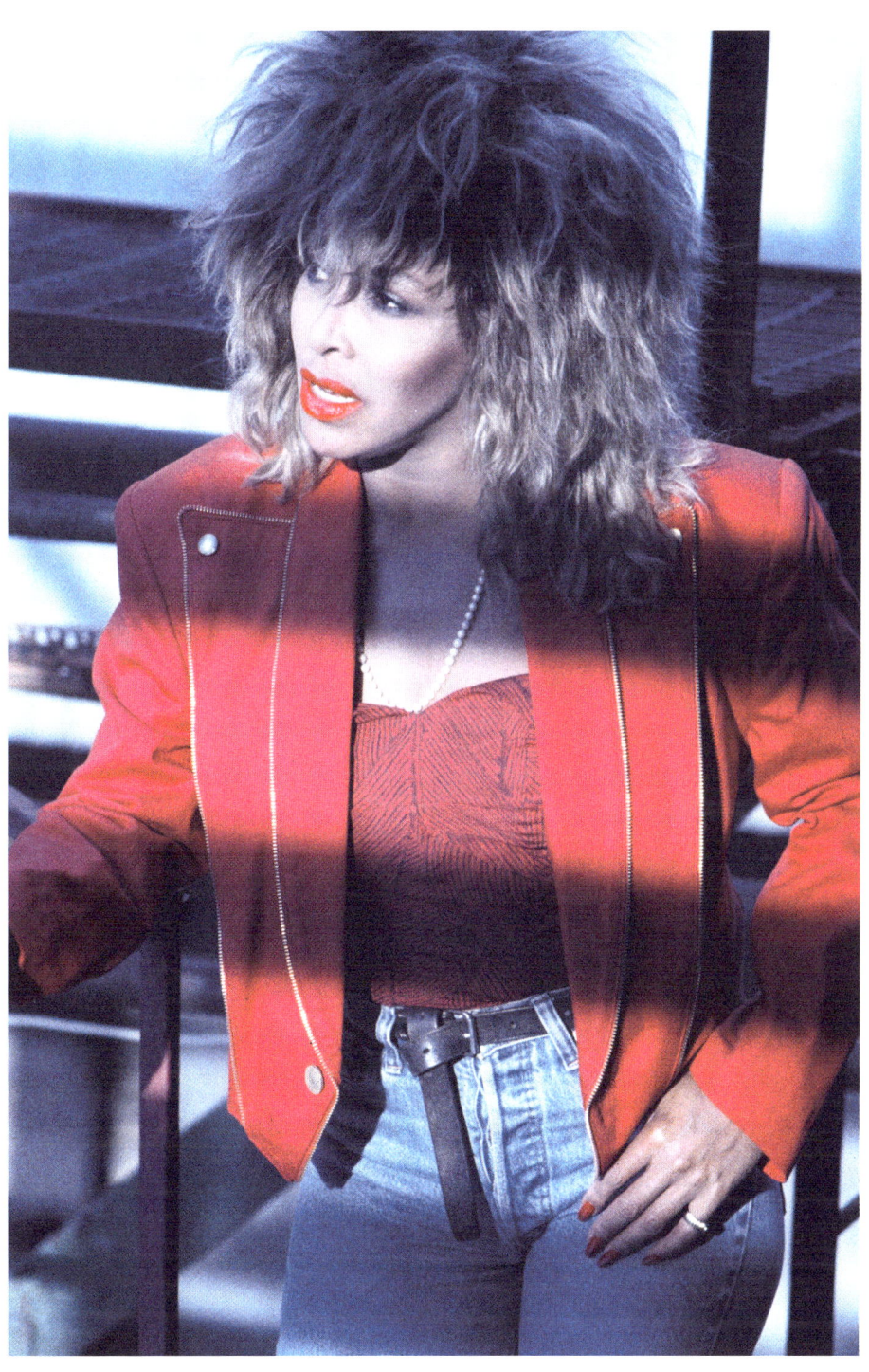

1986

'GIRLS' photo session on video shoot

'Tina would sometimes play up to the camera, it depended
on the situation,' Paul states. 'She was so happy with
what she was doing, but in this black-and-white she
looks solemn, which I actually think is quite nice, because
like everybody, you can't be happy all the time.'

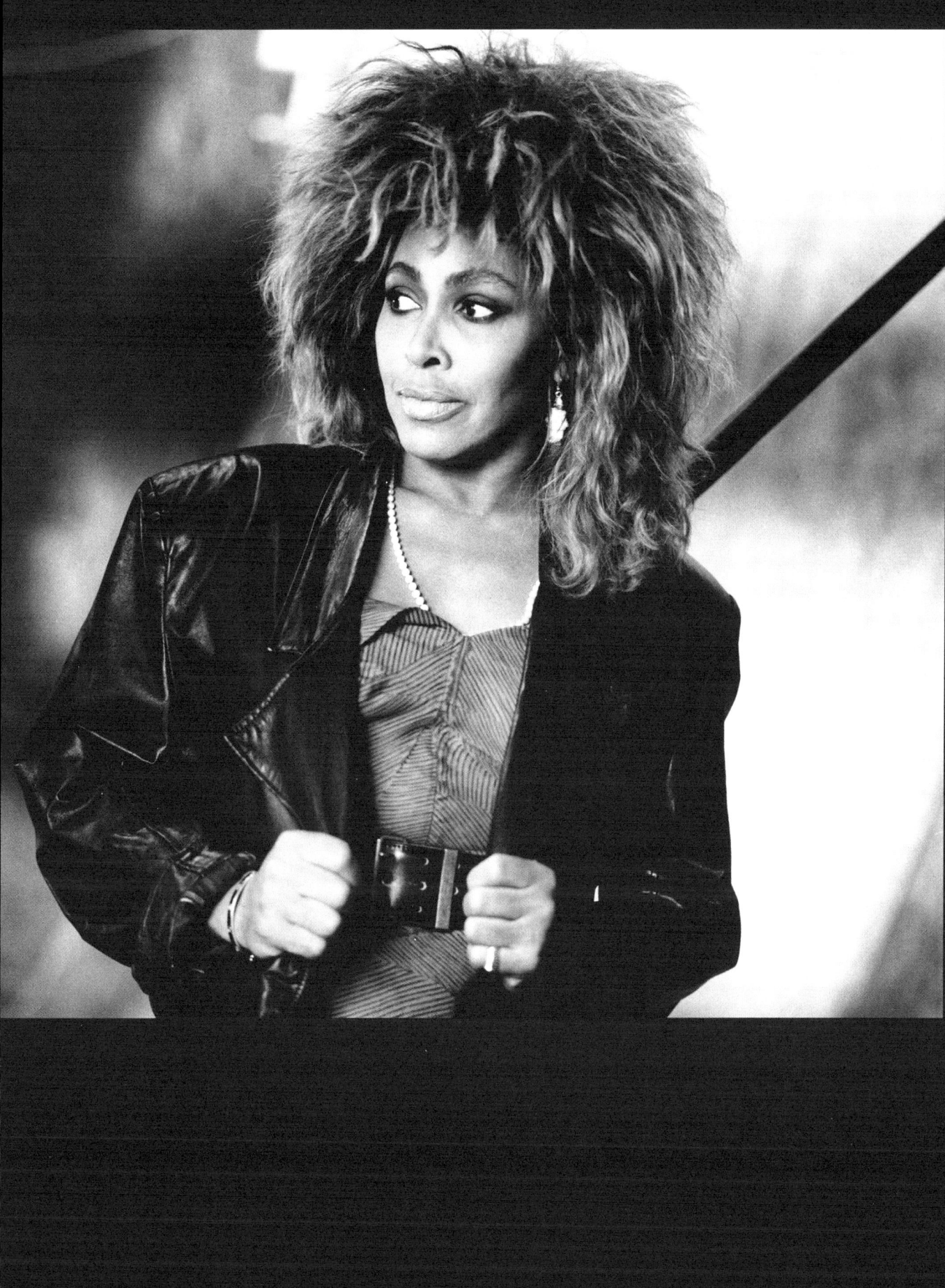

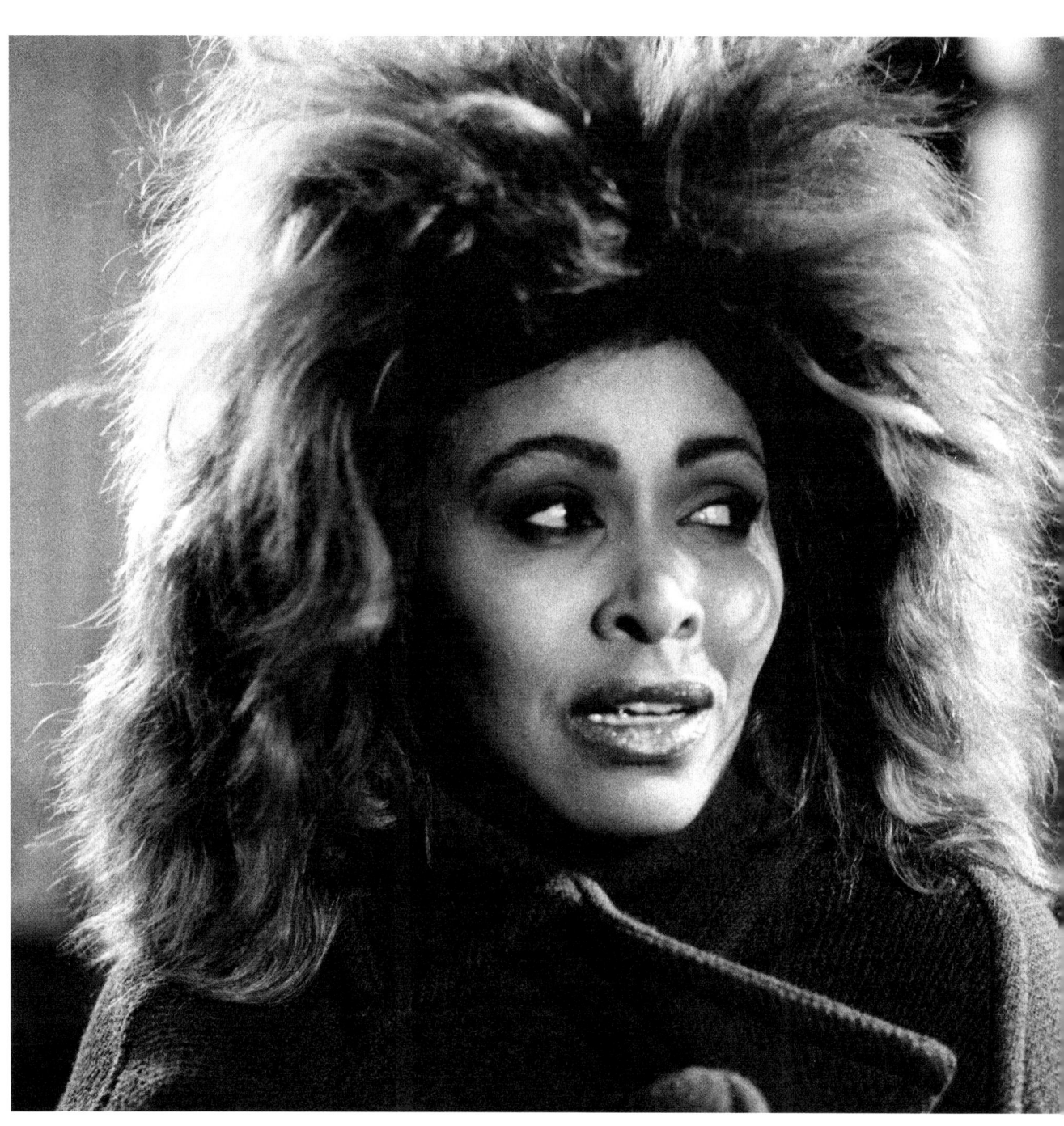

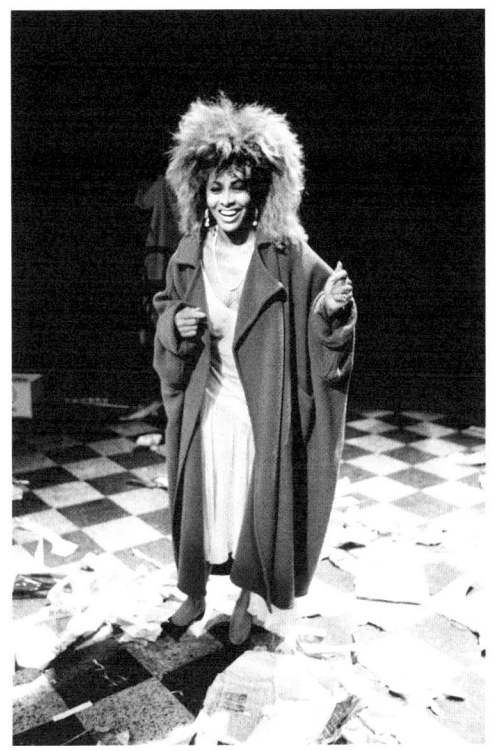

1986

'TWO PEOPLE' **video shoot**

Directed by David Mallet, there were two versions of
the promo for 'Two People', both shot at London's East
India Docks. The first was a typically moody, mid-eighties
narrative: brass beds, wistful looks to camera, pouring
rain. The second, 'Tina's Hollywood Version', was intercut
with Tina dressing as movie icons. Paul: 'They had a rain
machine and so she's soaked, in a phone box with really
wet hair. The lighting team had brollies, yet she was getting
drenched. She was a trooper. I love the night shot [the
black-and-white of which was used for the single sleeve].
She took a bit of persuading, but I knew that it was a great
picture. It literally took two minutes.'

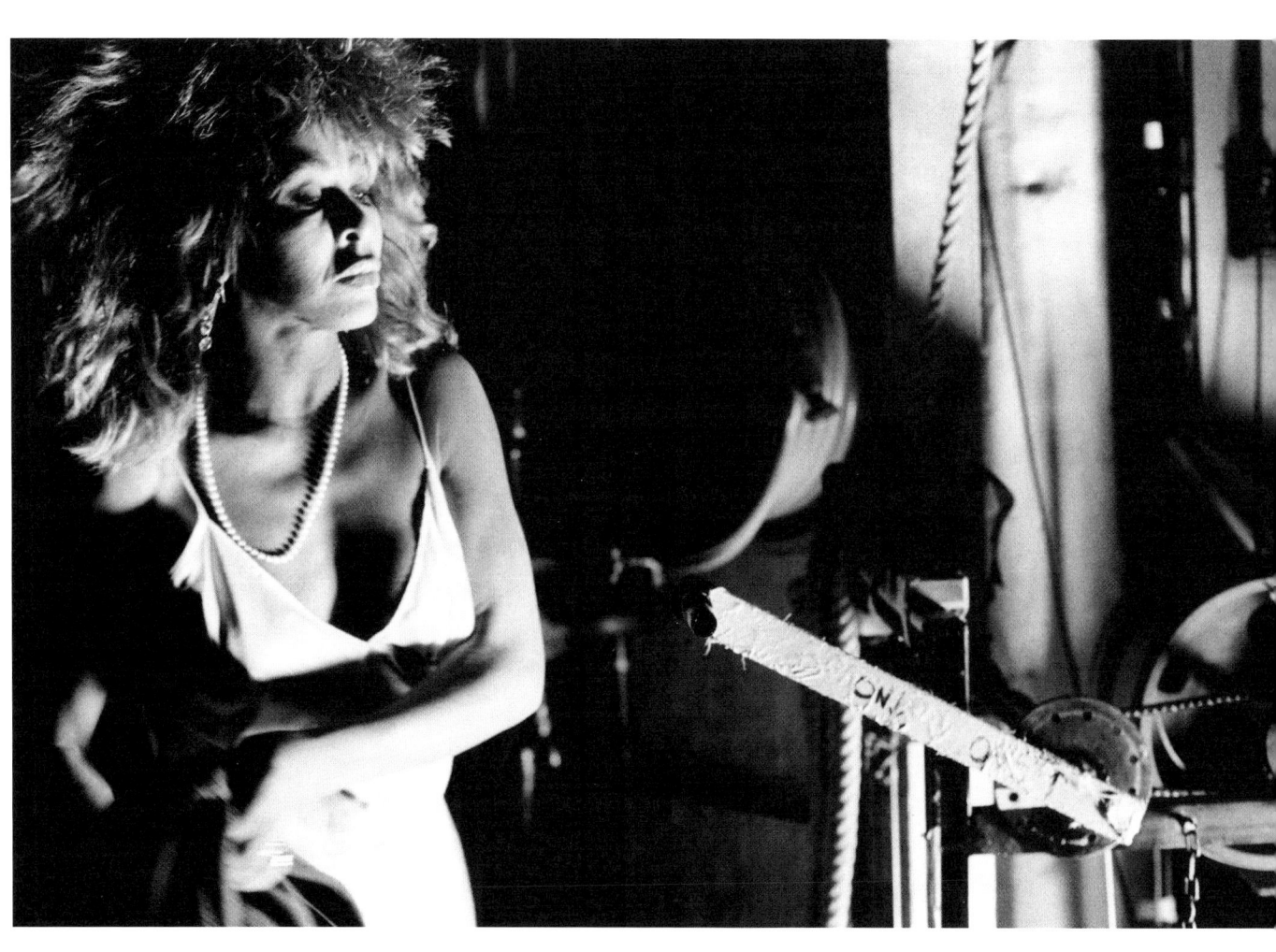

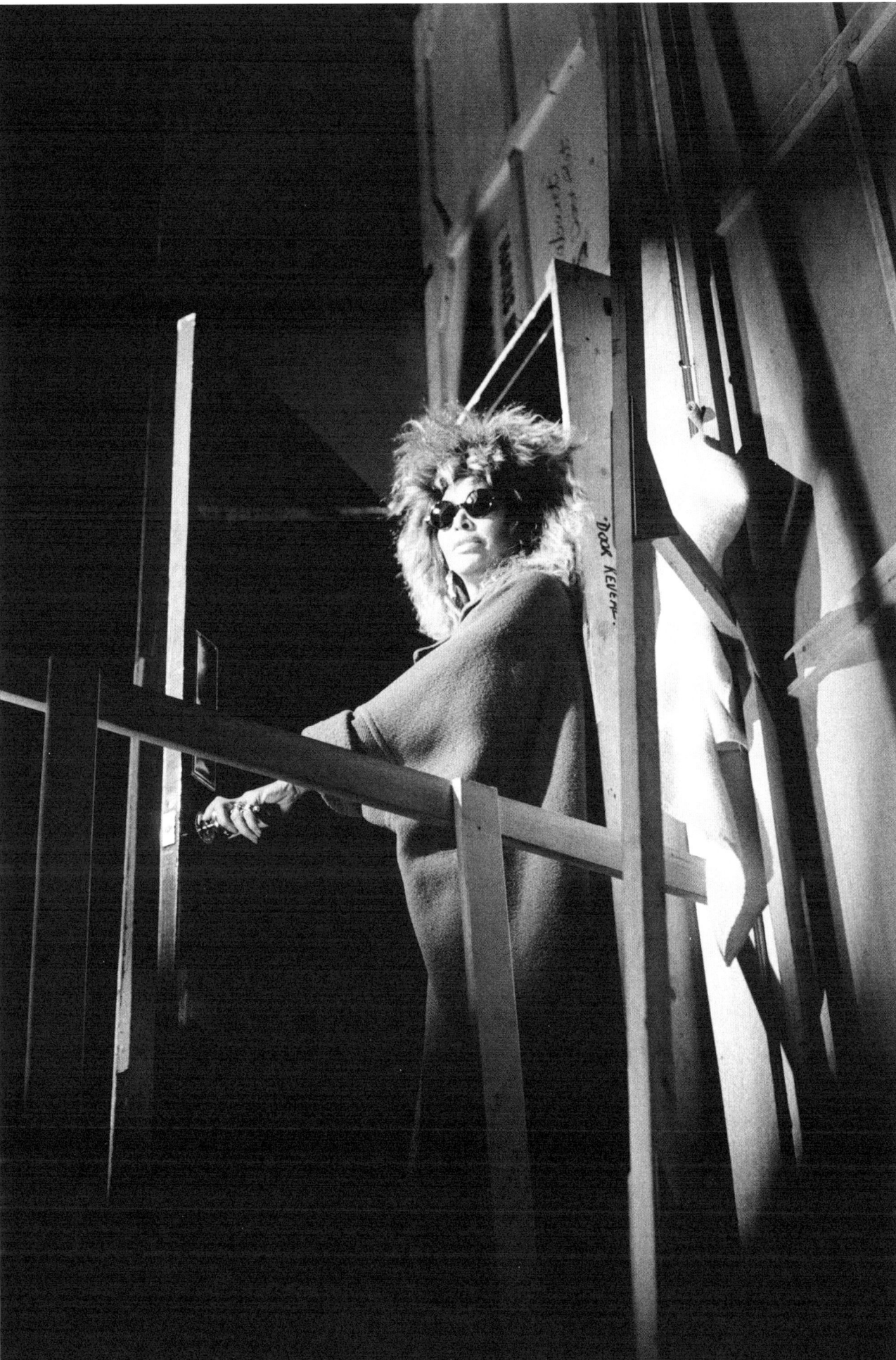

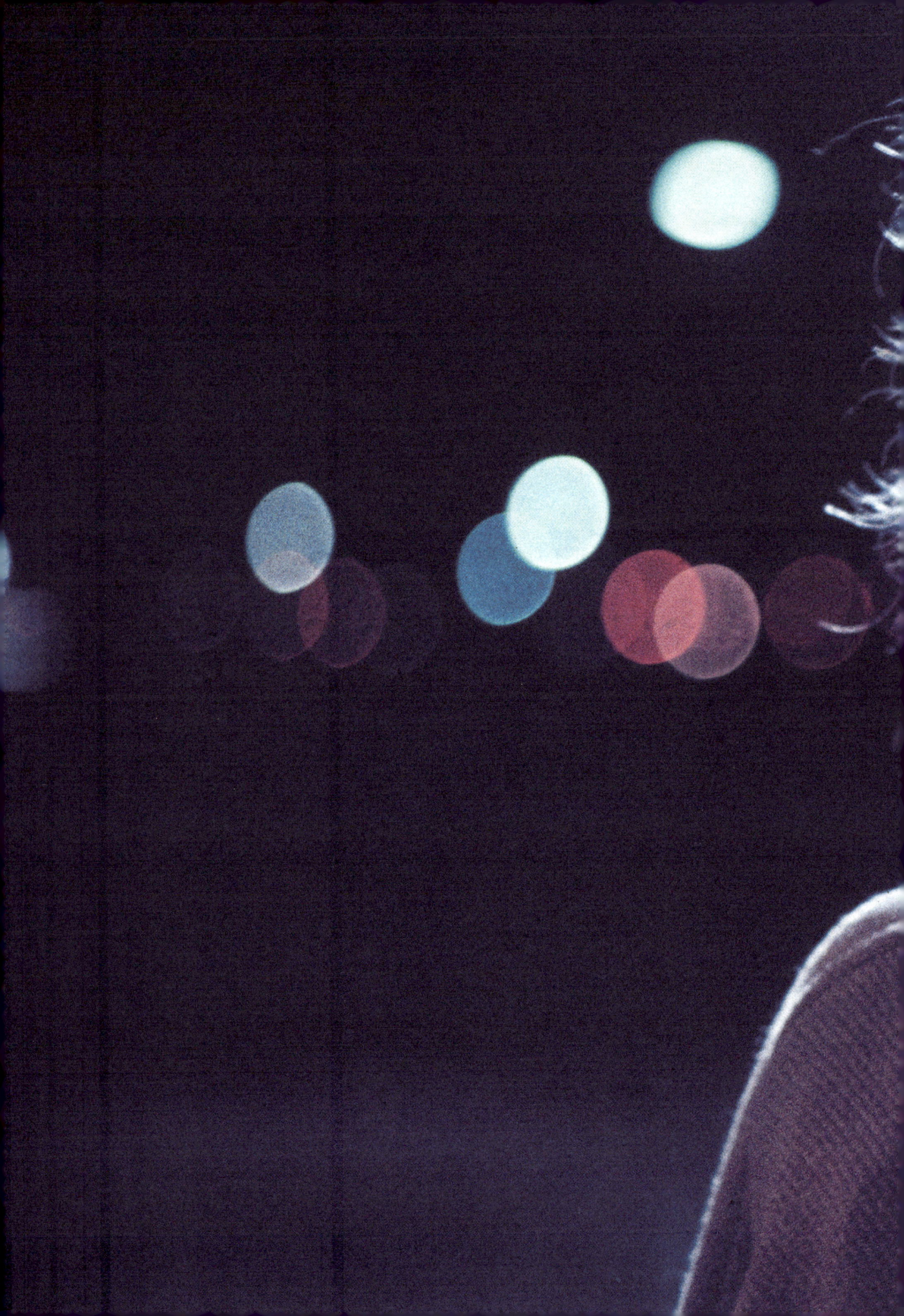

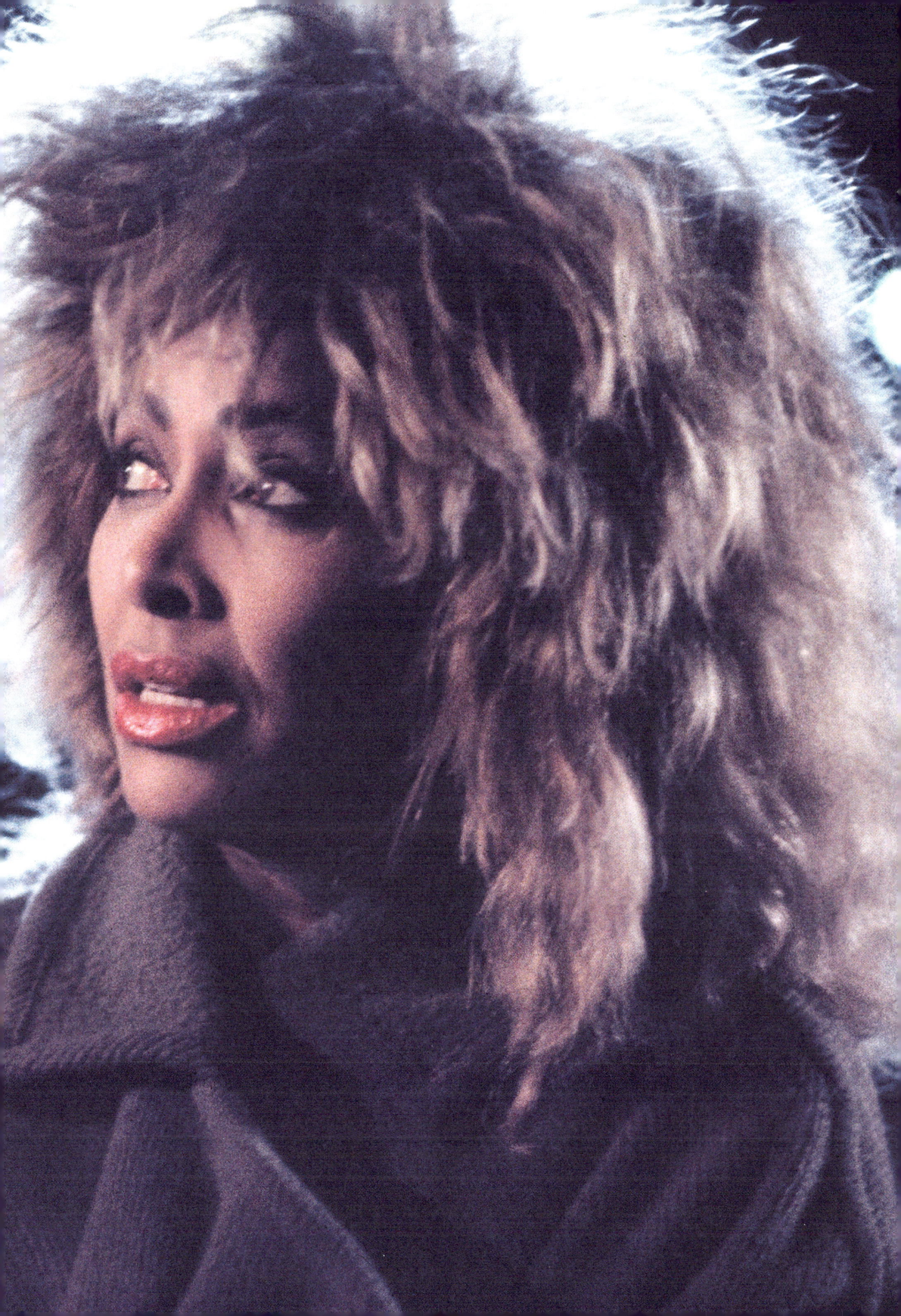

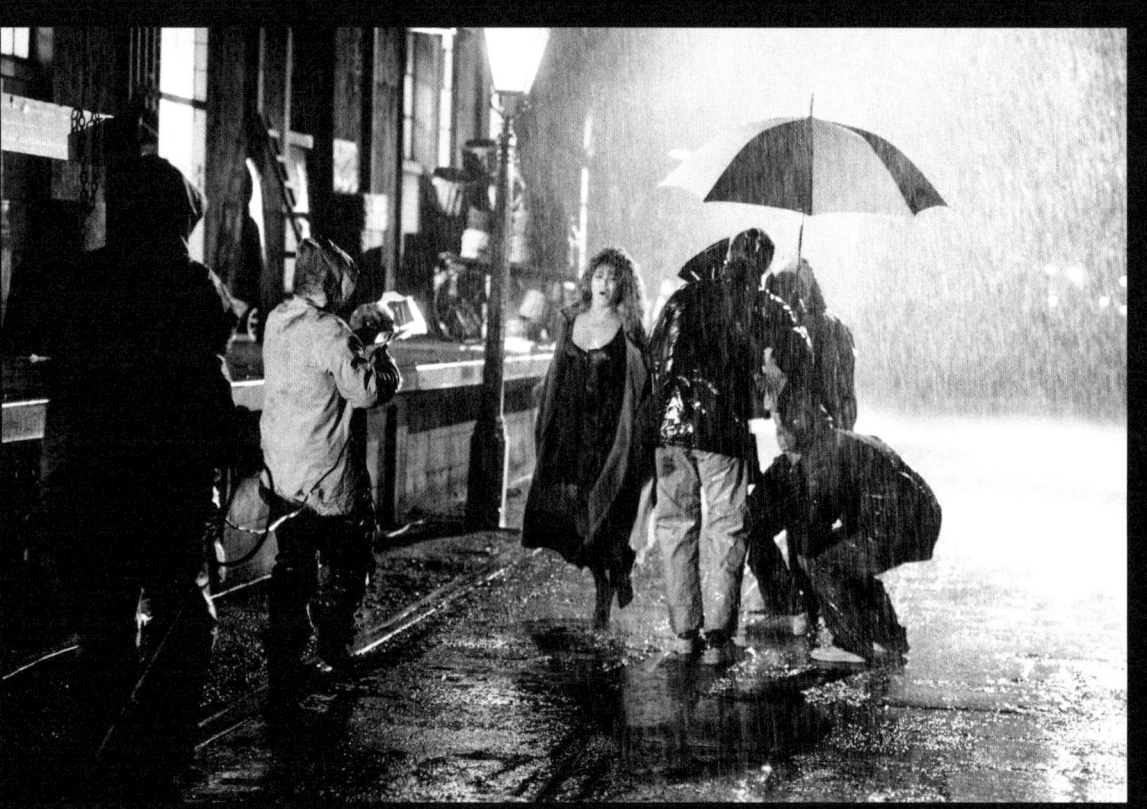

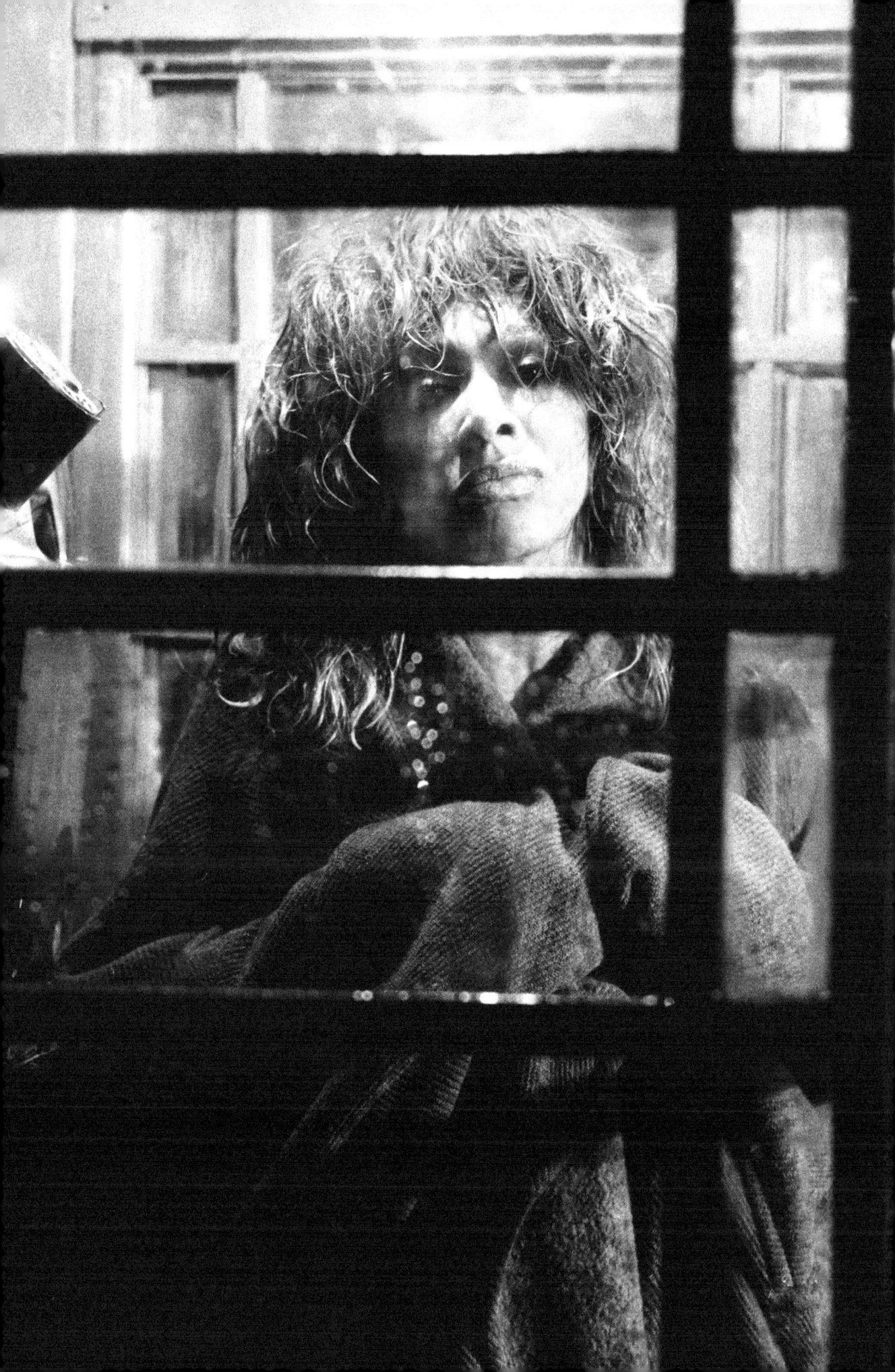

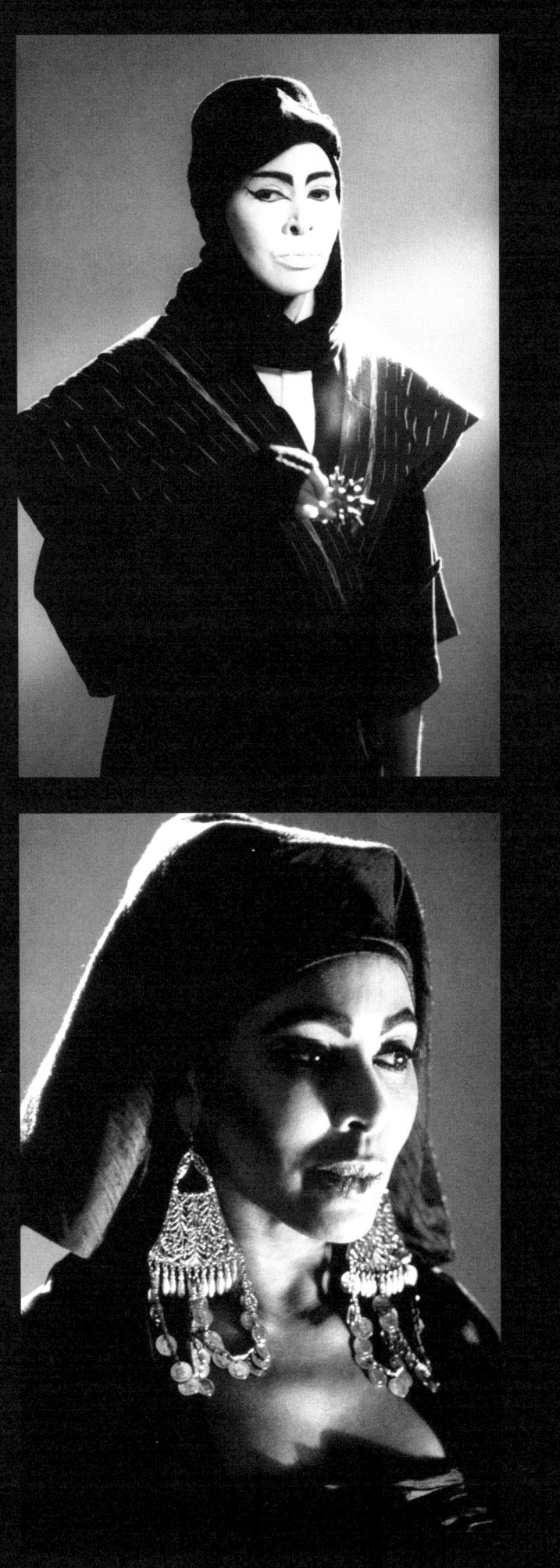

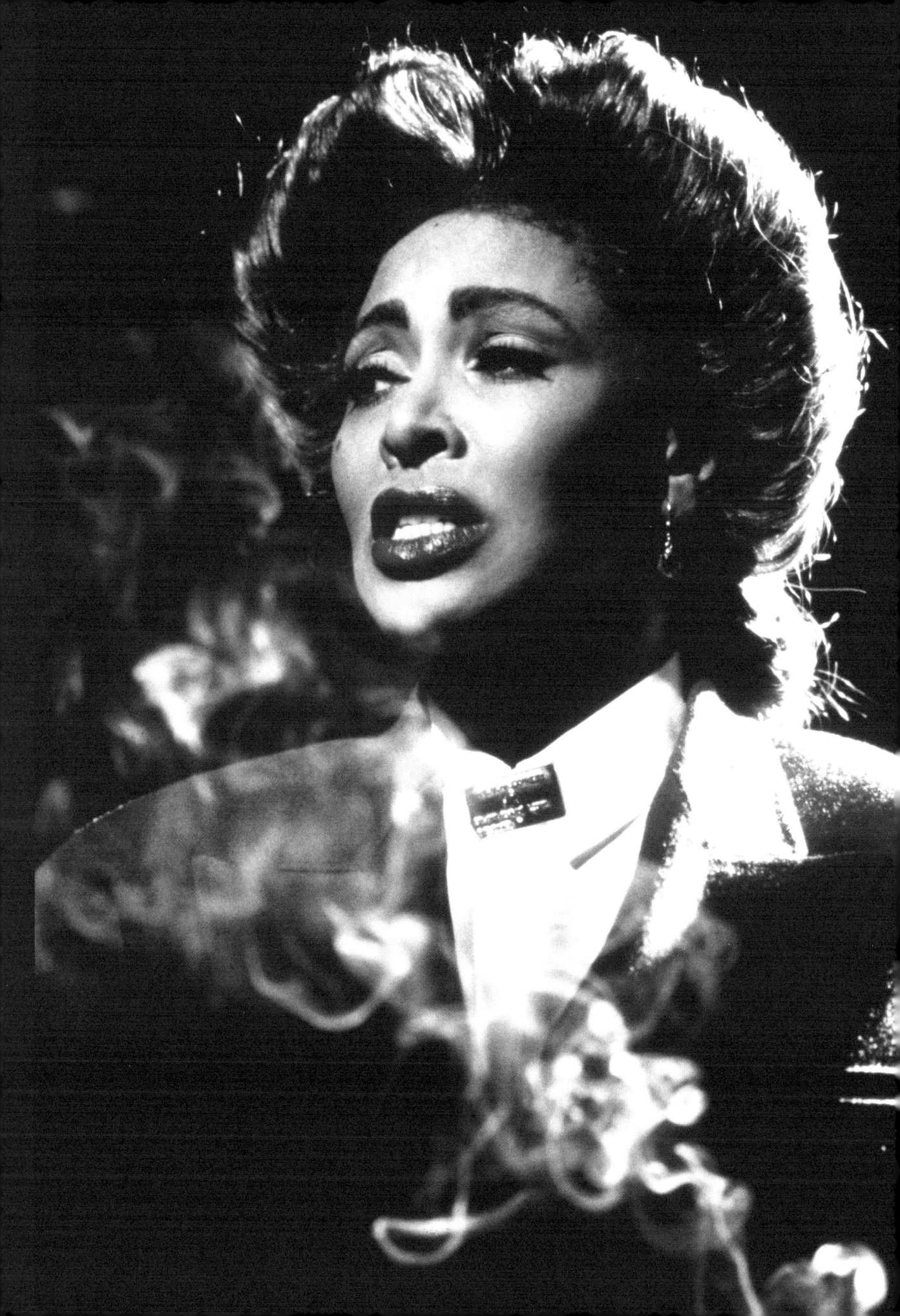

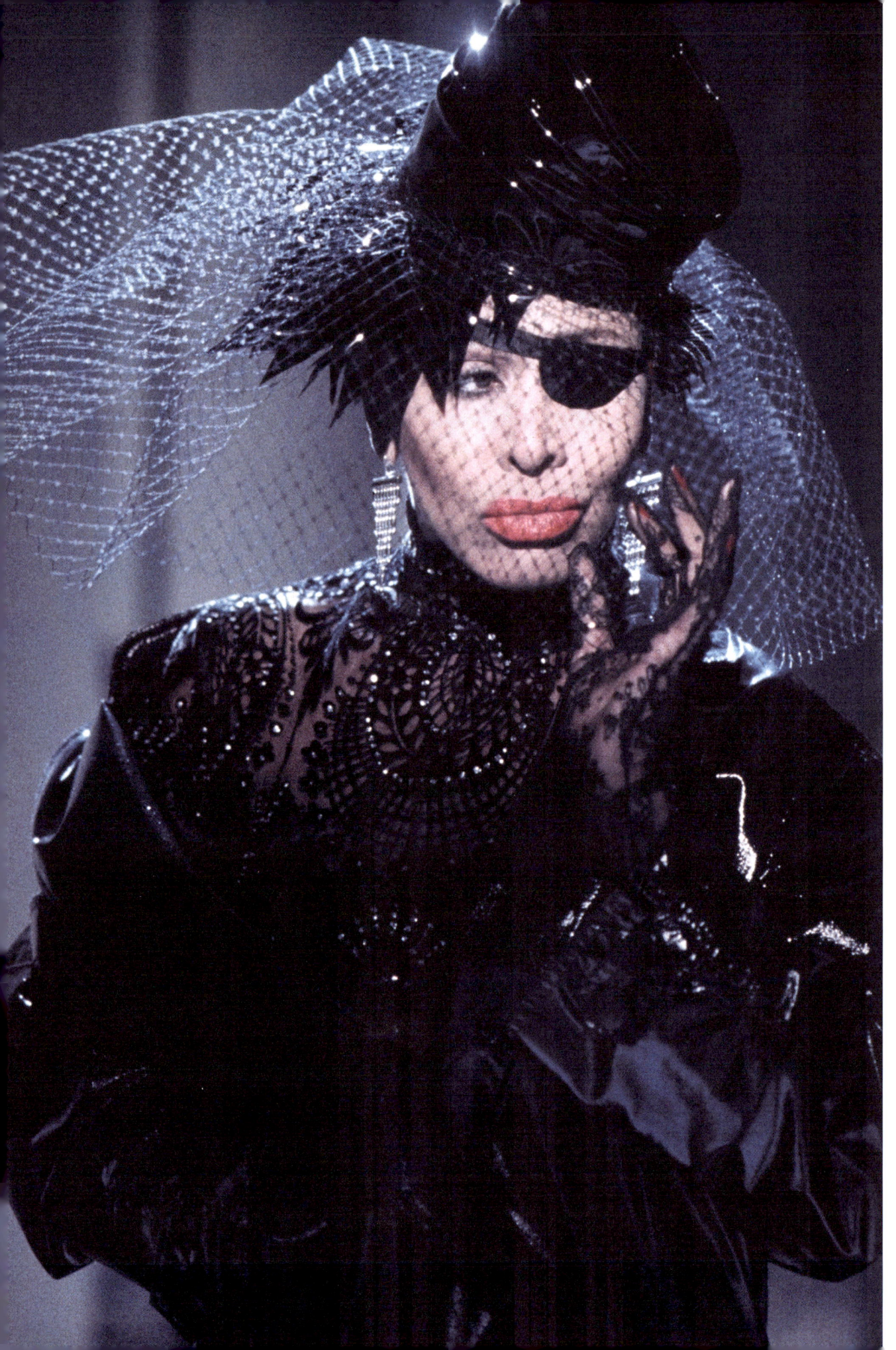

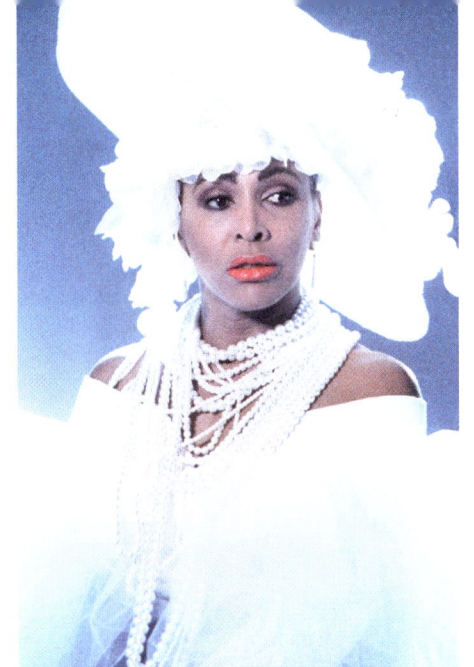

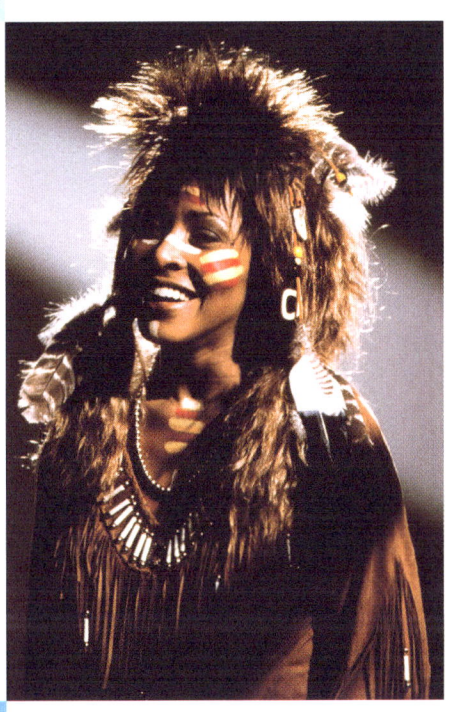

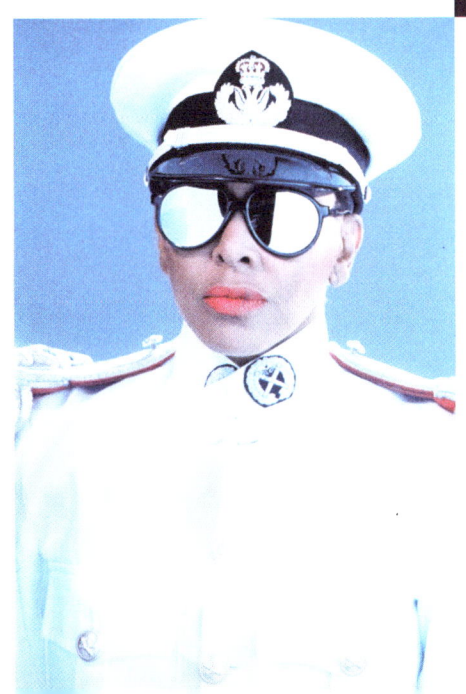

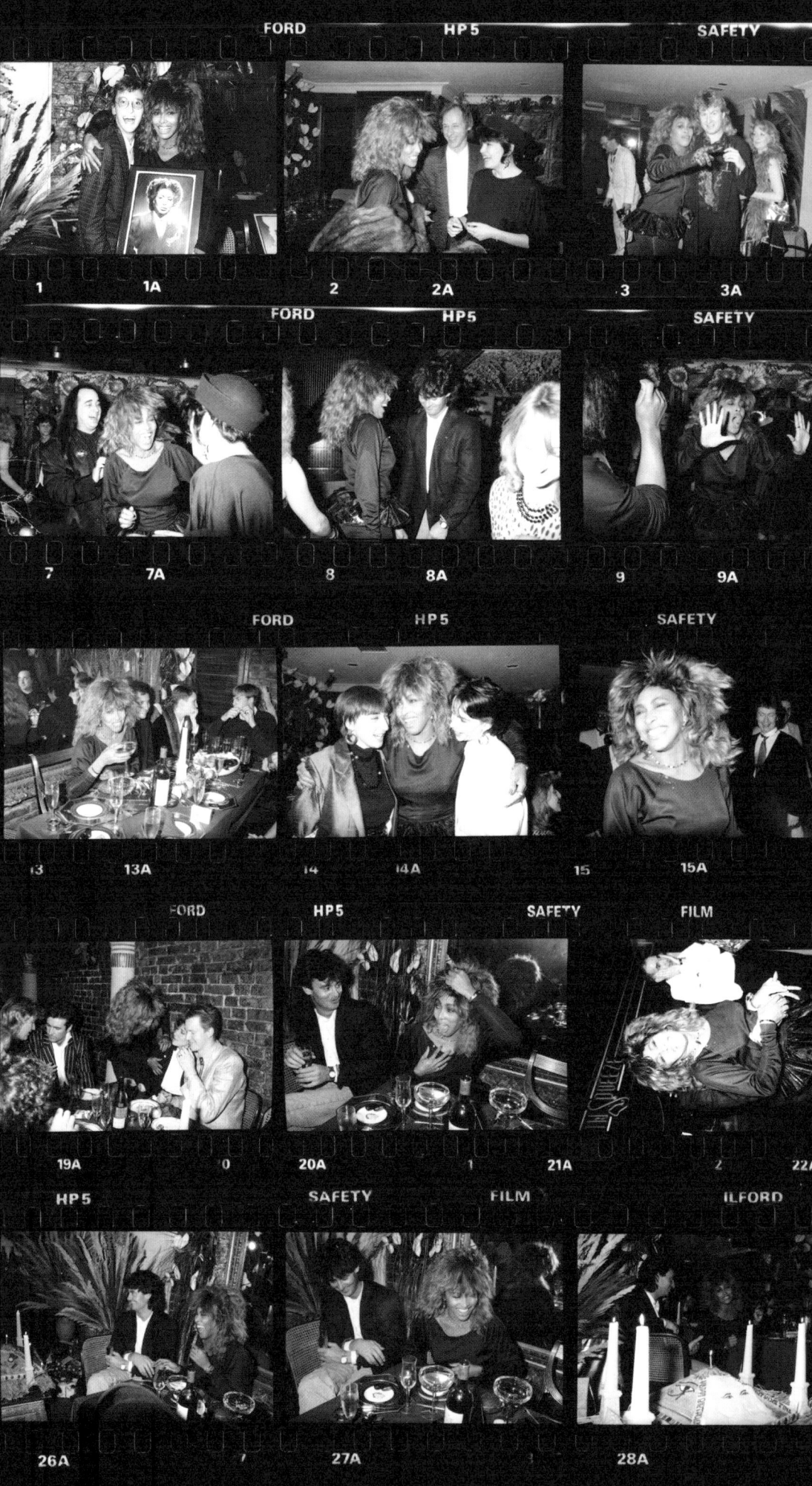

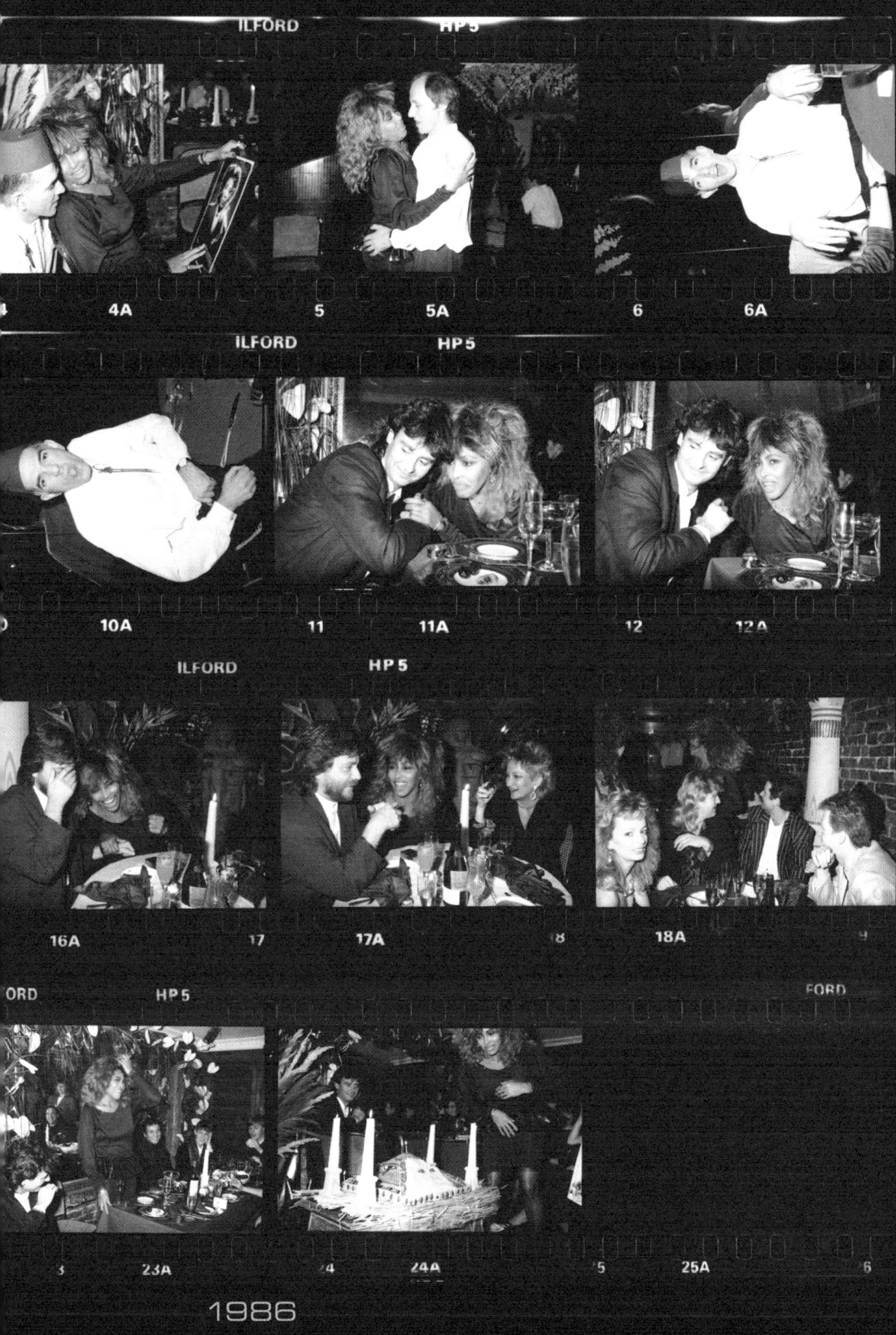

1986
BIRTHDAY PARTY contact sheet

'We went to the Main Squeeze on Kings Road for her birthday,' Paul says. 'I'd taken a black-and-white photo of her as Marlene Dietrich, [from the Hollywood 'Two People' video] had it framed and gave it to her as a birthday present. There's a picture of us together – no one recognises me because of the long hair I had back then. It was one the first nights when she was with her husband-to-be, Erwin Bach, and there are pictures of them together. Mark Knopfler's having a dance with Tina and Bernard Doherty, her PR, is wearing a fez as it was an Egyptian-themed party [as can be seen from the splendid pyramid cake, contact bottom-right].'

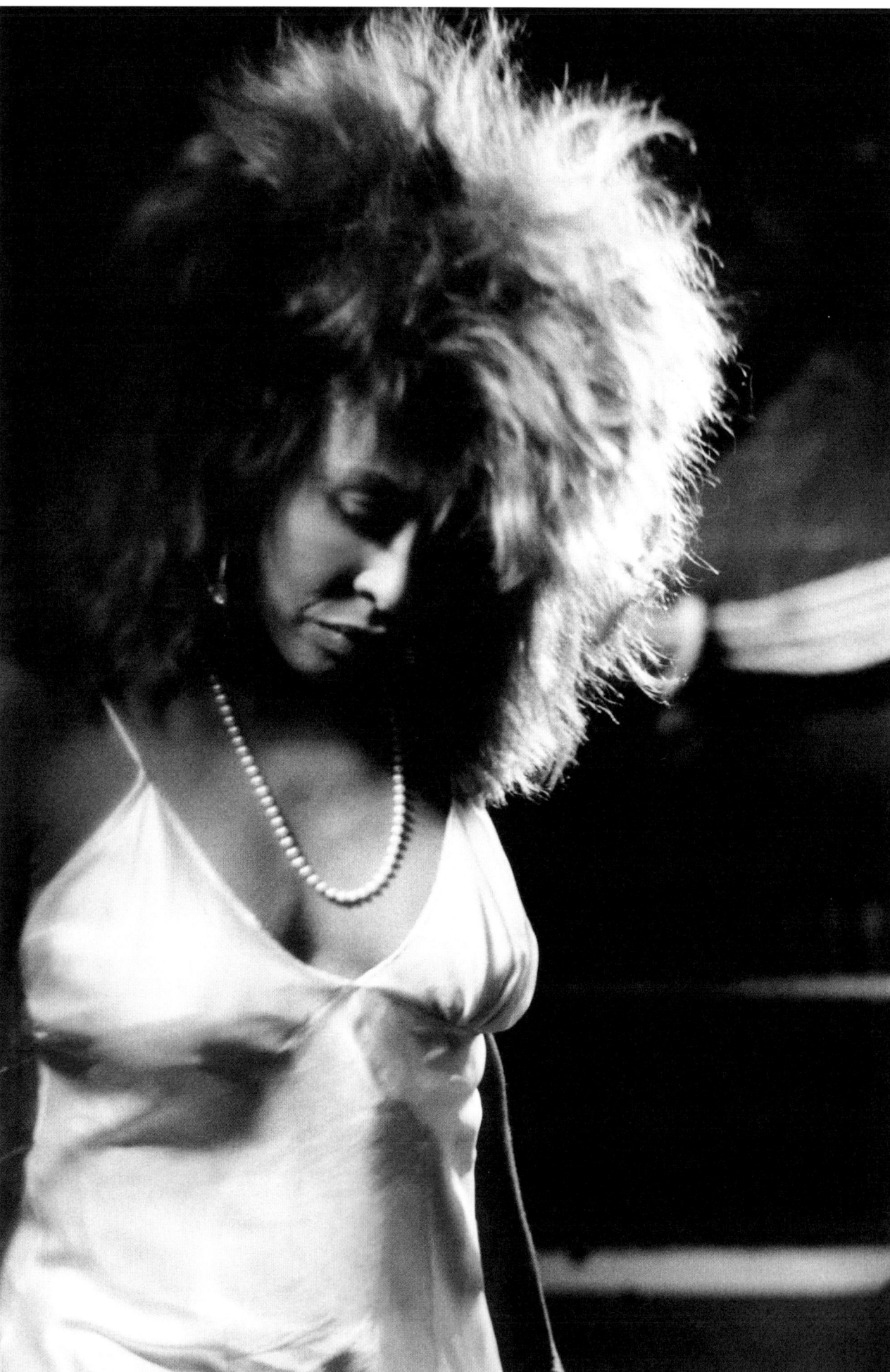

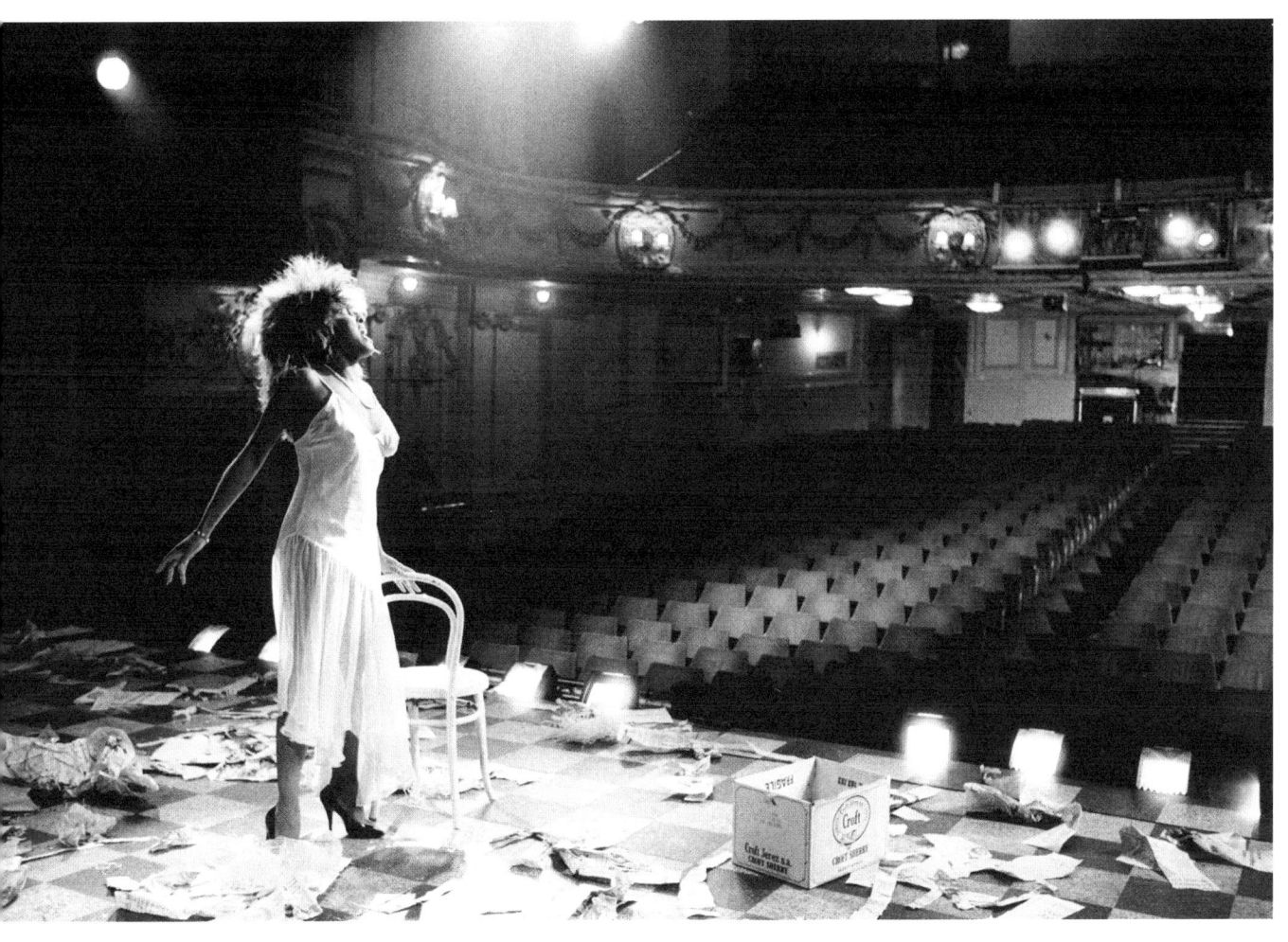

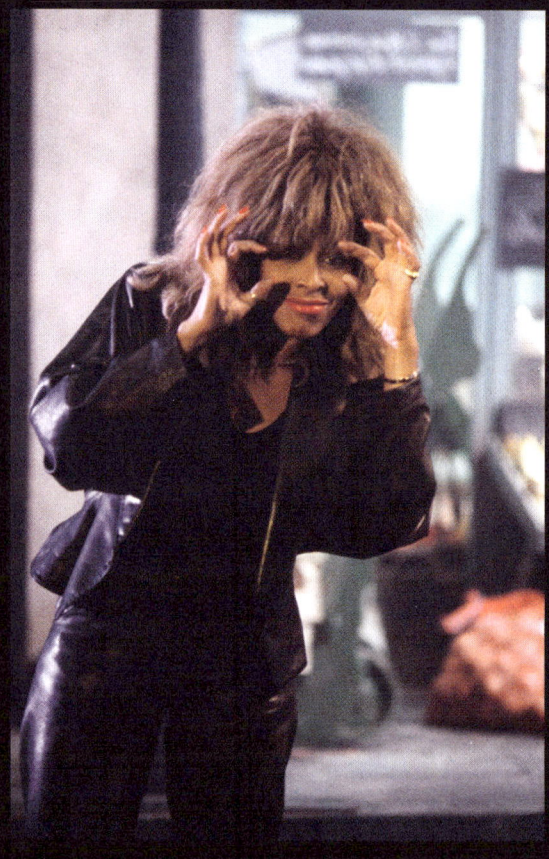

1986

LE ZERO, CAMDEN PALACE, LONDON

'By 1986, things were changing – most people were dressed in black, and Tina's hair was getting bigger,' Paul laughs. The *Tina Turner: Break Every Rule* special captured this perfectly. It was filmed at London's Camden Palace in November 1986 for HBO, the idea to present Tina as a 'chanteuse' in the fictional setting of Le Club Zero from Paris, performing a concert, intercut with various scenes. 'There was a whole scenario going on [nuns, gendarmes, vespas etc] with some acting, which she liked doing. That was her thing. She liked a little bit of a storyline.' The TV special was aired in March 1987 as a taster for her upcoming world tour.

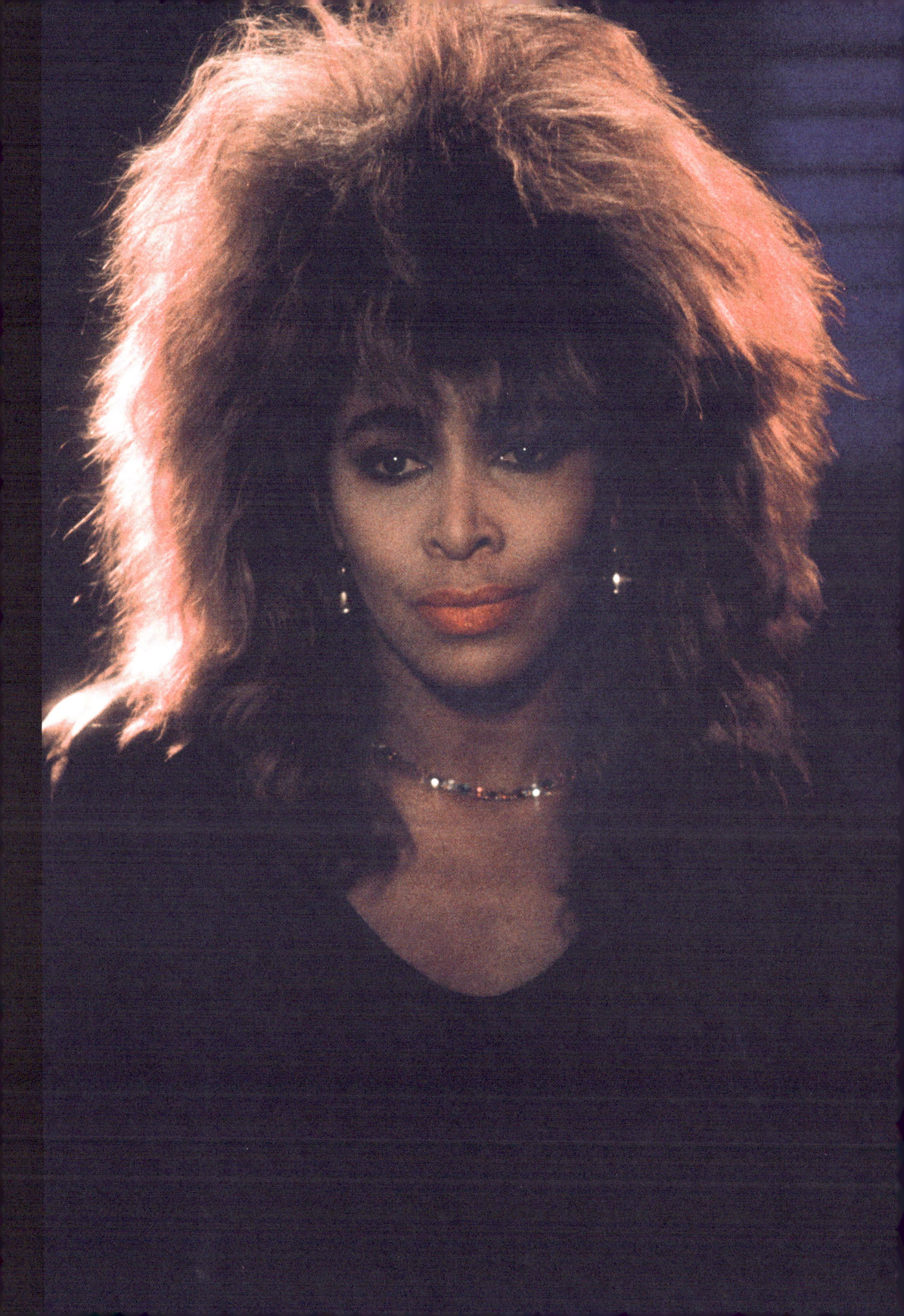

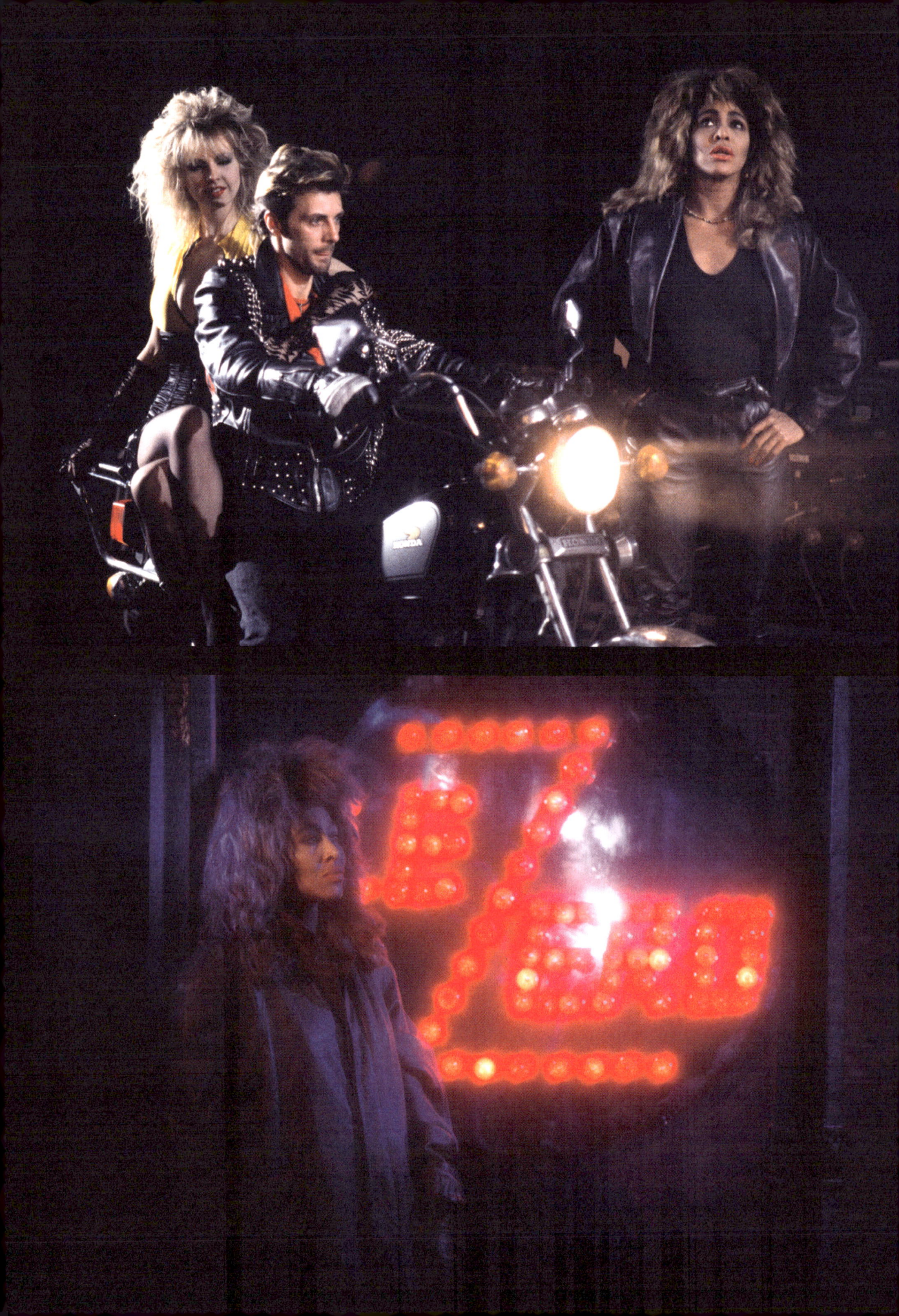

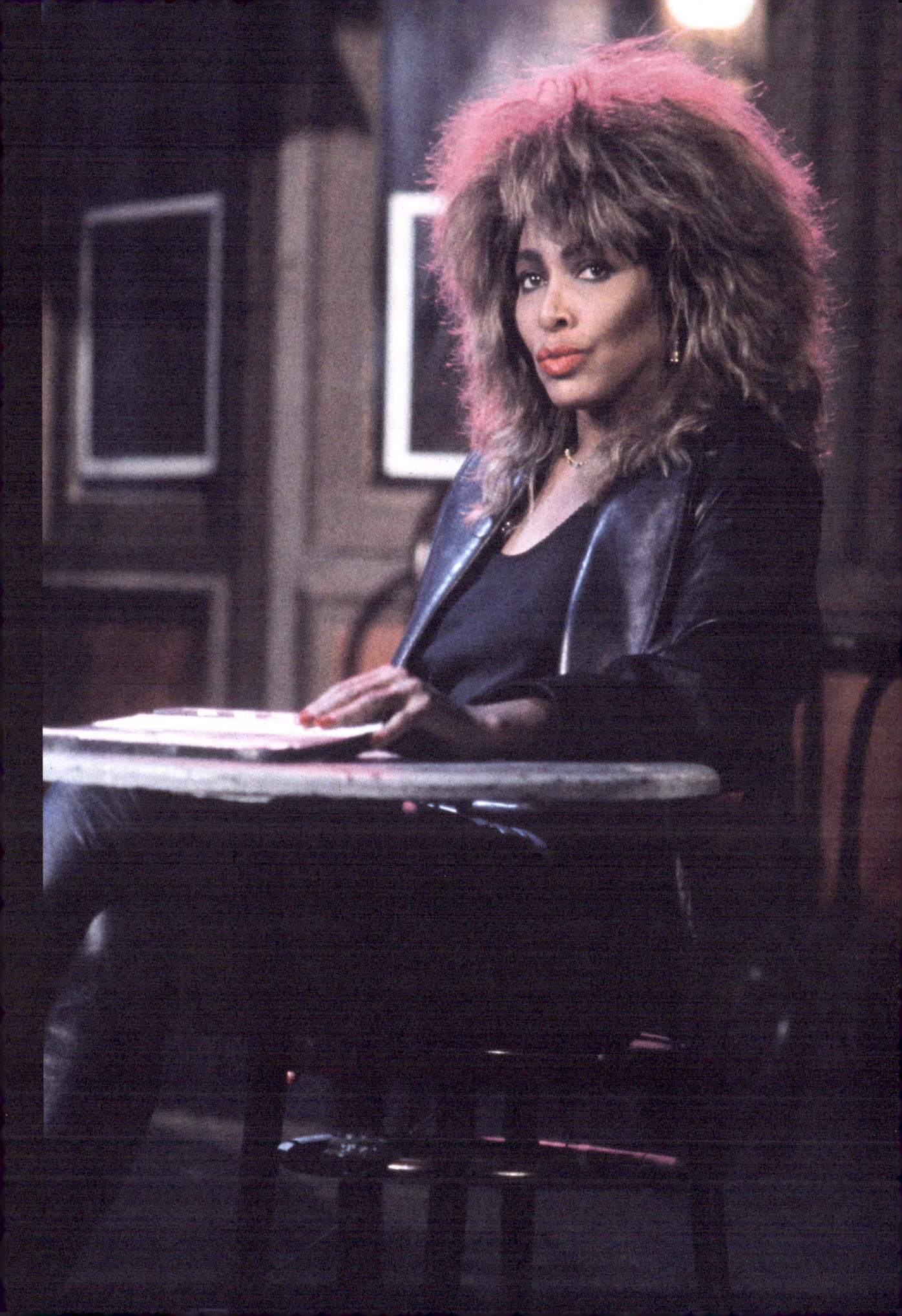

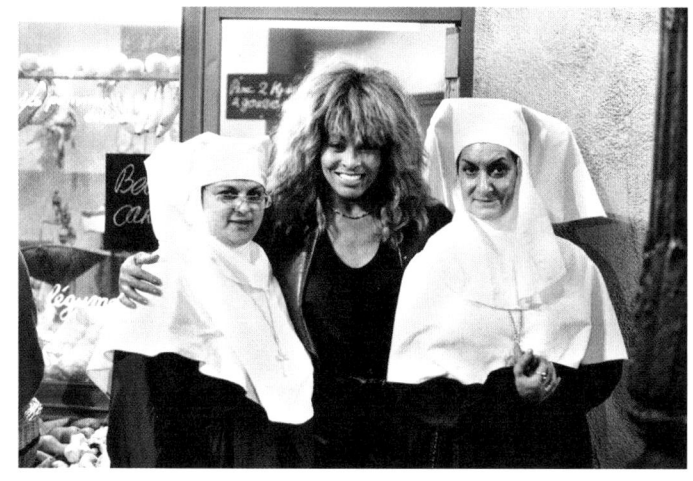

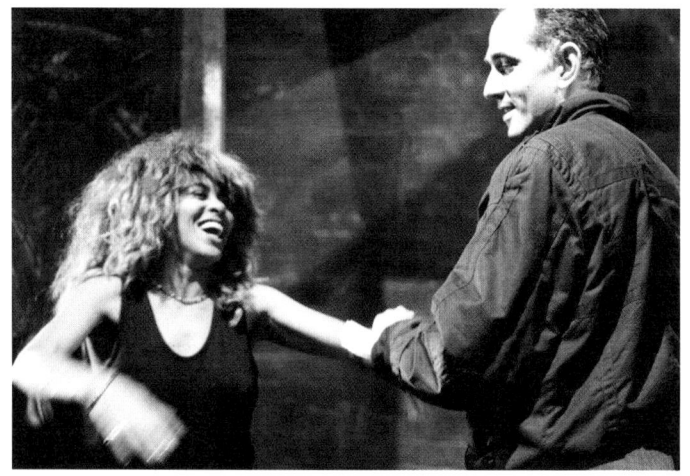

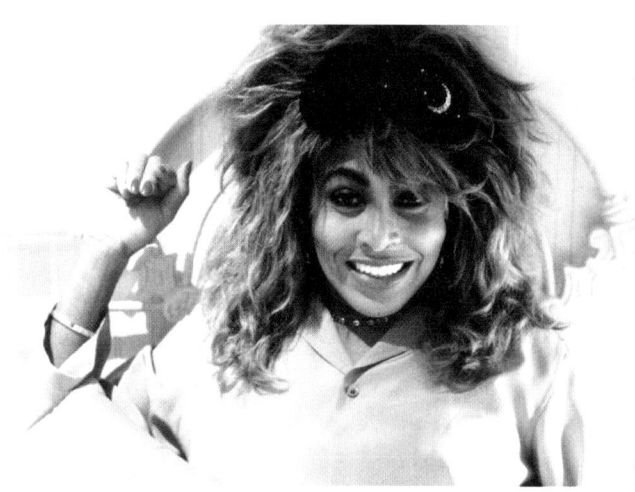

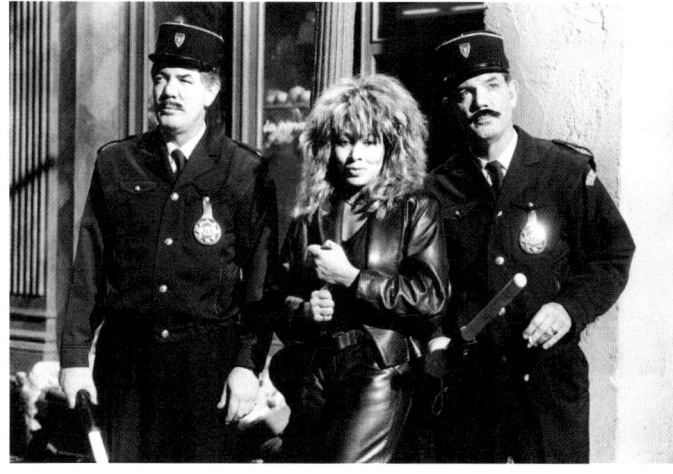

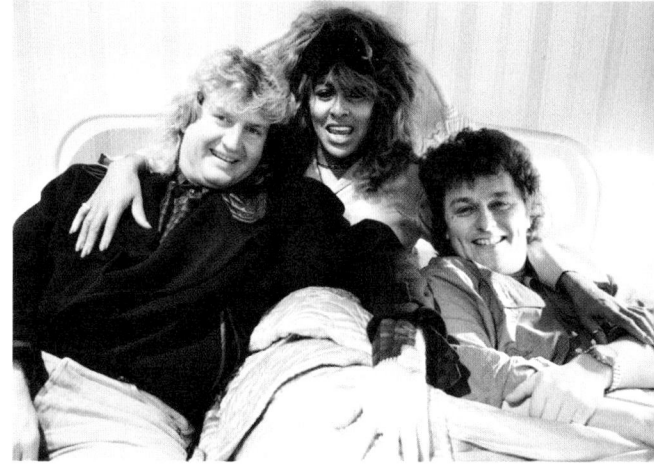

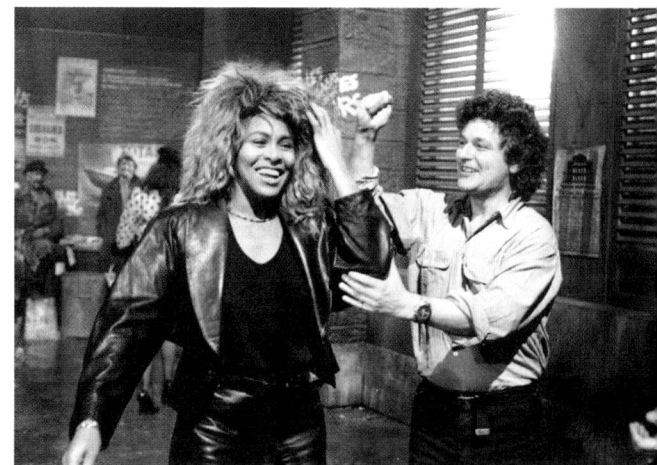

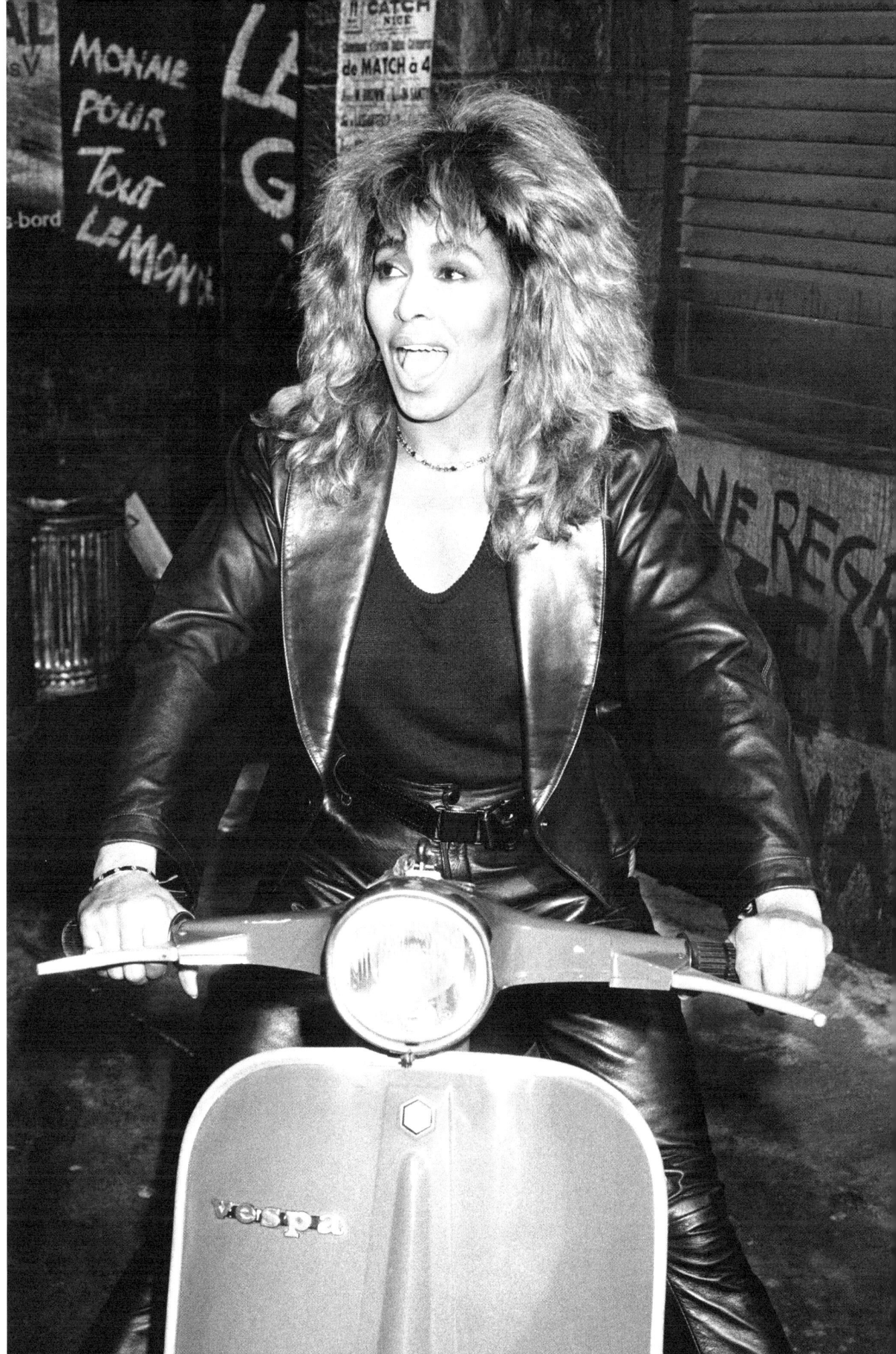

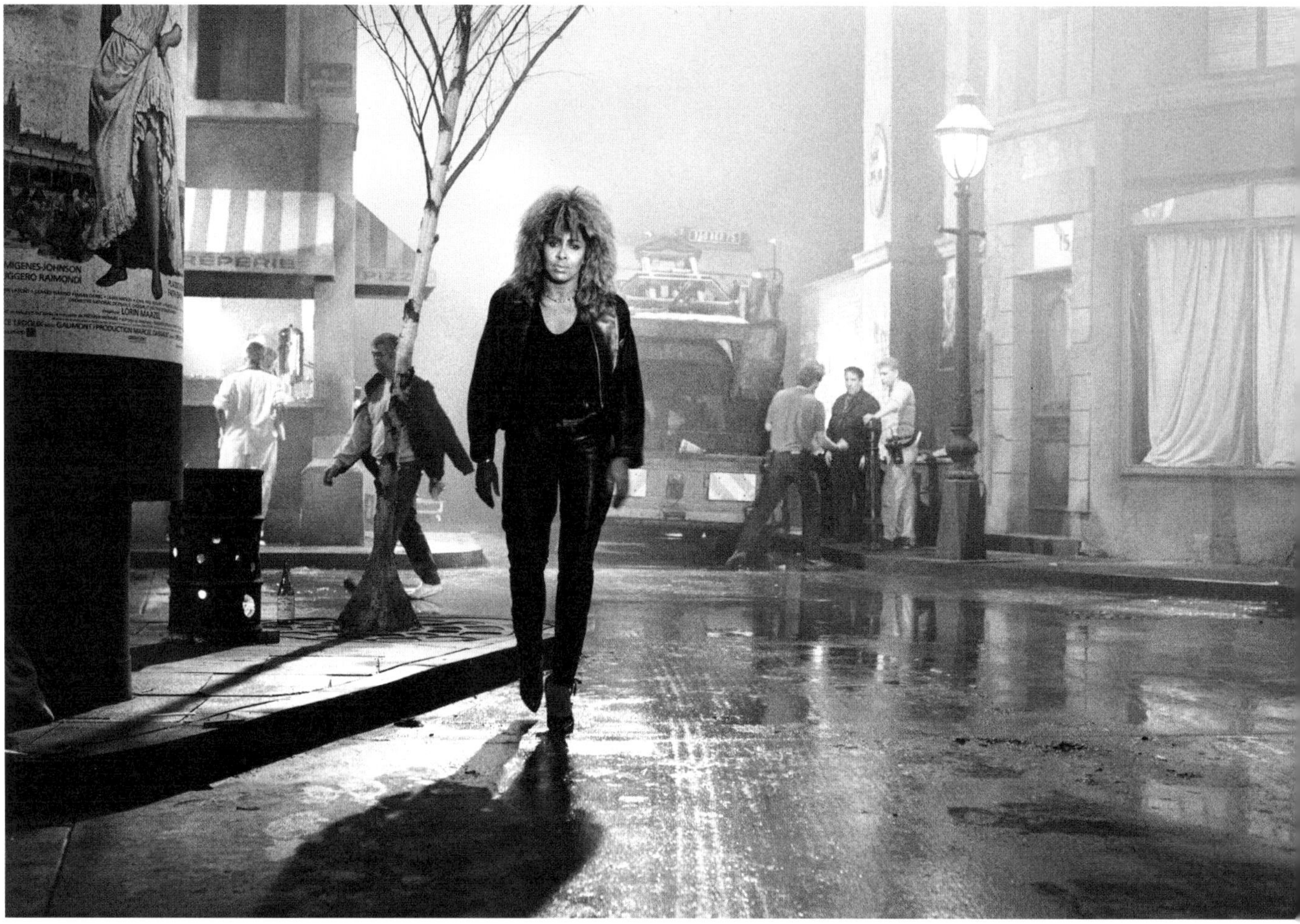

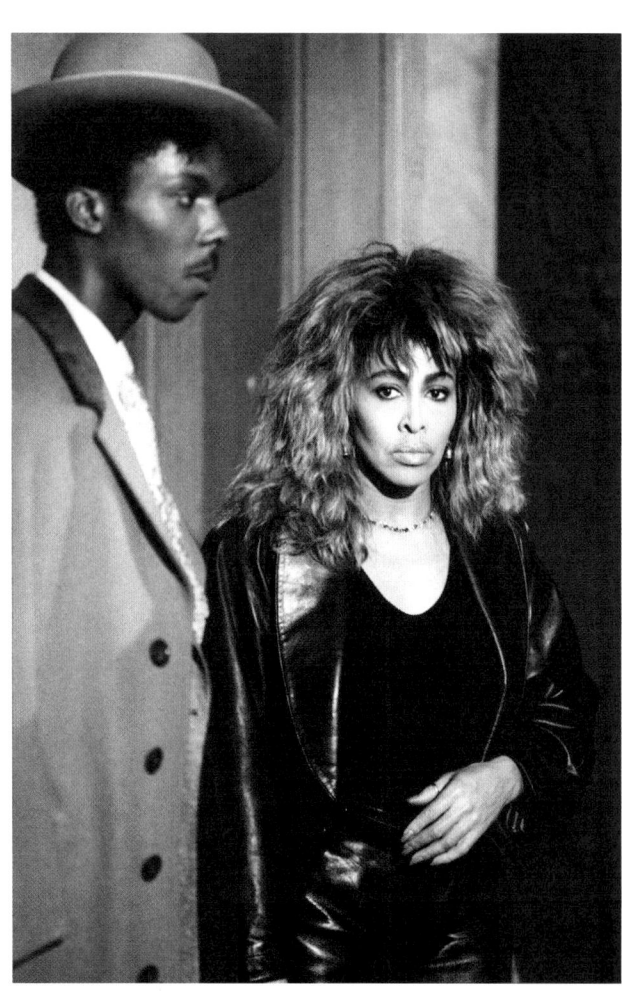

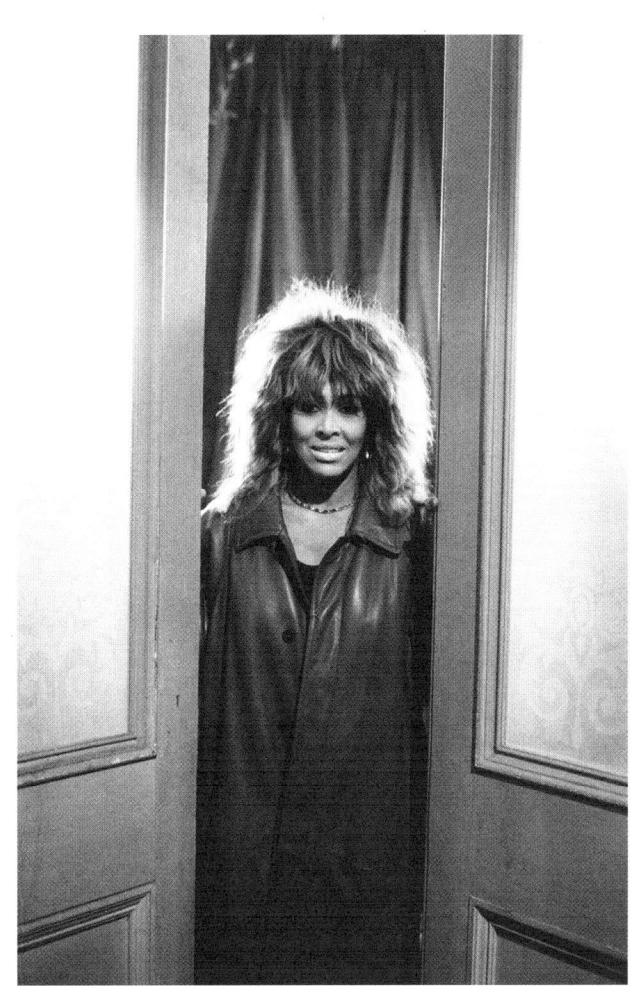

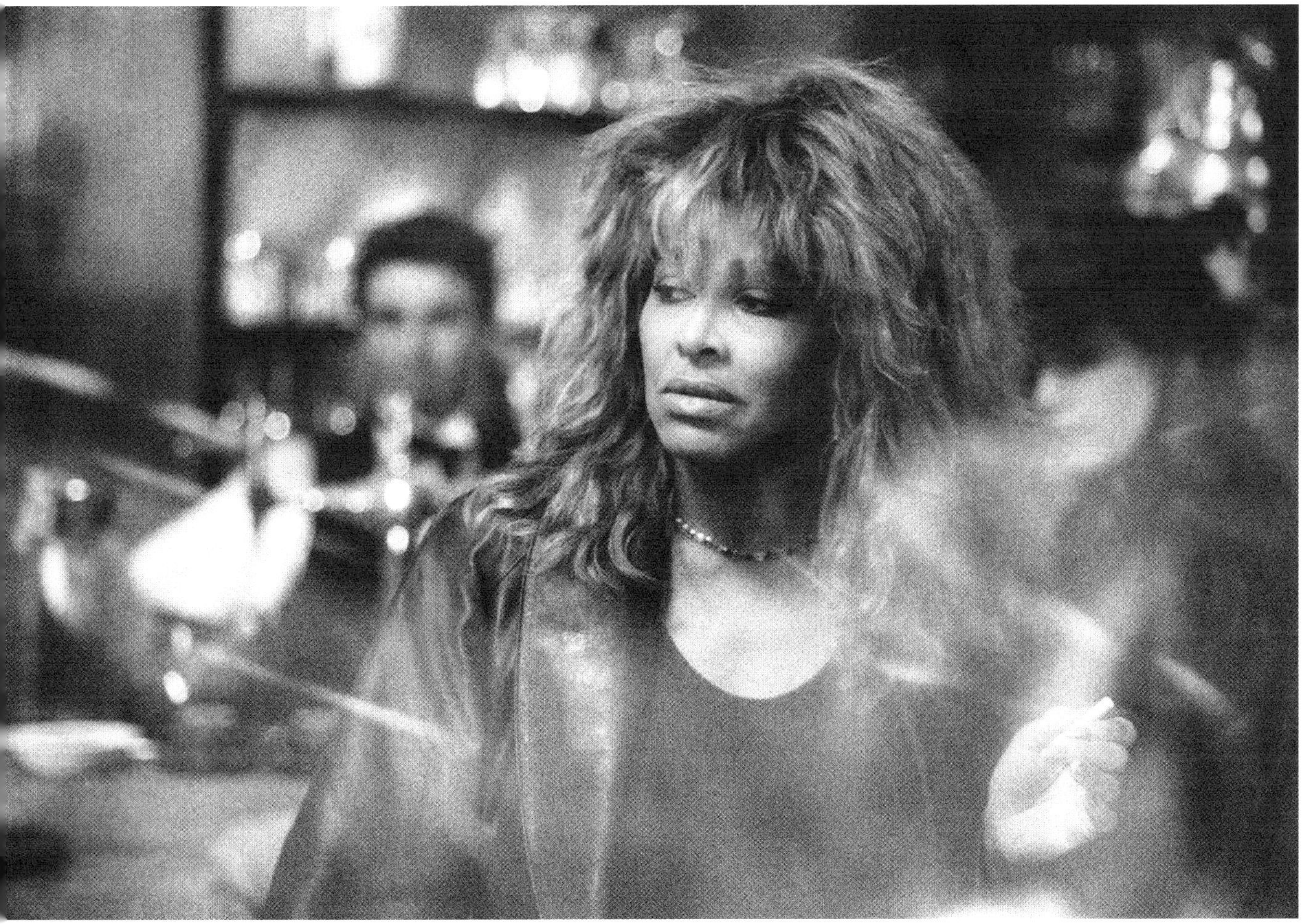

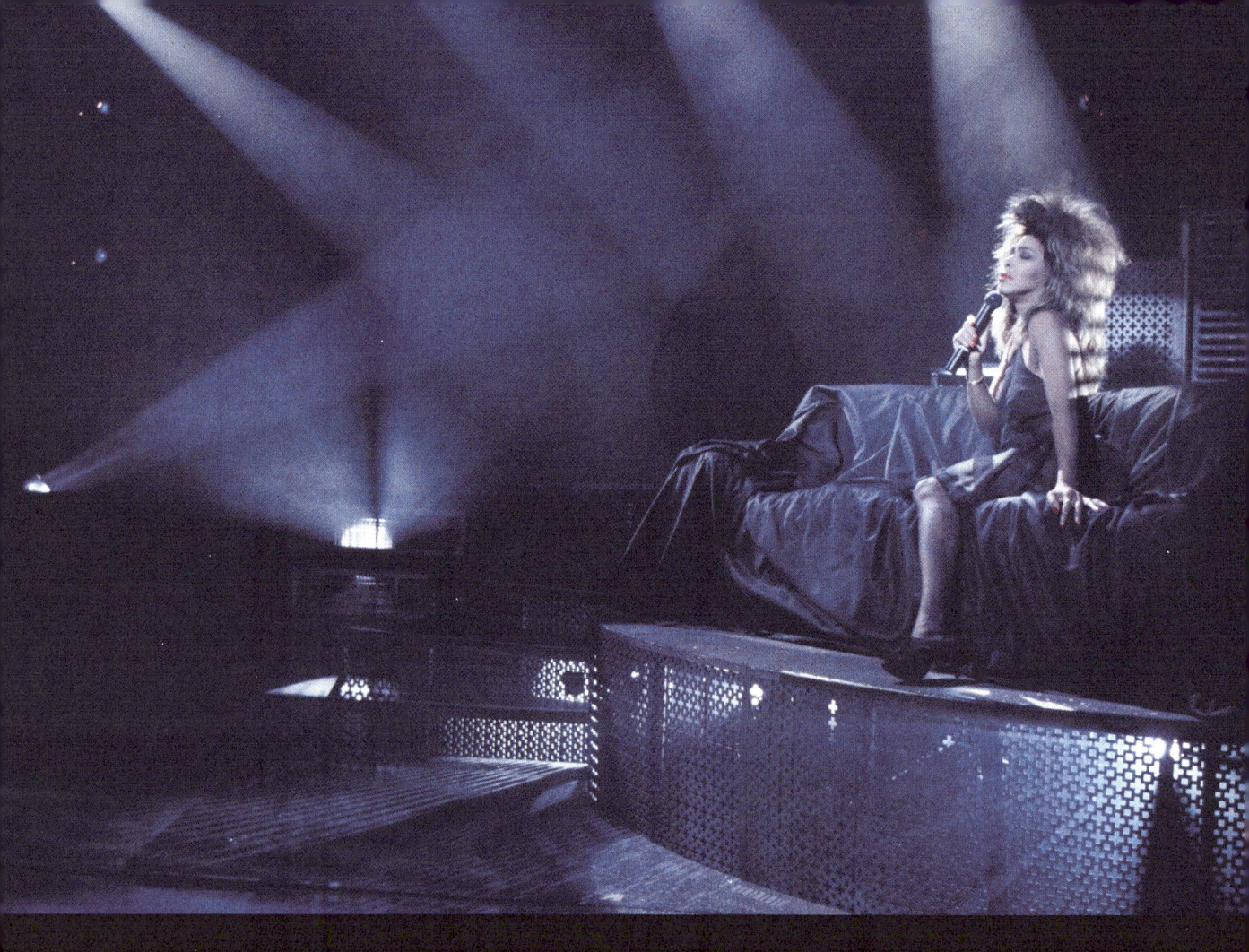

1986
'GIRLS' video shoot

During the filming of the promotional video for 'Girls' – the fourth single (written by David Bowie and Erdal Kızılçay) from the *Break Every Rule* album – Paul was able to frame Tina perfectly standing above the six models in the video, including a young Naomi Campbell (second from right in the picture overleaf) and Jeny Howorth to her left ('Me and my girls,' Paul remembers Tina saying). To add to the effect, he took the backlit shot in front of the blinds, with the light radiating from Tina. 'If there was a break, she'd disappear to her dressing room. If she was in the mood, I'd encourage her out to take some pictures.'

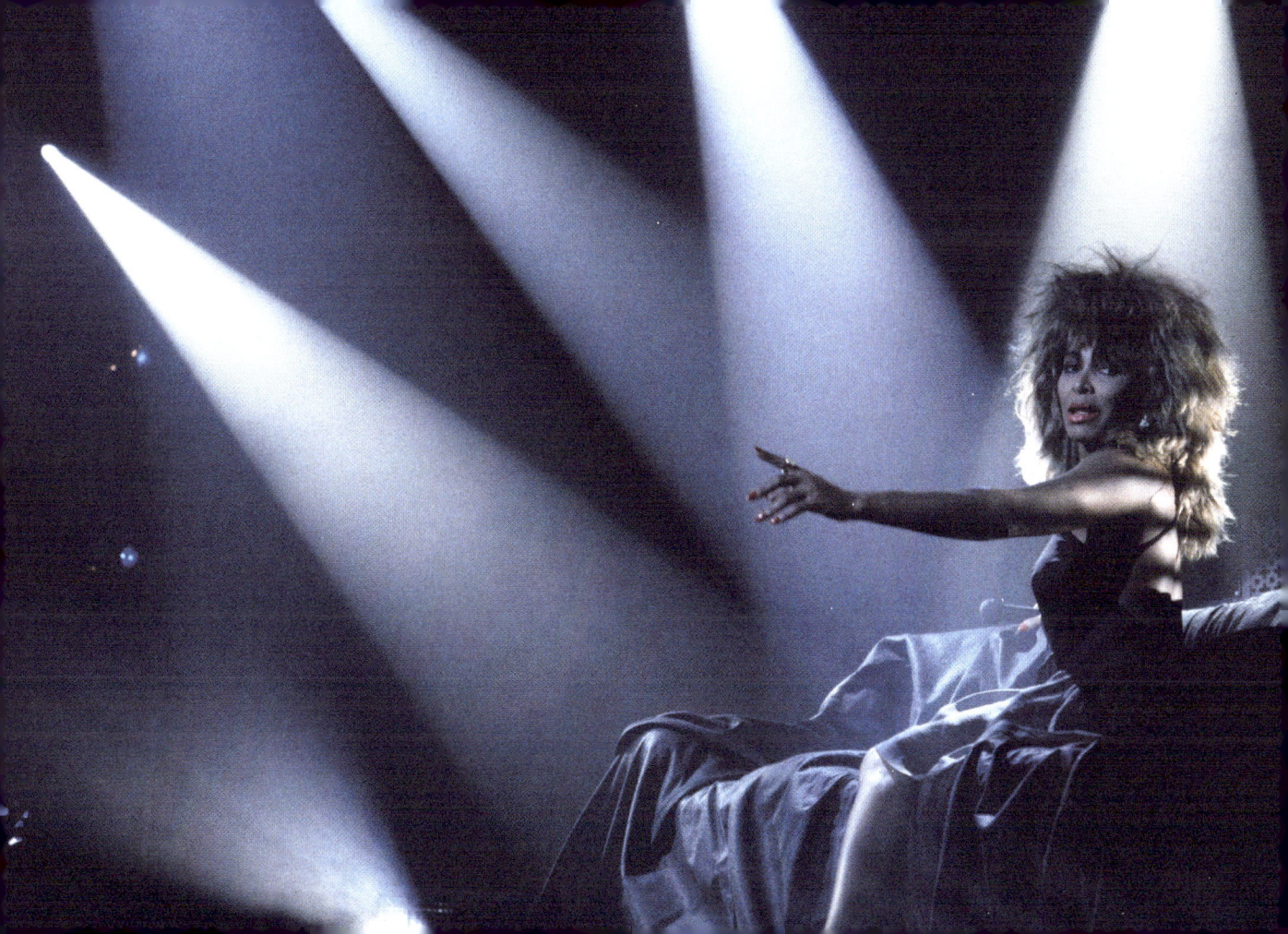

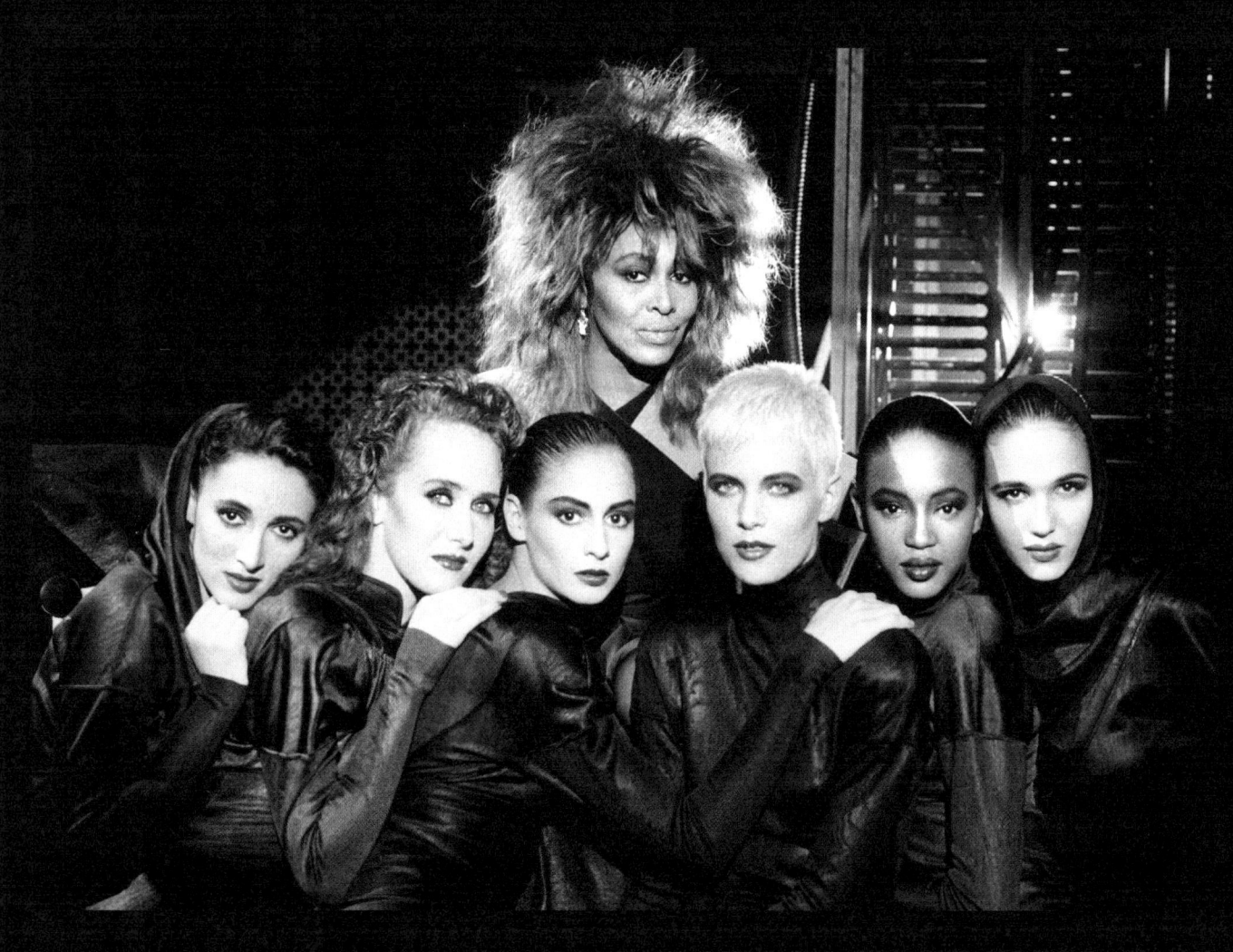

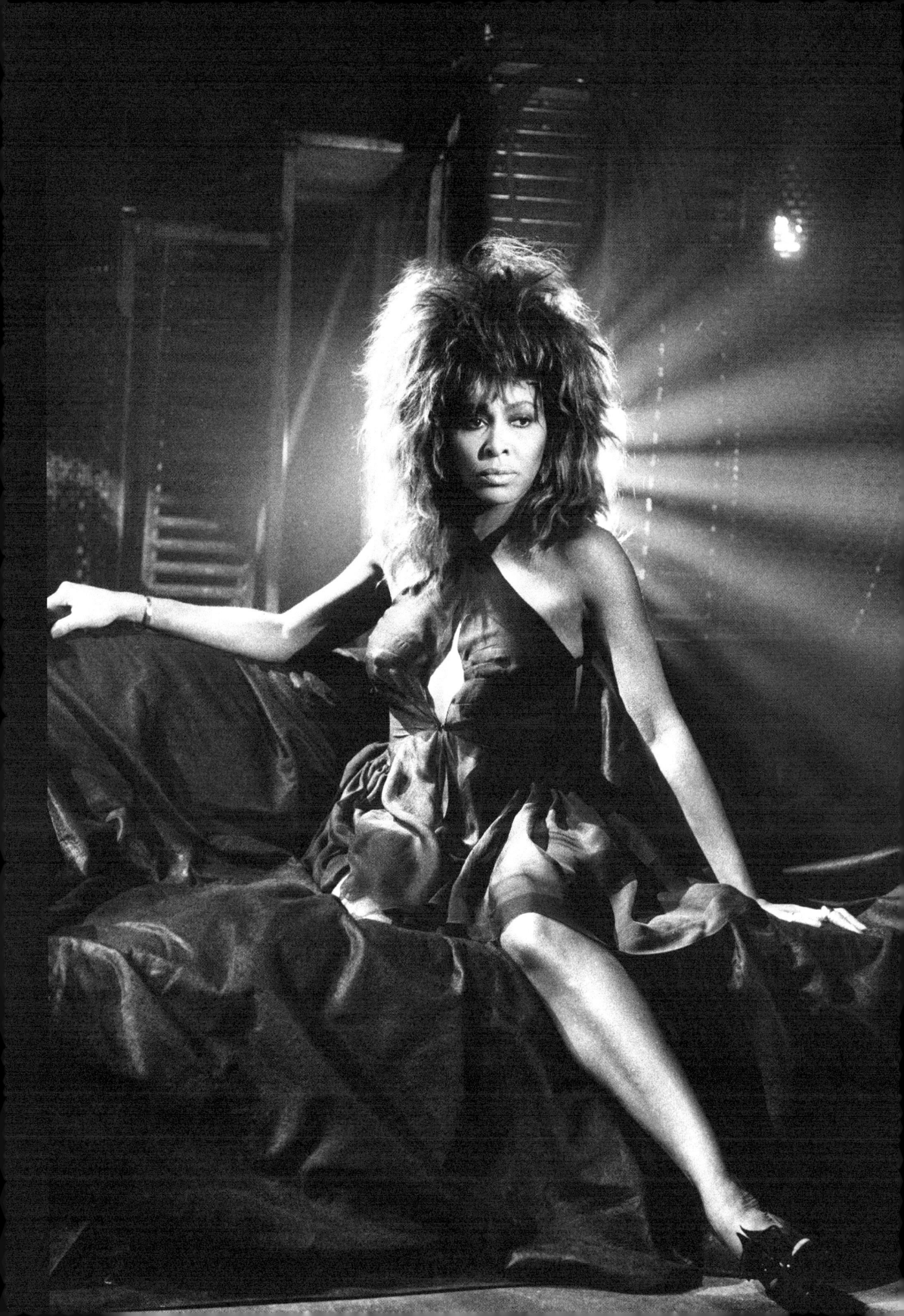

ILFORD   HP5   SAFETY

31   31A   32   32A   33   33A

1986

TINA TURNER:
BREAK EVERY RULE **special**

The HBO special caught Tina at close range and showcased her accomplished players, including Gary Barnacle on saxophone, Steve Scales (Talking Heads) on percussion, Don Snow (Squeeze) on keyboards and Laurie Wisefield (Wishbone Ash) on guitar. The electricity of the performance was heightened by Tina's special guest, Robert Cray, who was the new sensation on the block. He joined her in a version of '634-5789', and soul legend Wilson 'Wicked' Pickett went full tilt with Tina on 'Land of 1000 Dances'. Anne Doherty designed and made the little red leather dress. Paul was able to capture the power, warmth and camaraderie of the performers.

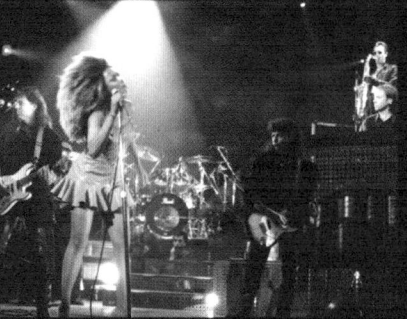

FILM

34   34A

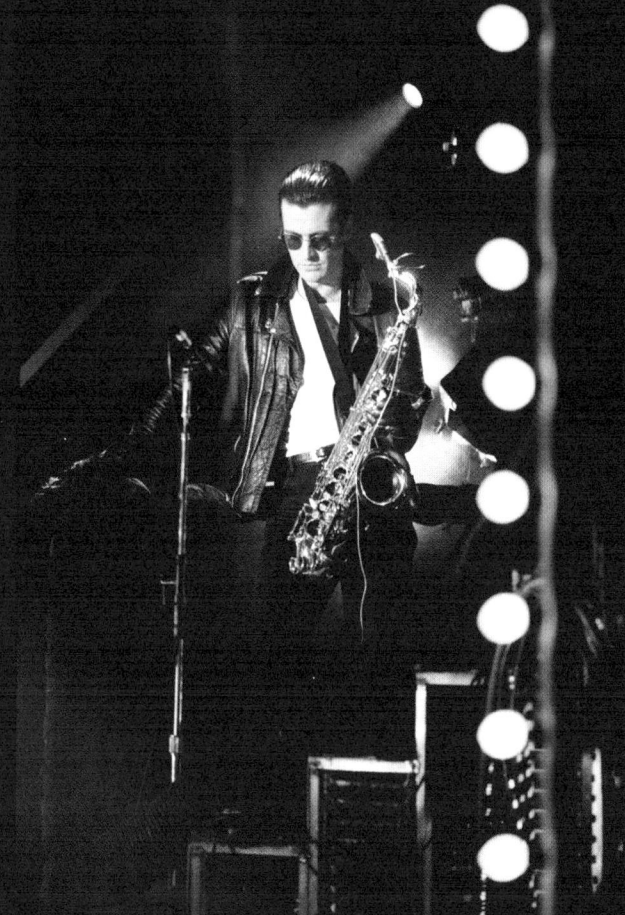

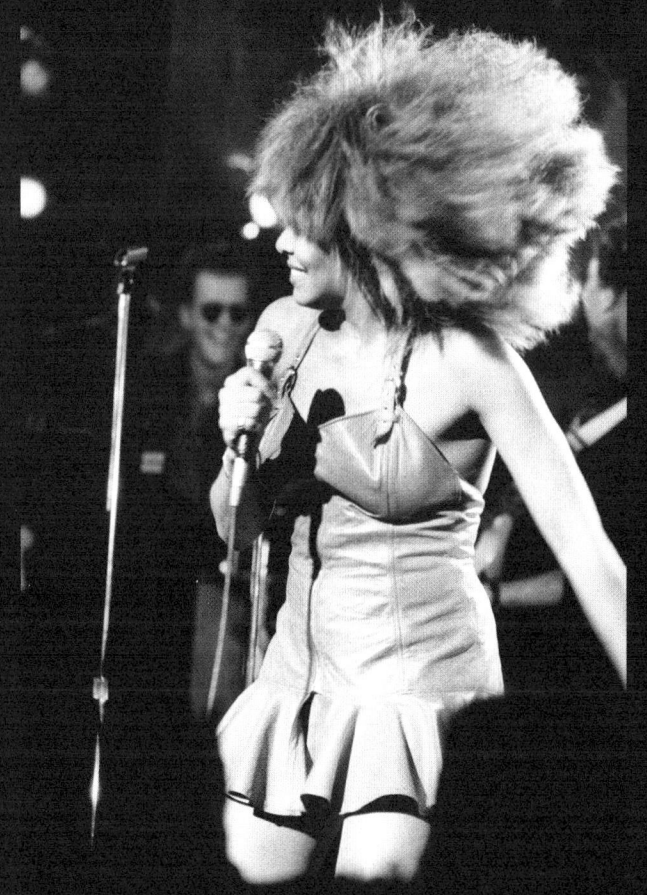

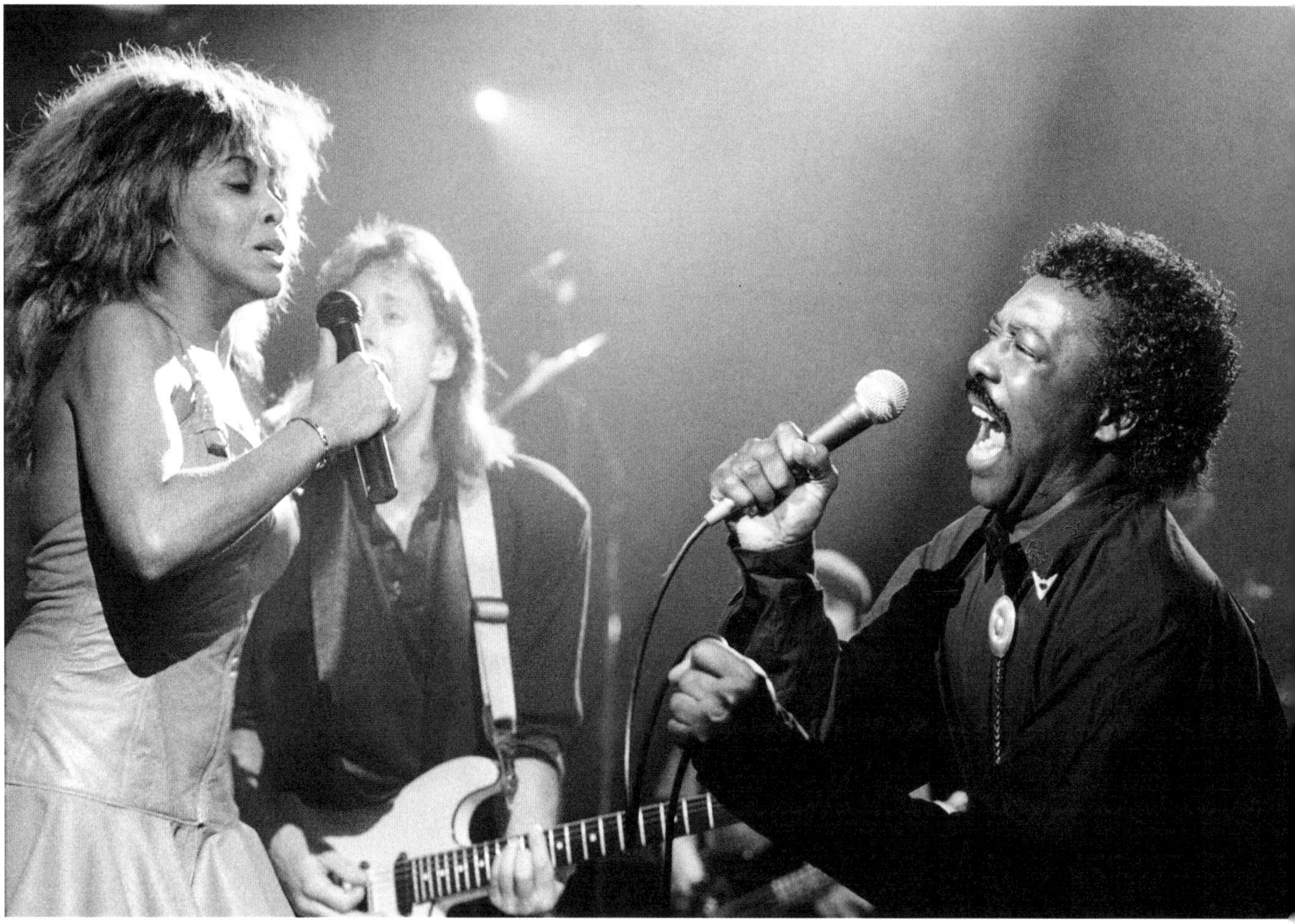

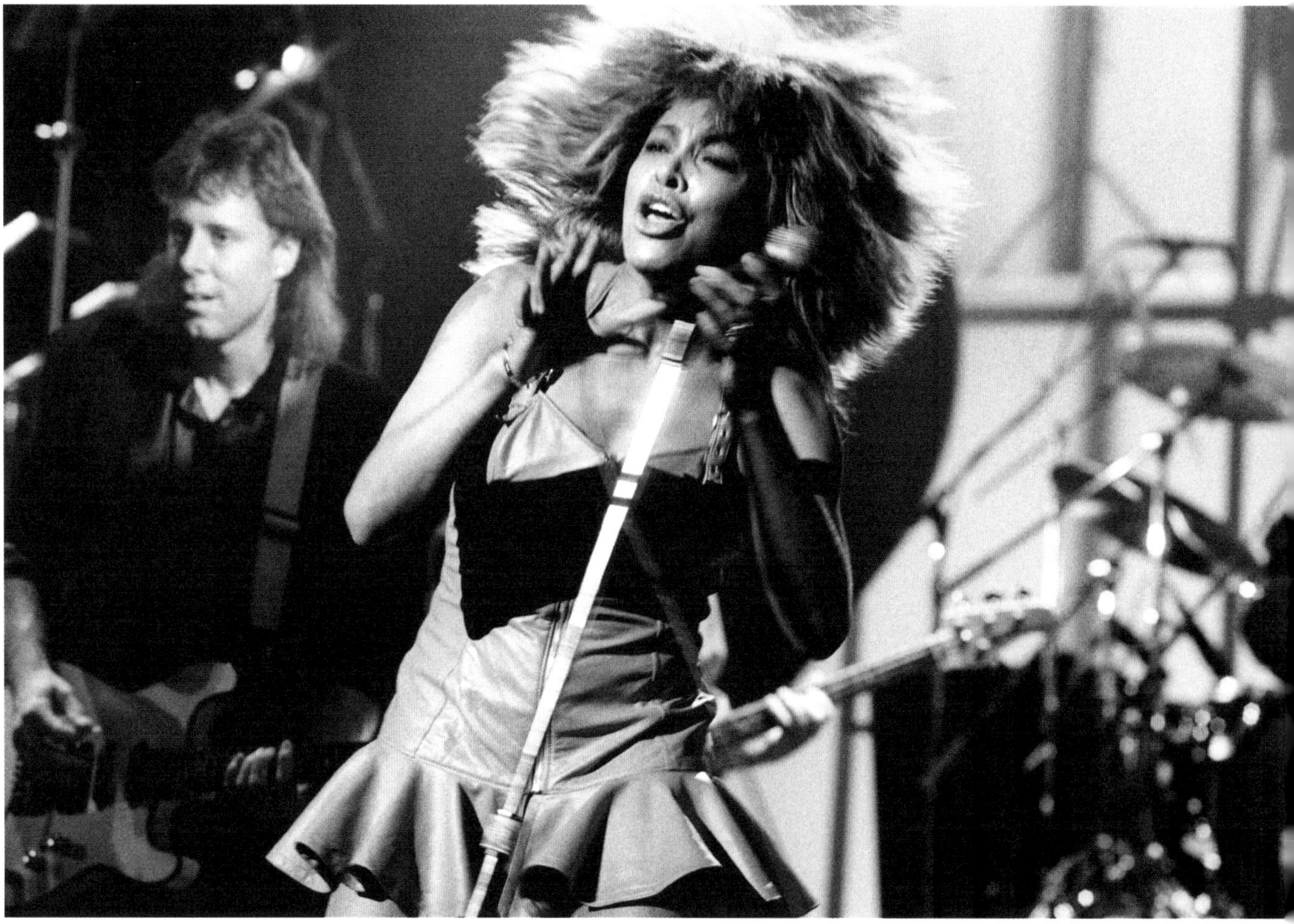

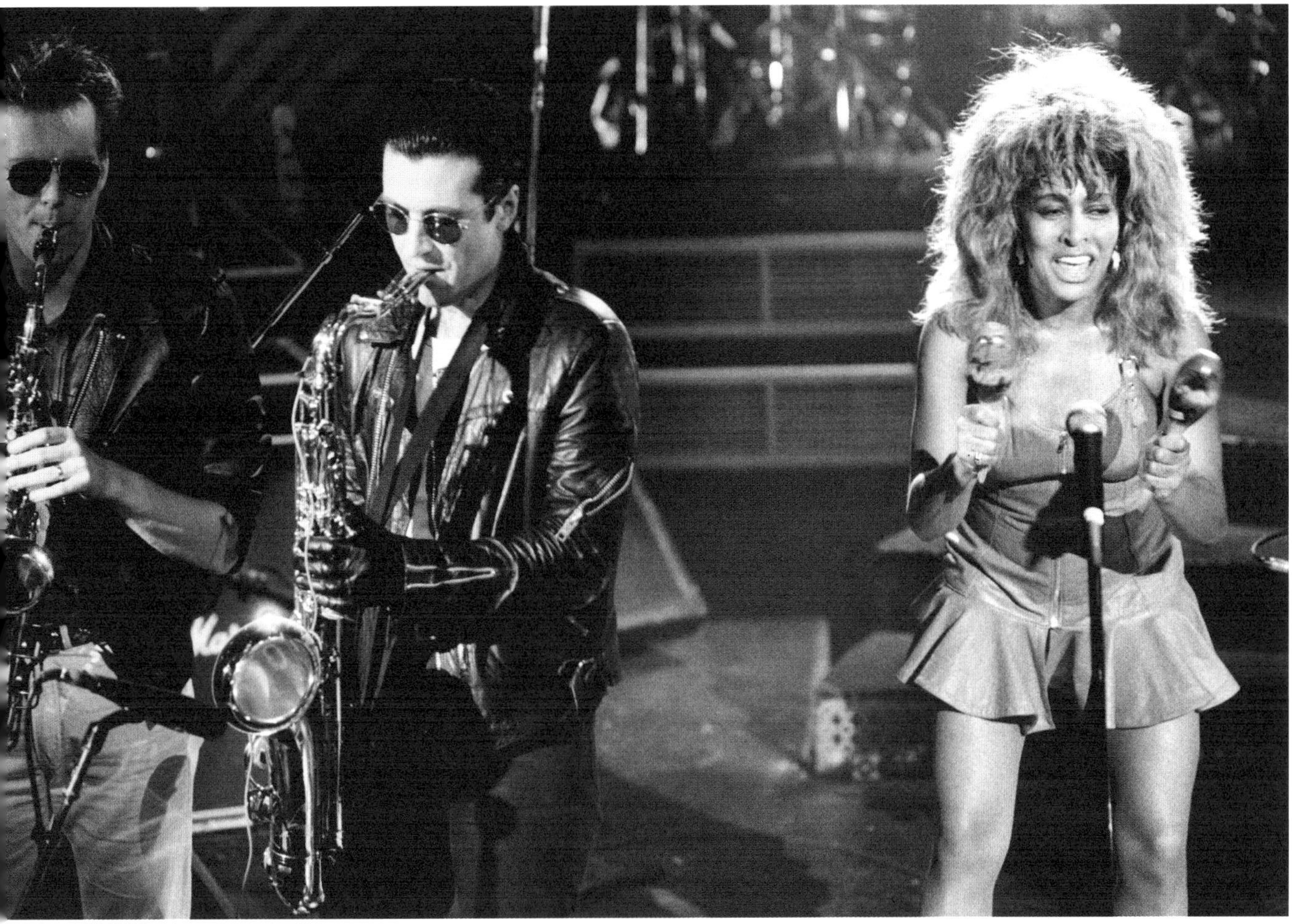

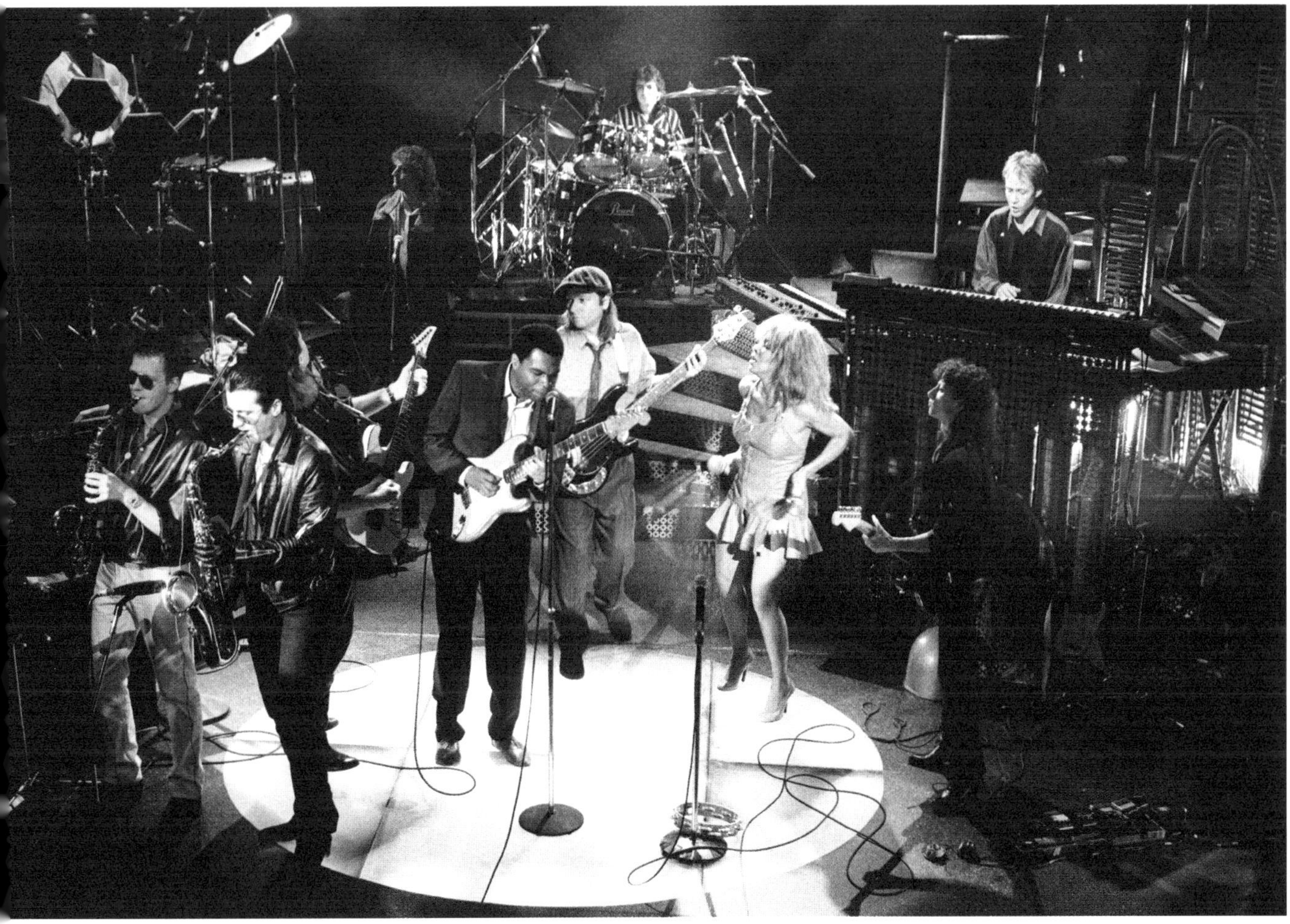

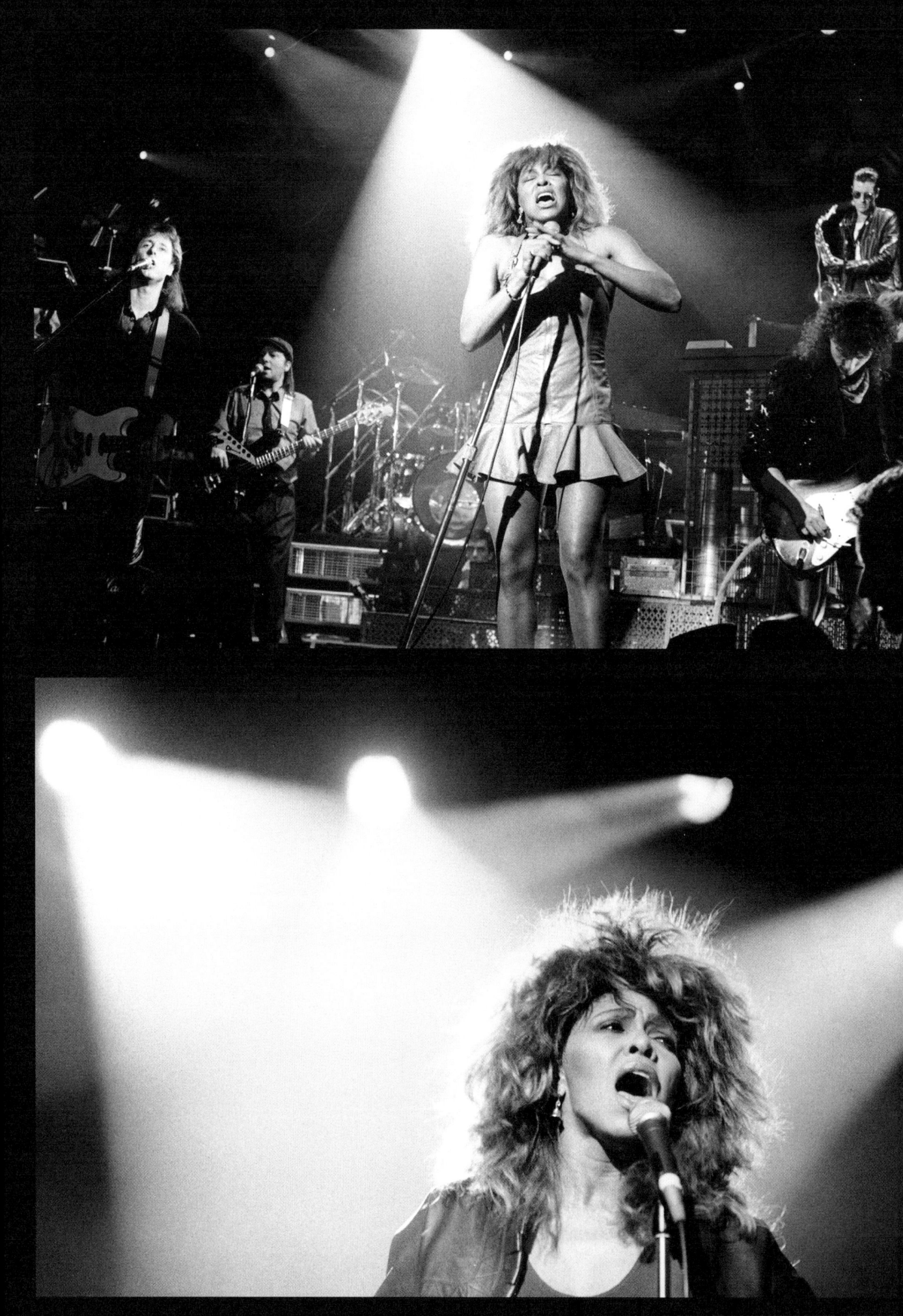

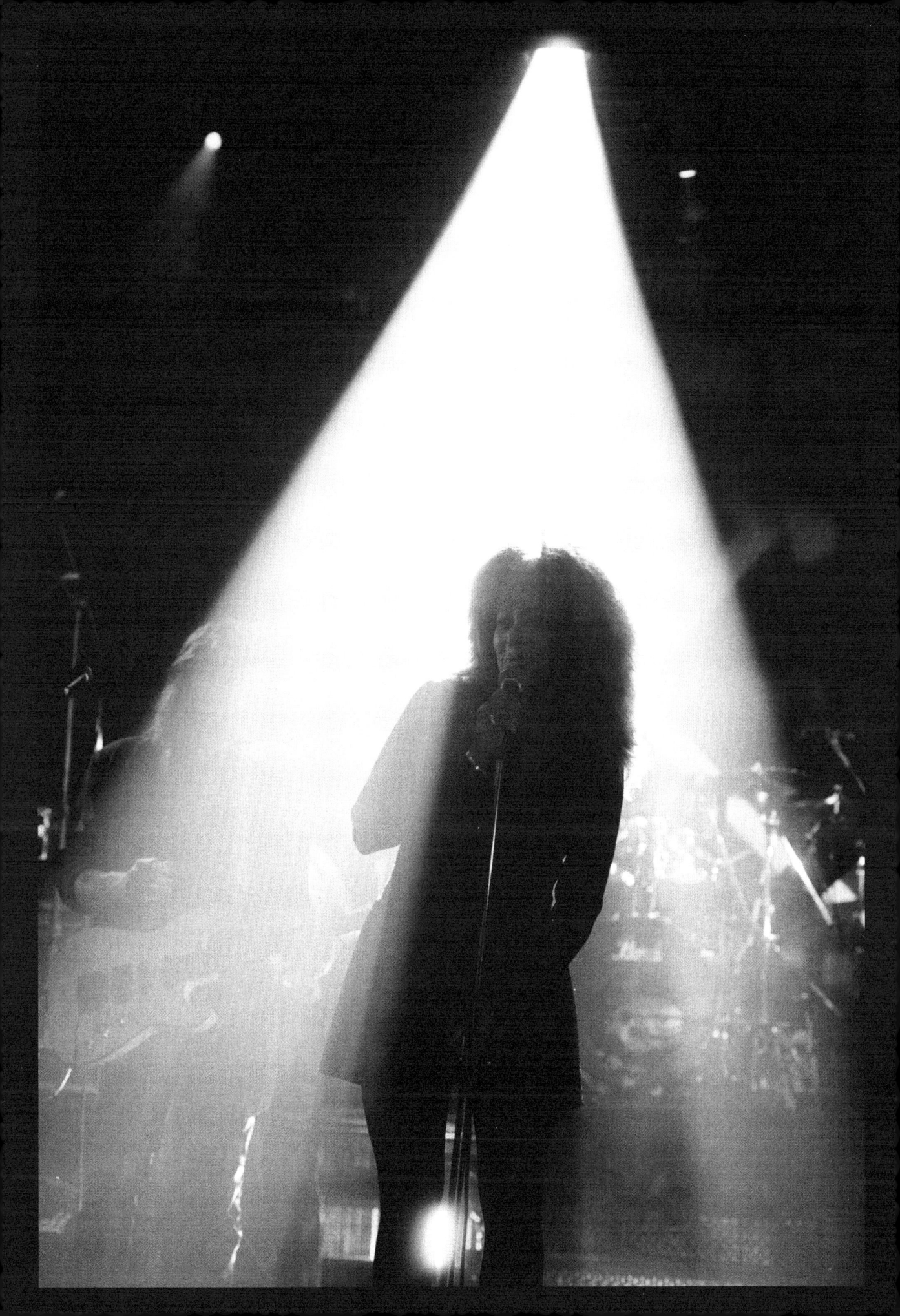

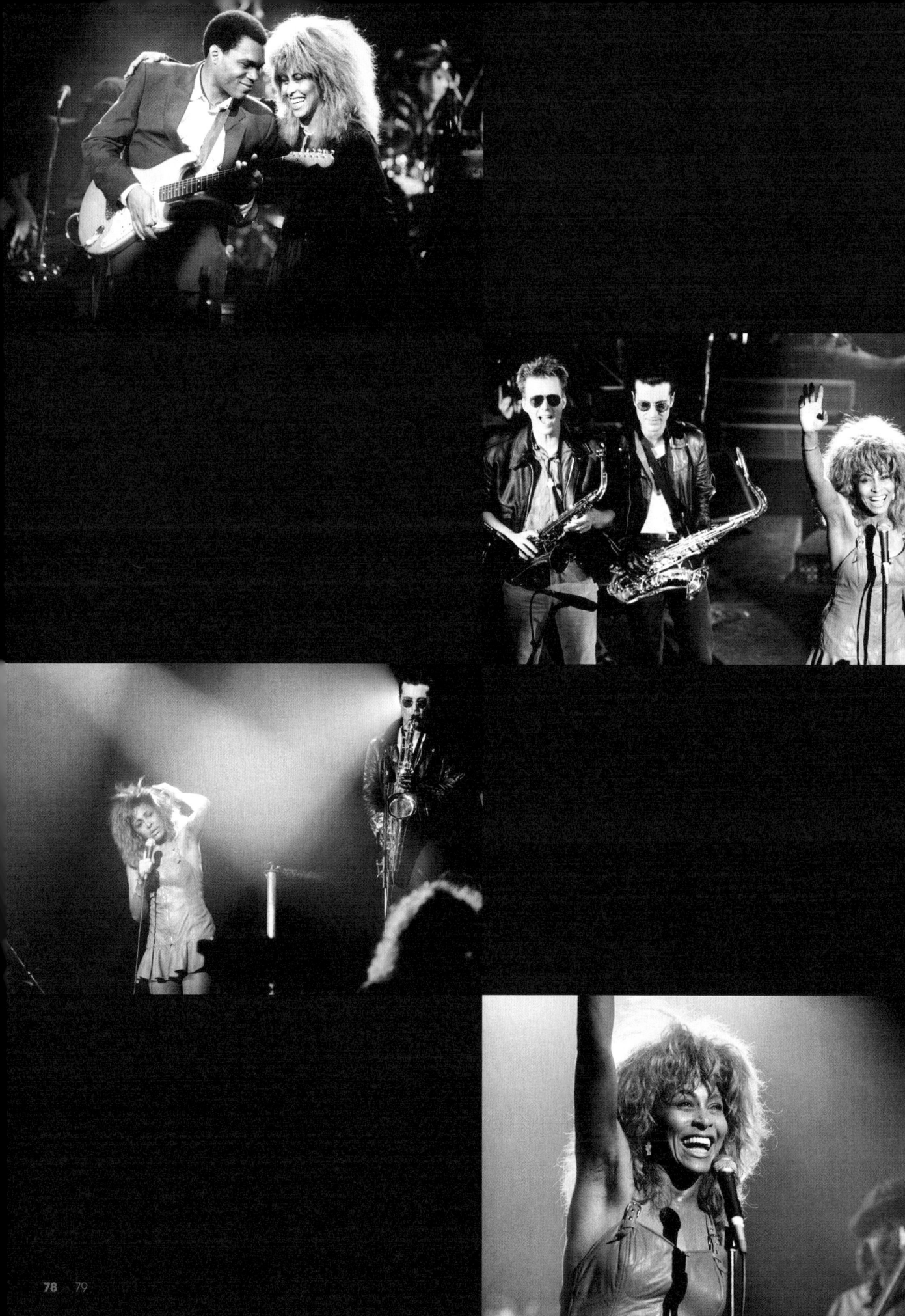

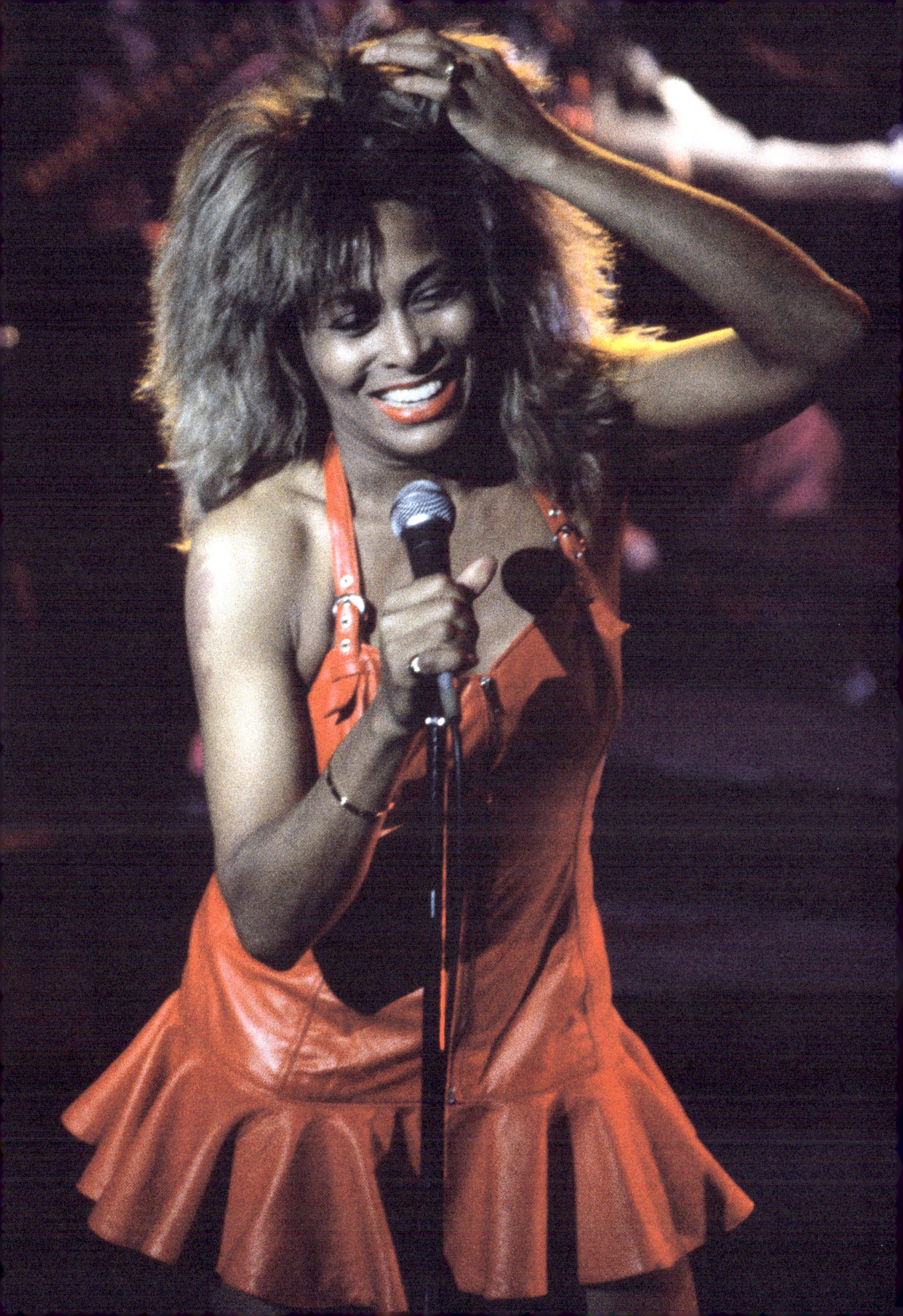

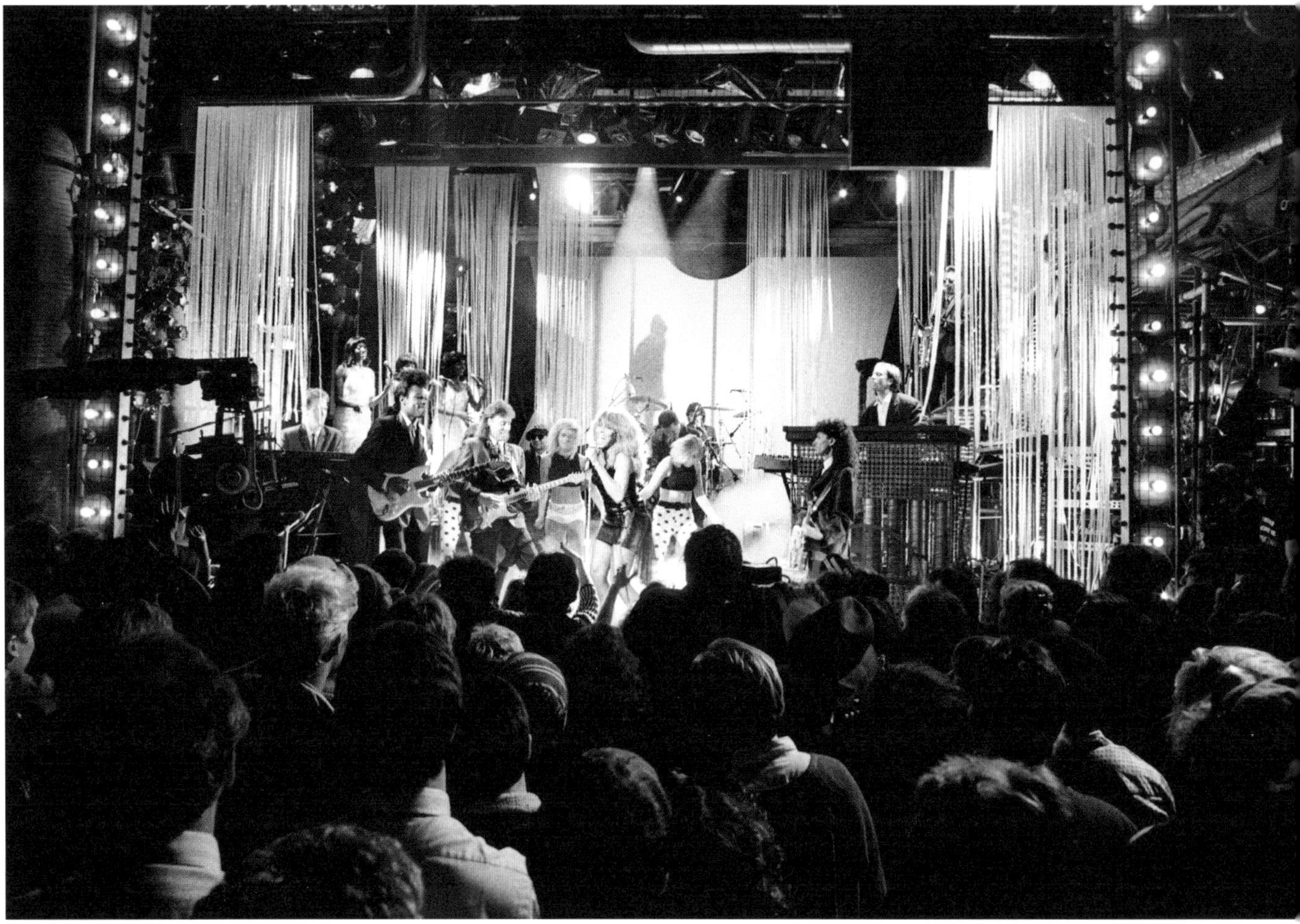

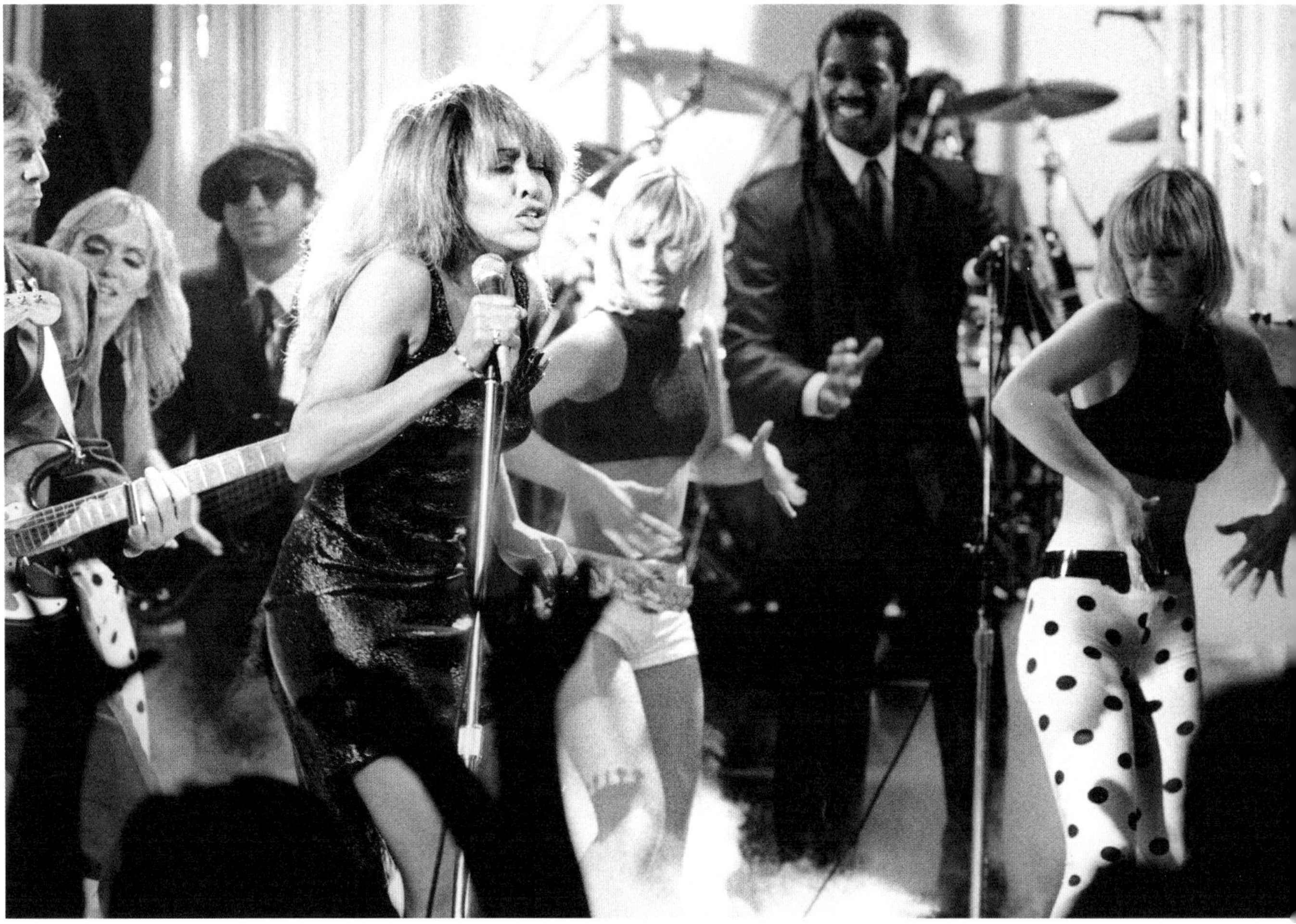

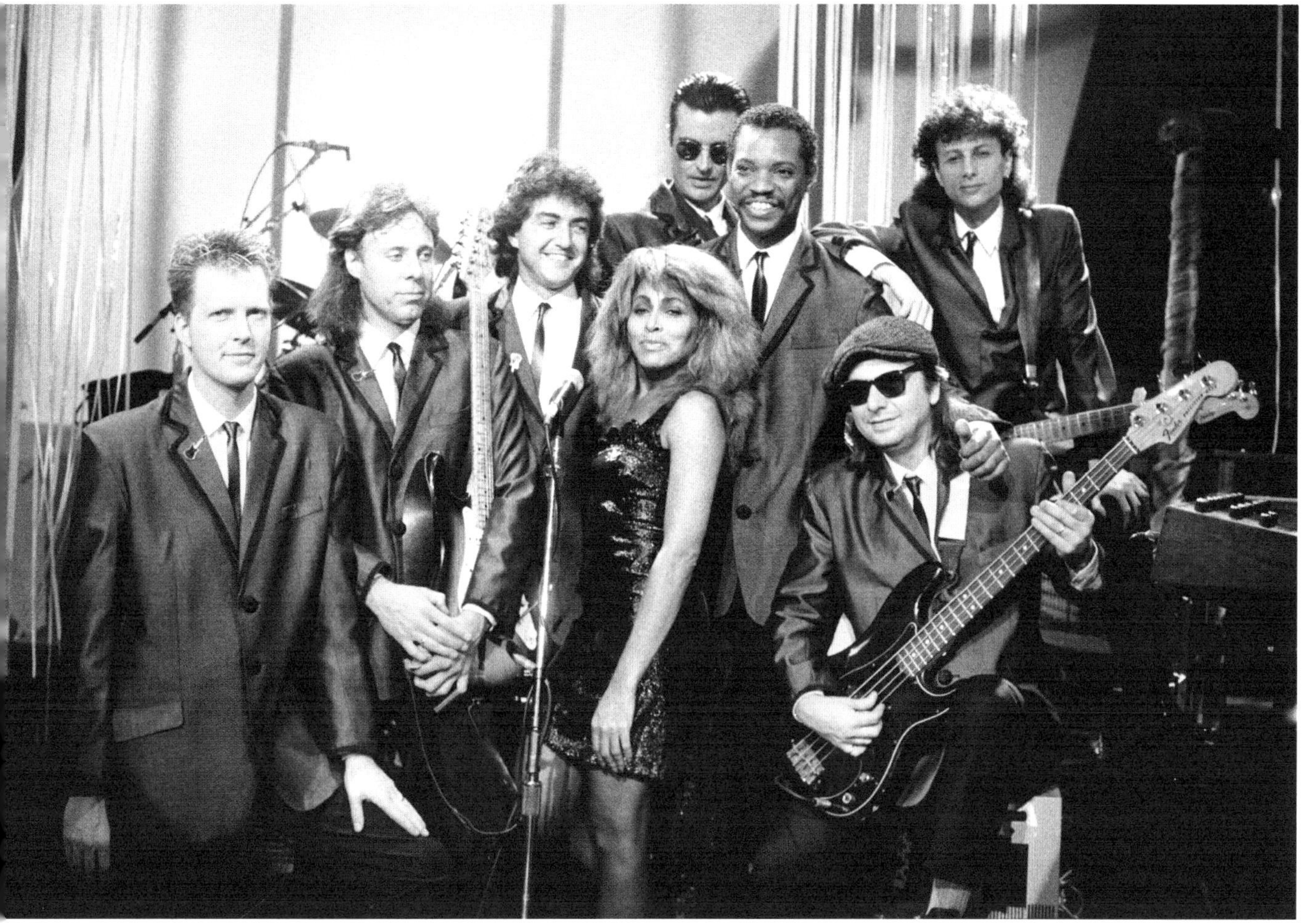

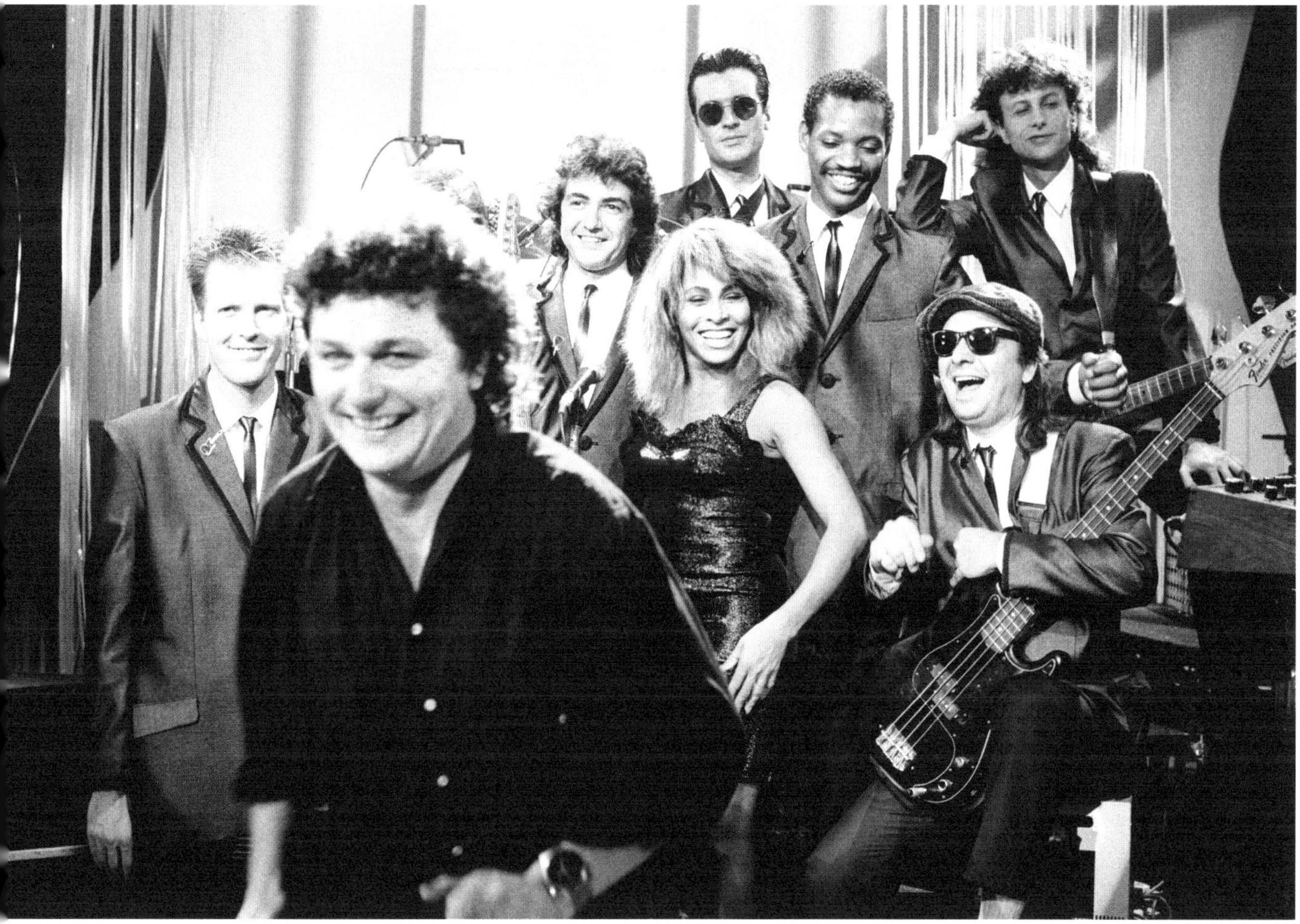

1987

'BREAK EVERY RULE' **video shoot**

The video for the fifth single taken from her *Break Every Rule* album took a different approach to its predecessors, catching Tina and her band in performance on her European tour. Paul went along and shot some memorable moments. 'I've got about 20 sheets of black-and-whites from that tour. It was great fun seeing her on the tour bus, interacting with her band. You can see Roger, her manager, stepping out from behind as they leave the coach.' The posed shots in denim and the jumper dress are iconic, yet there is also the lovely informality of the shot of Tina and her touring band together outside the venue in Munich.

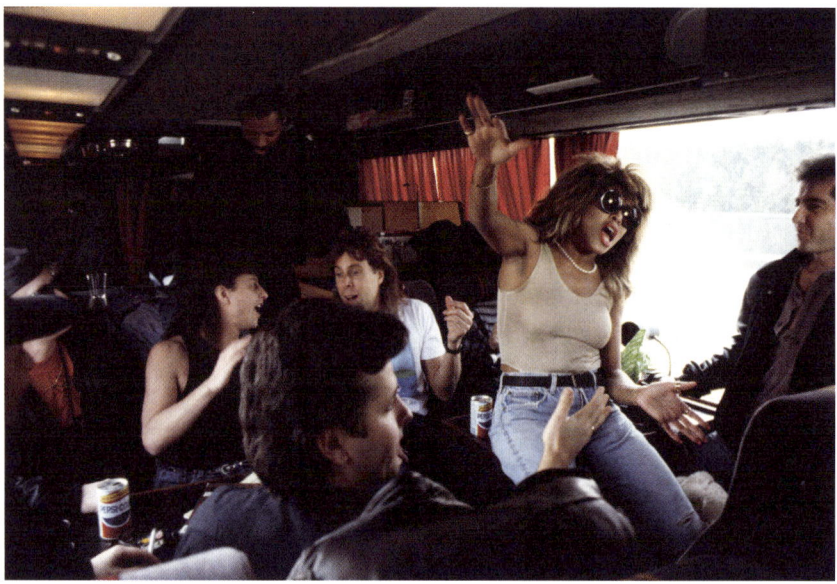

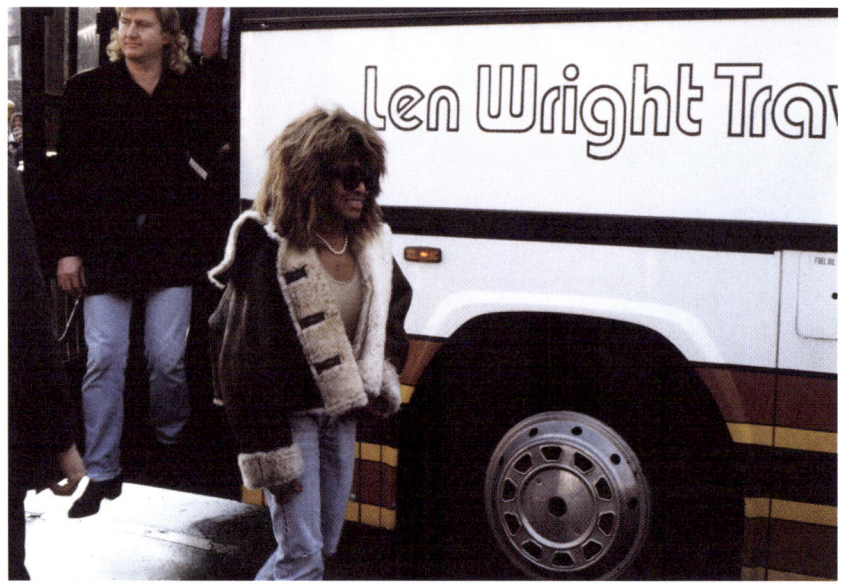

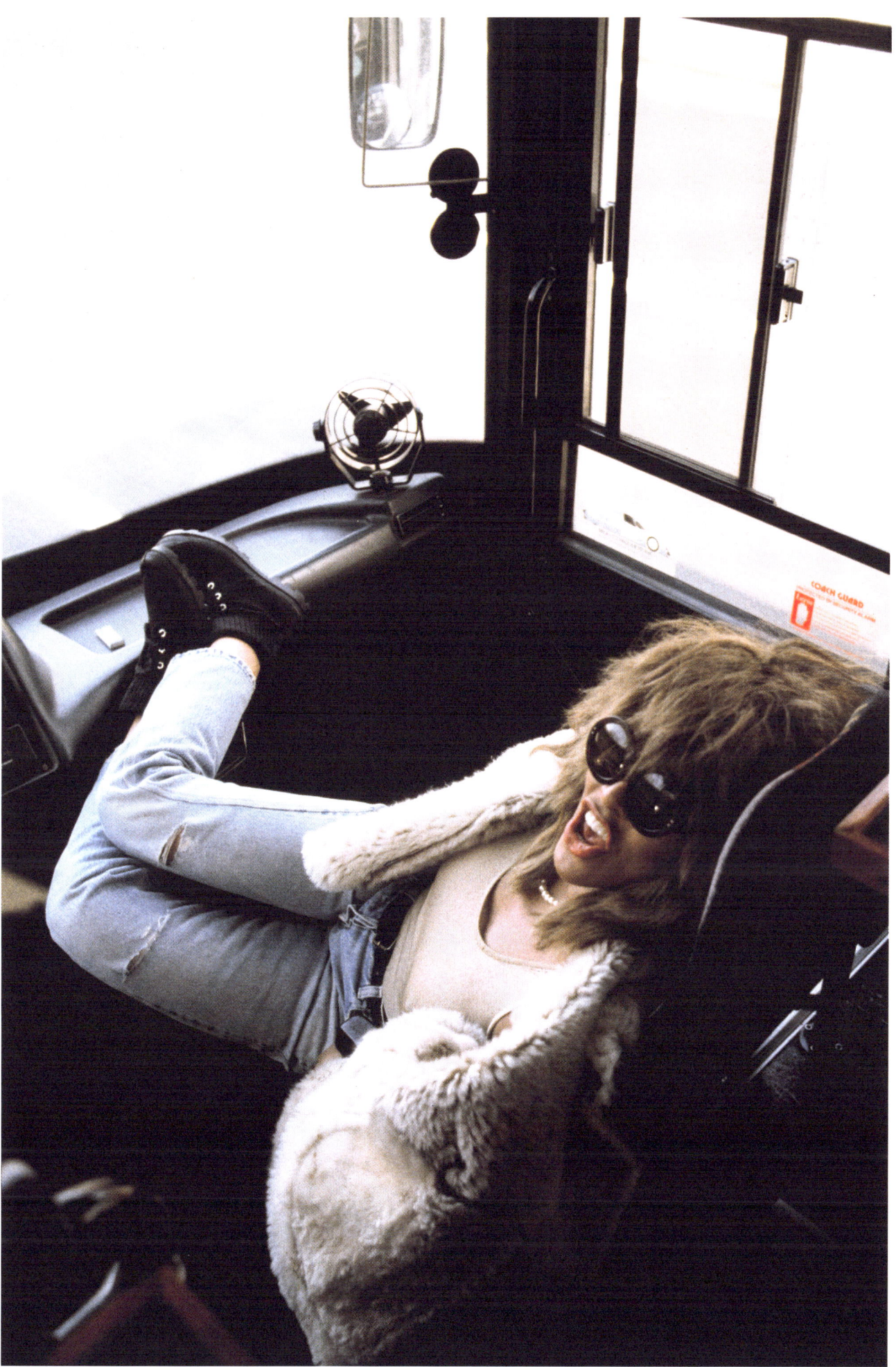

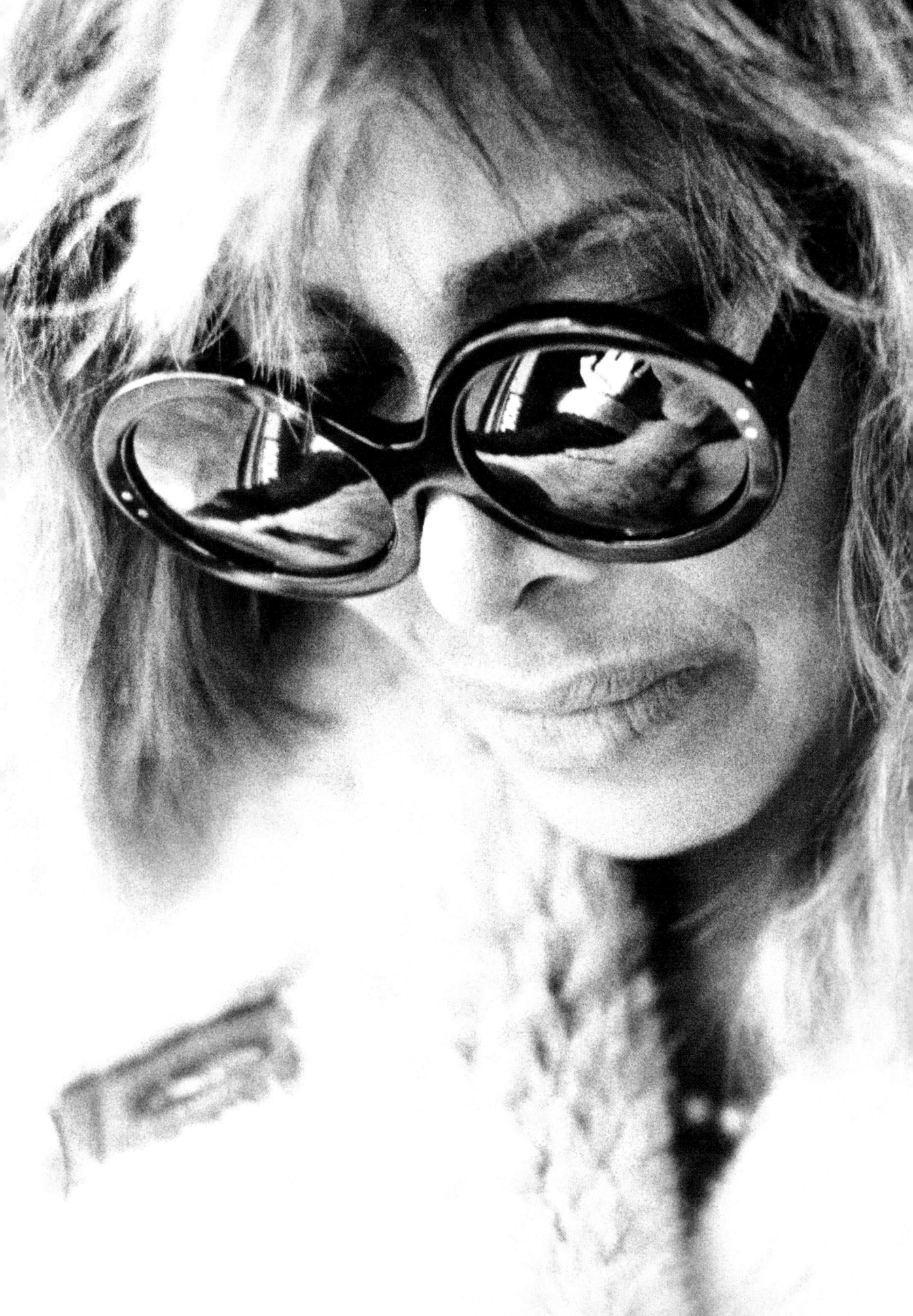

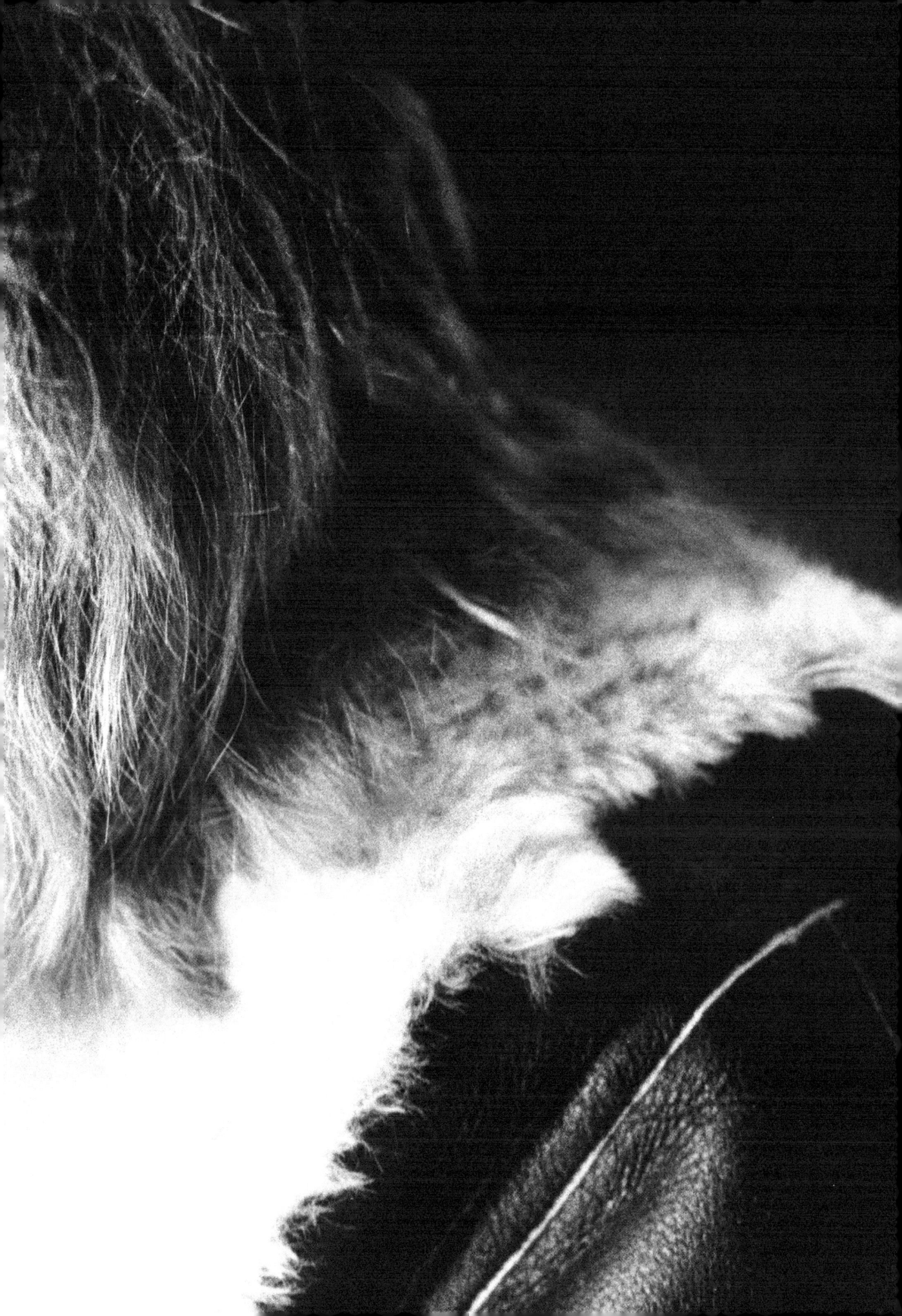

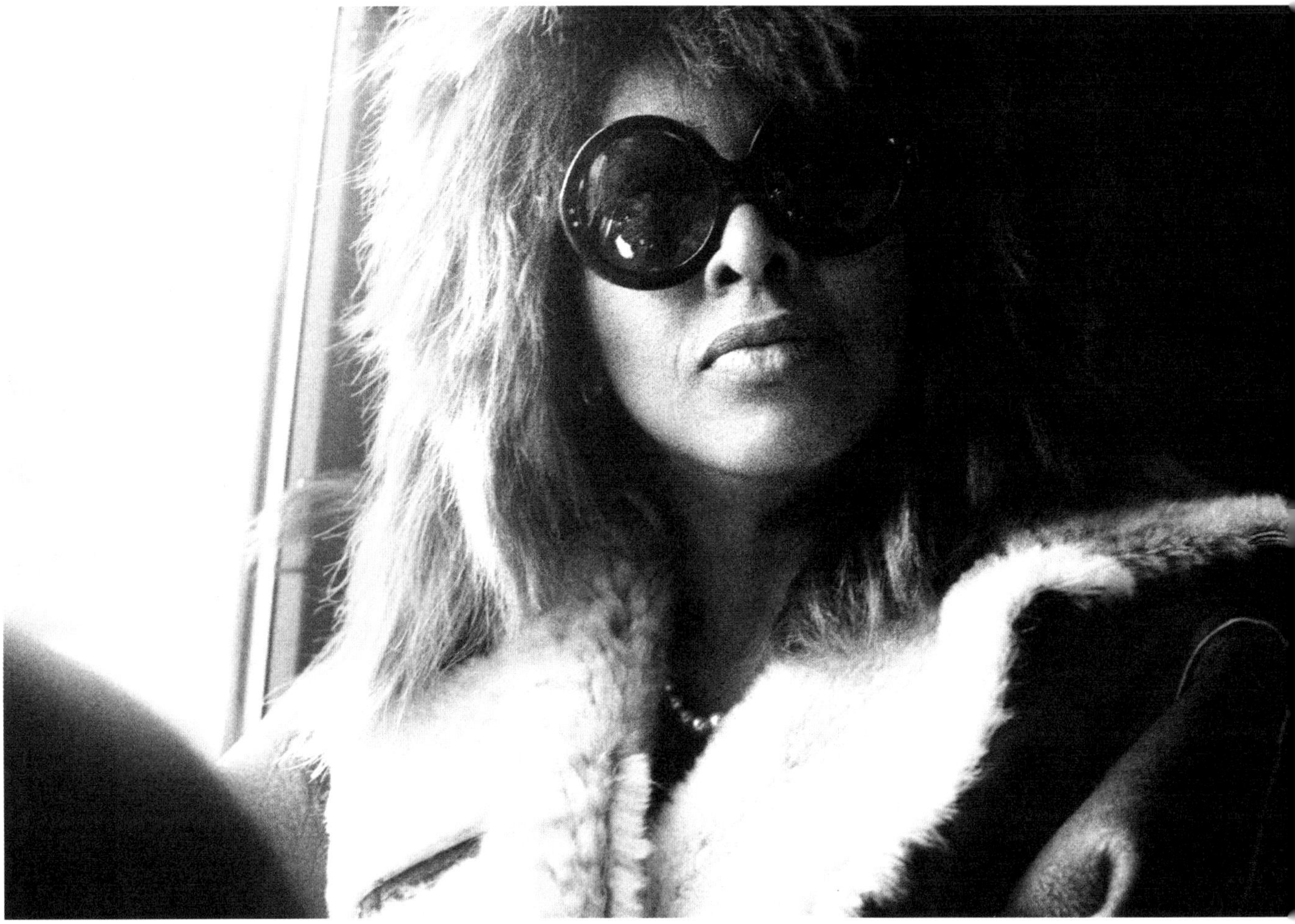

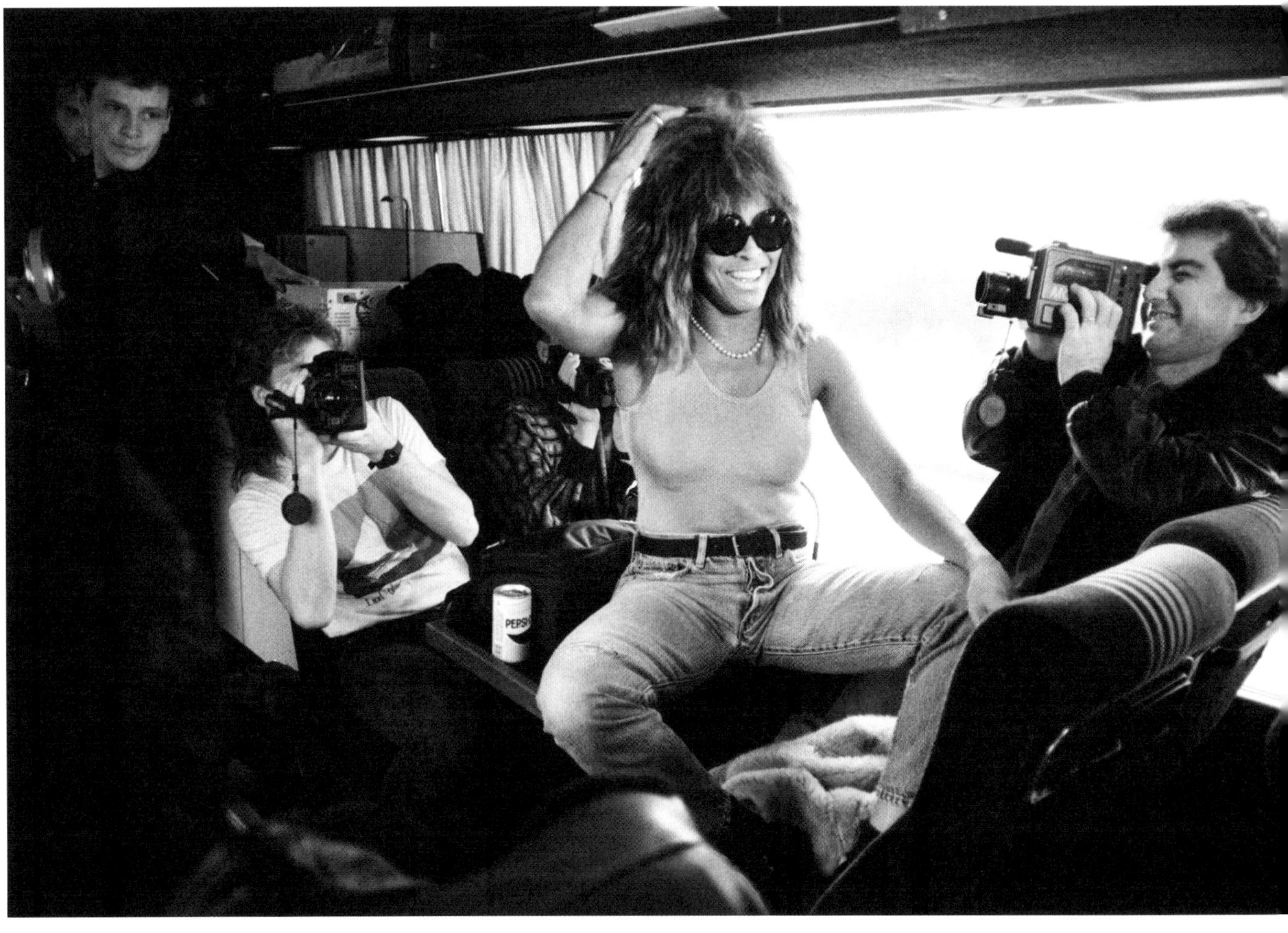

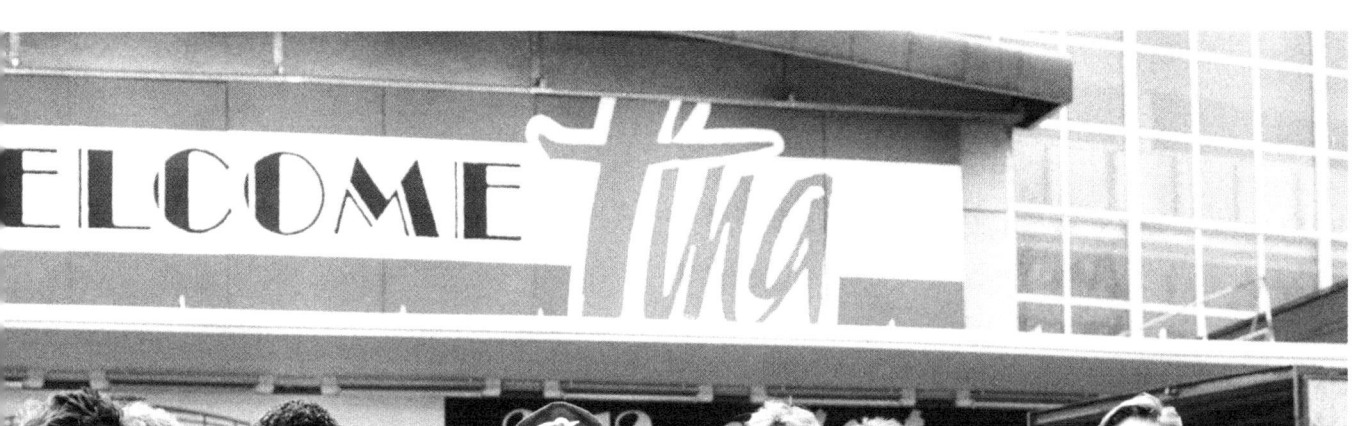

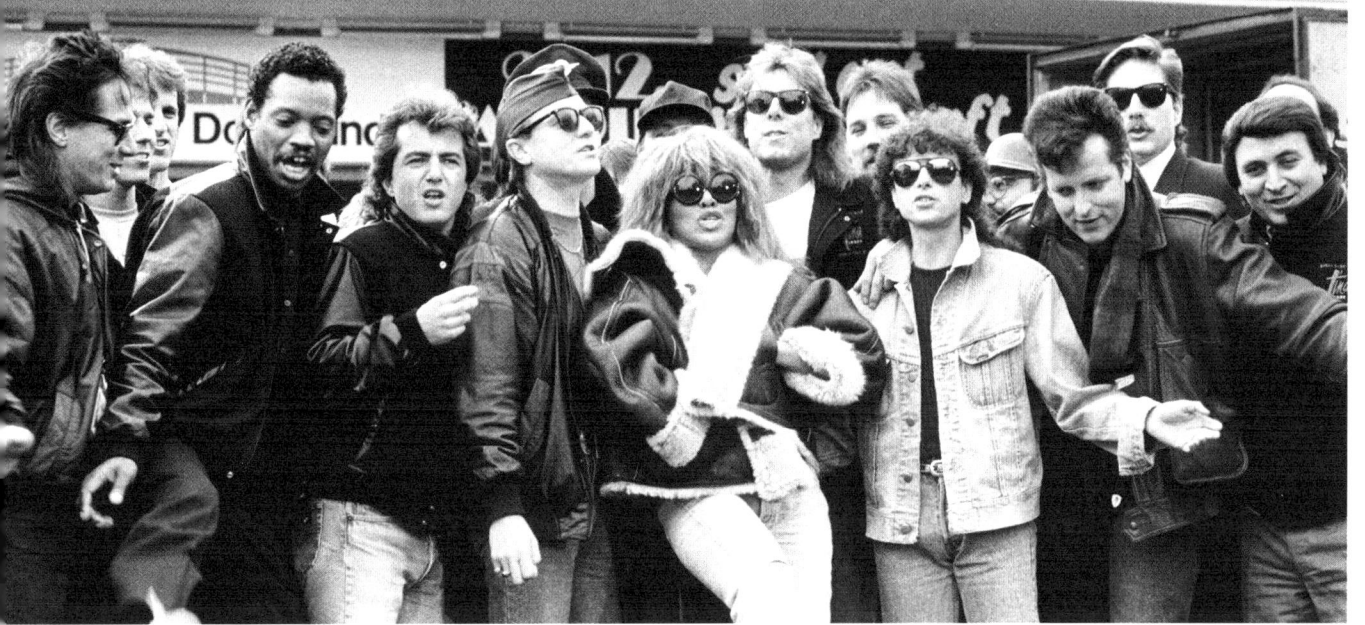

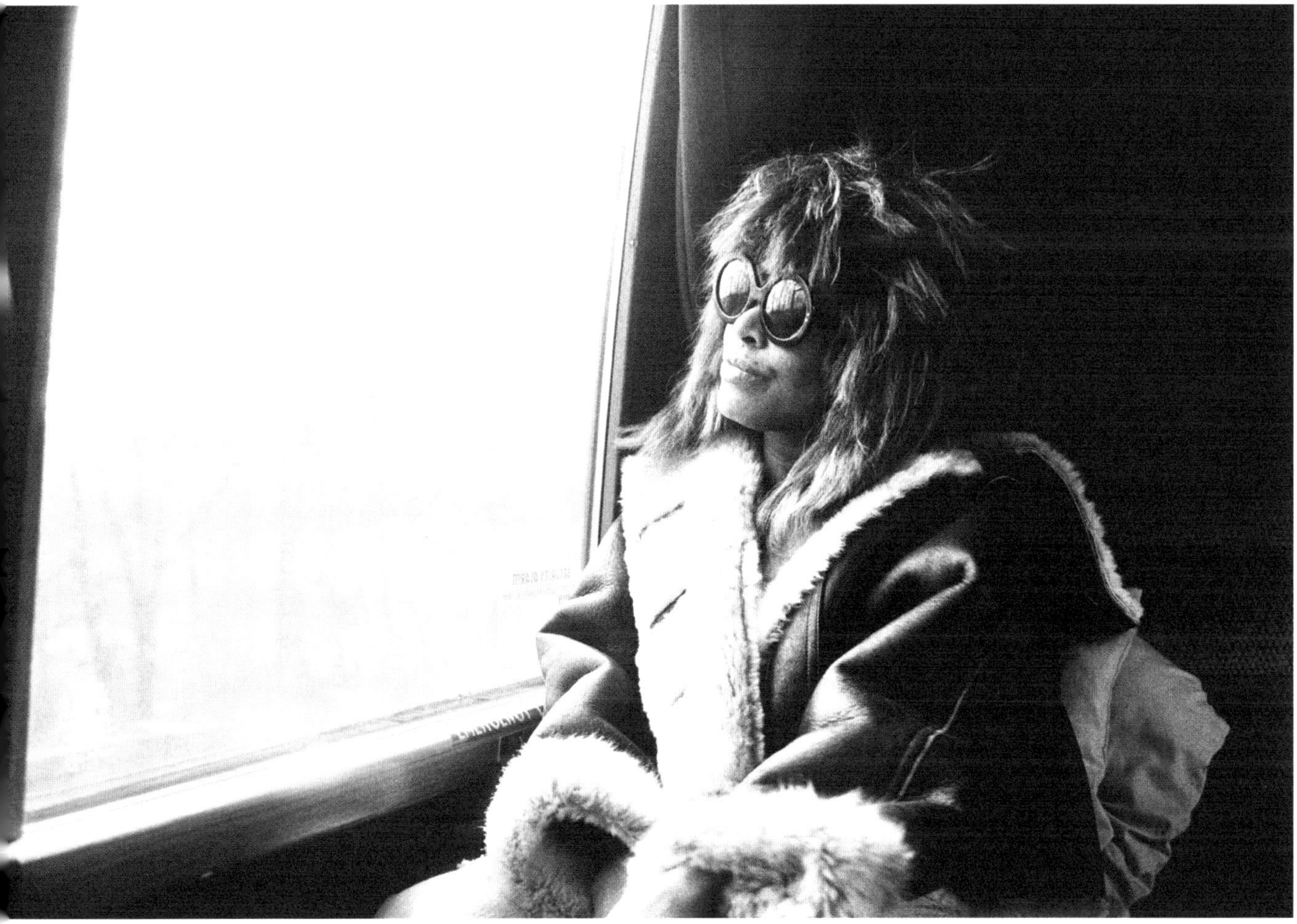

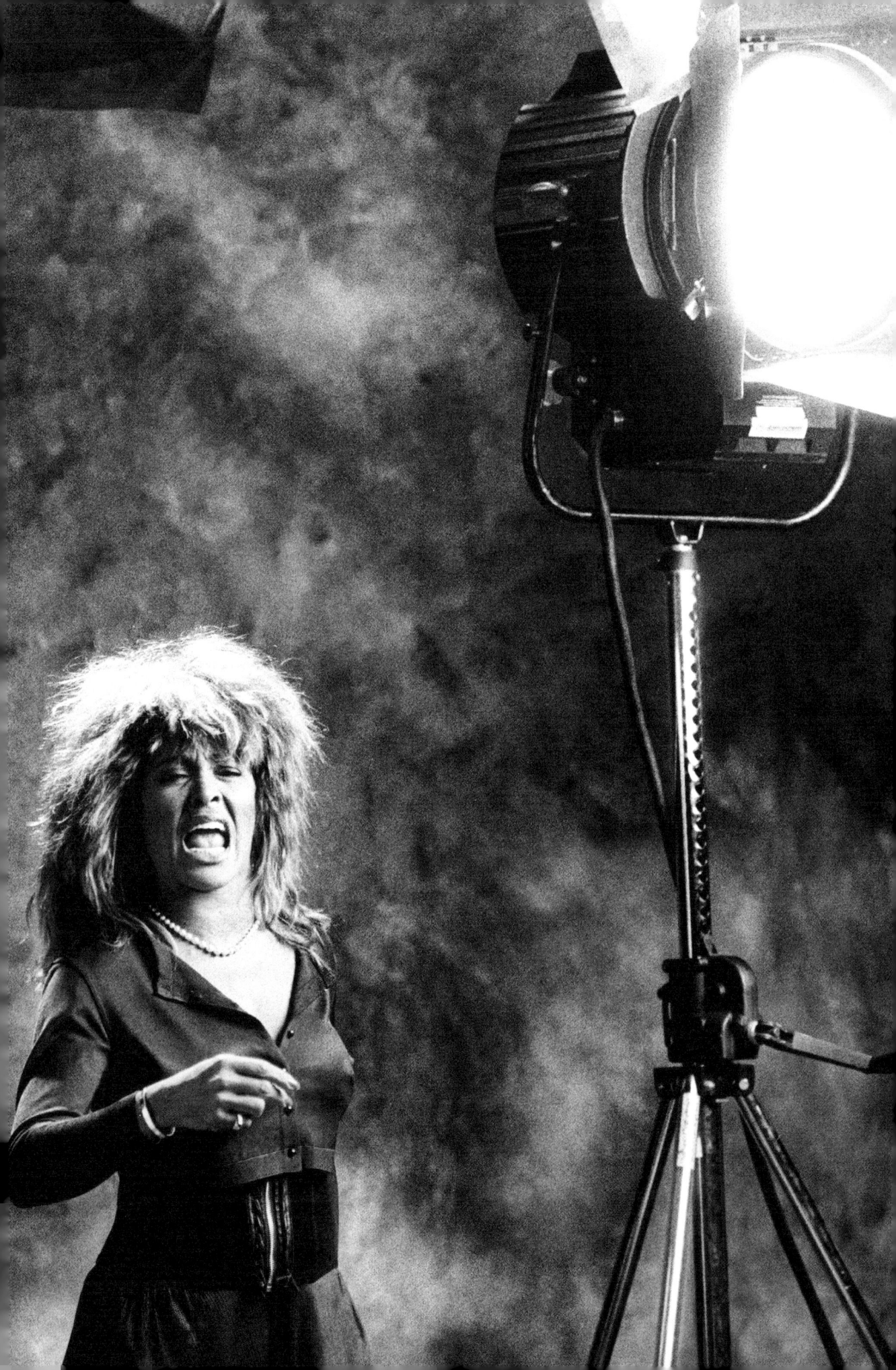

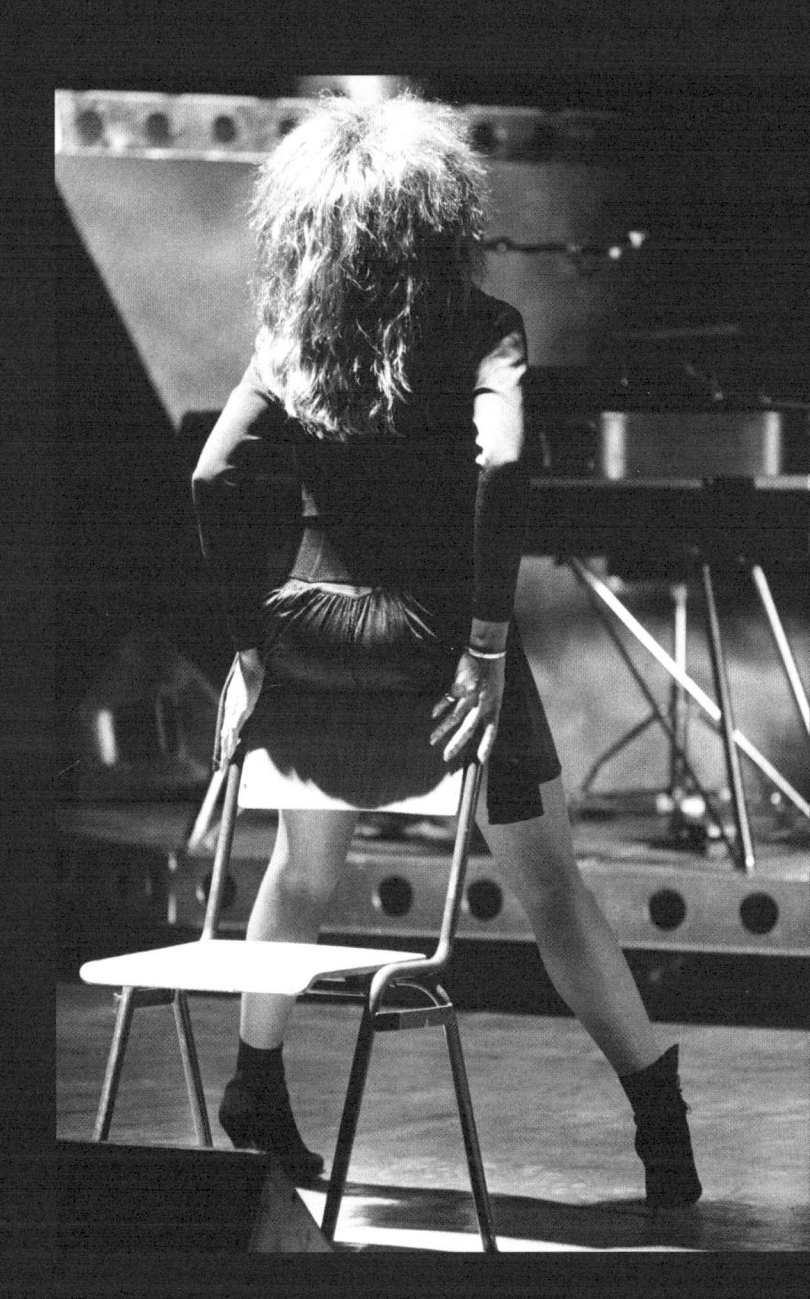

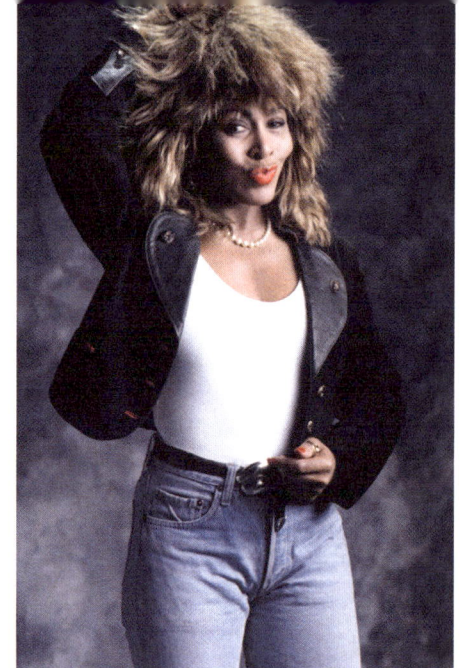

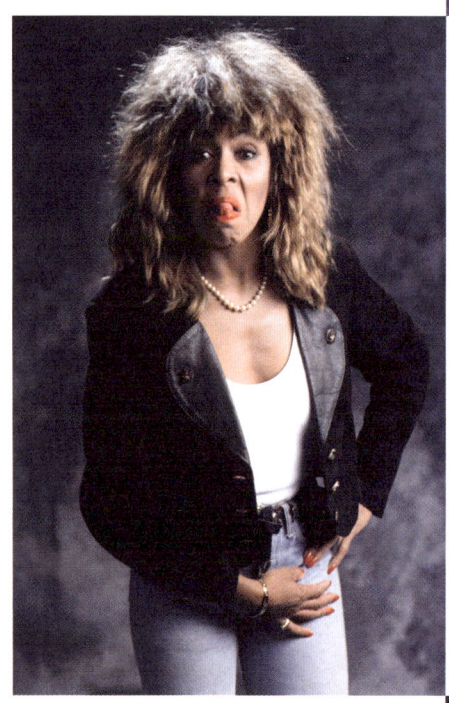

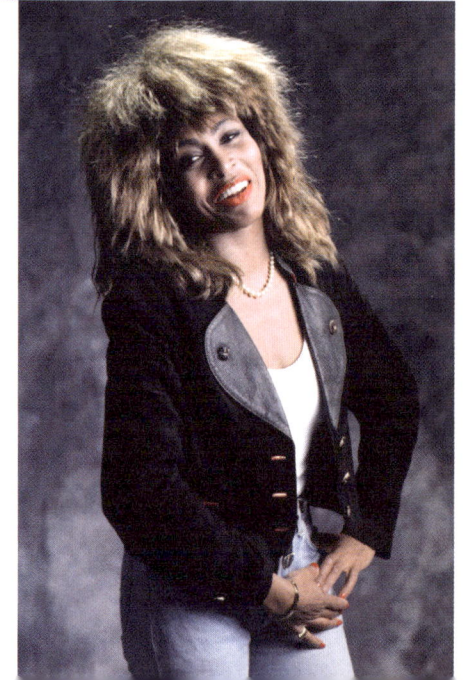

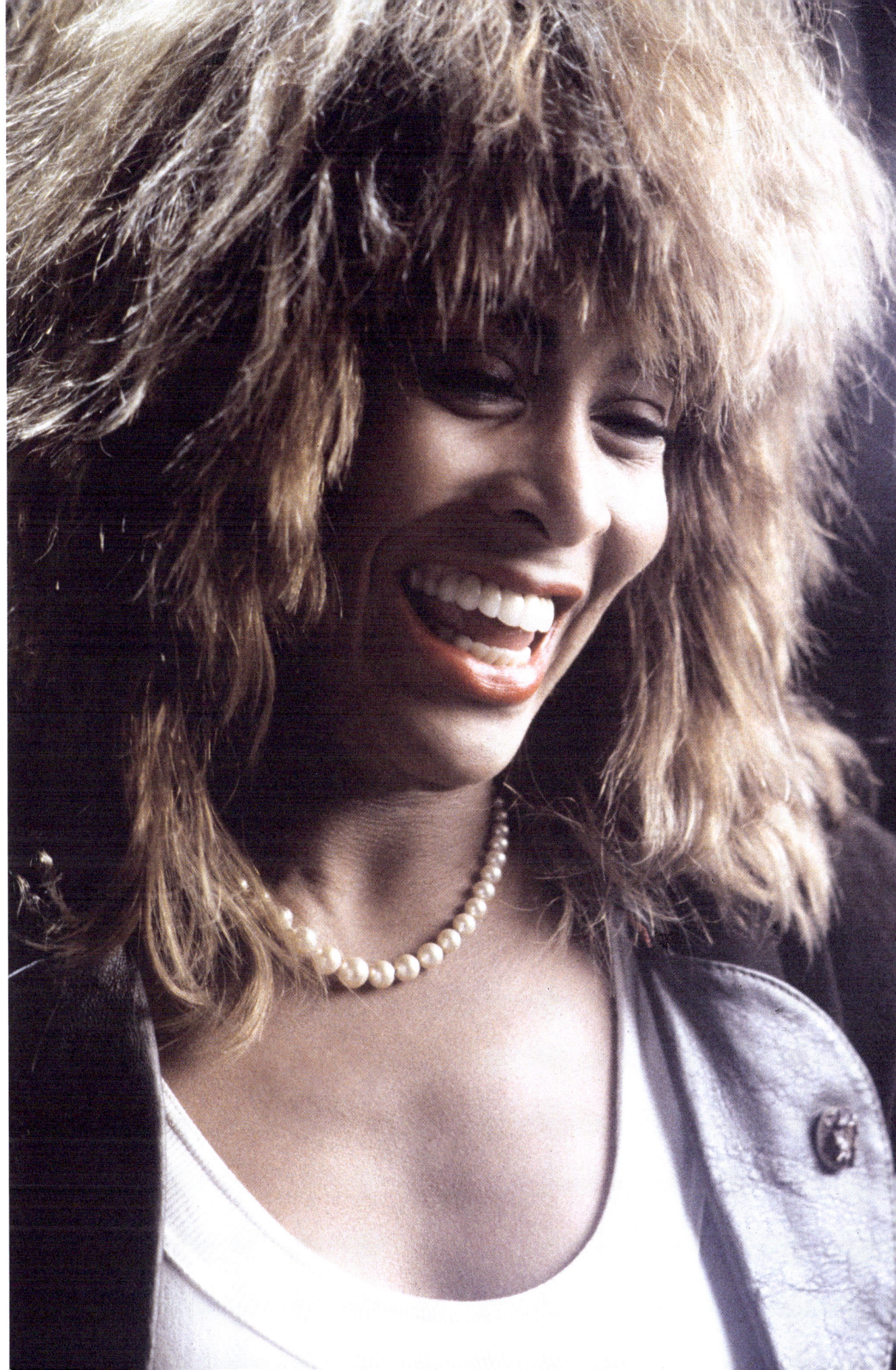

KODAK TX 5063

KODAK TX

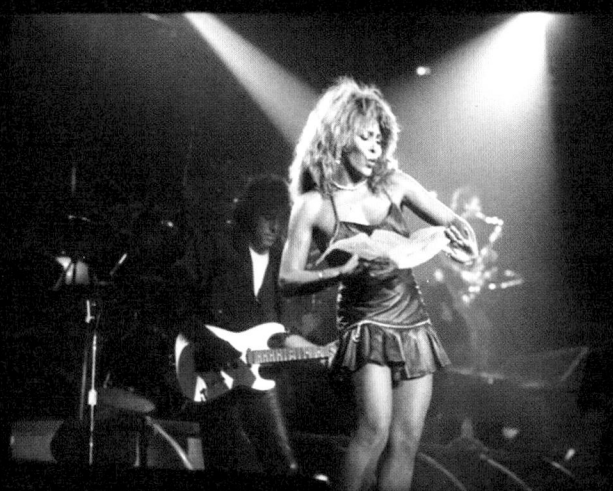

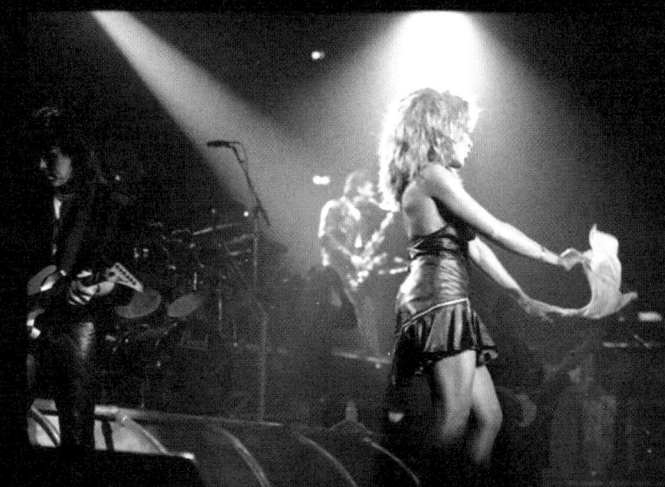

▷2A — 3 ▷3A 4

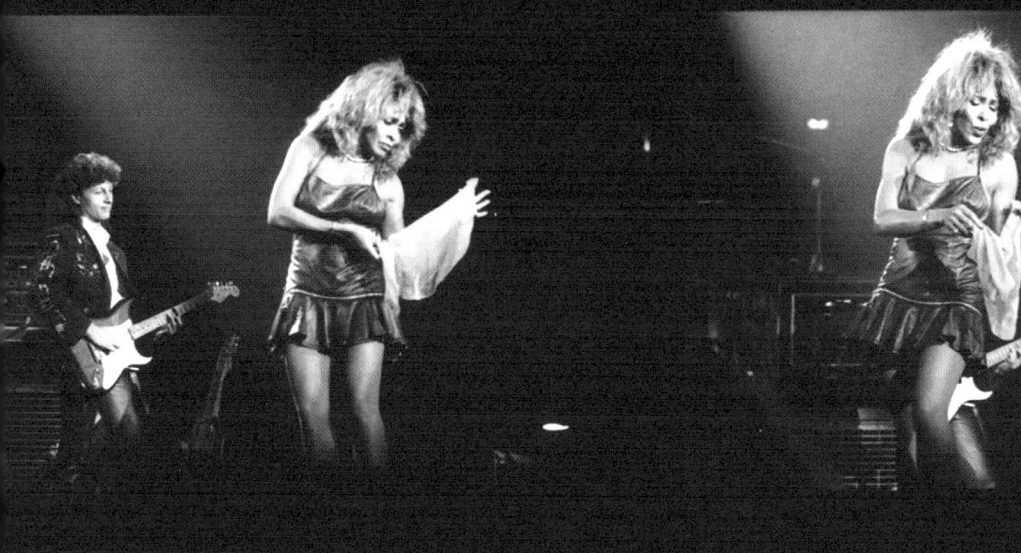

KODAK TX 5063

4A   5   ▷5A   6

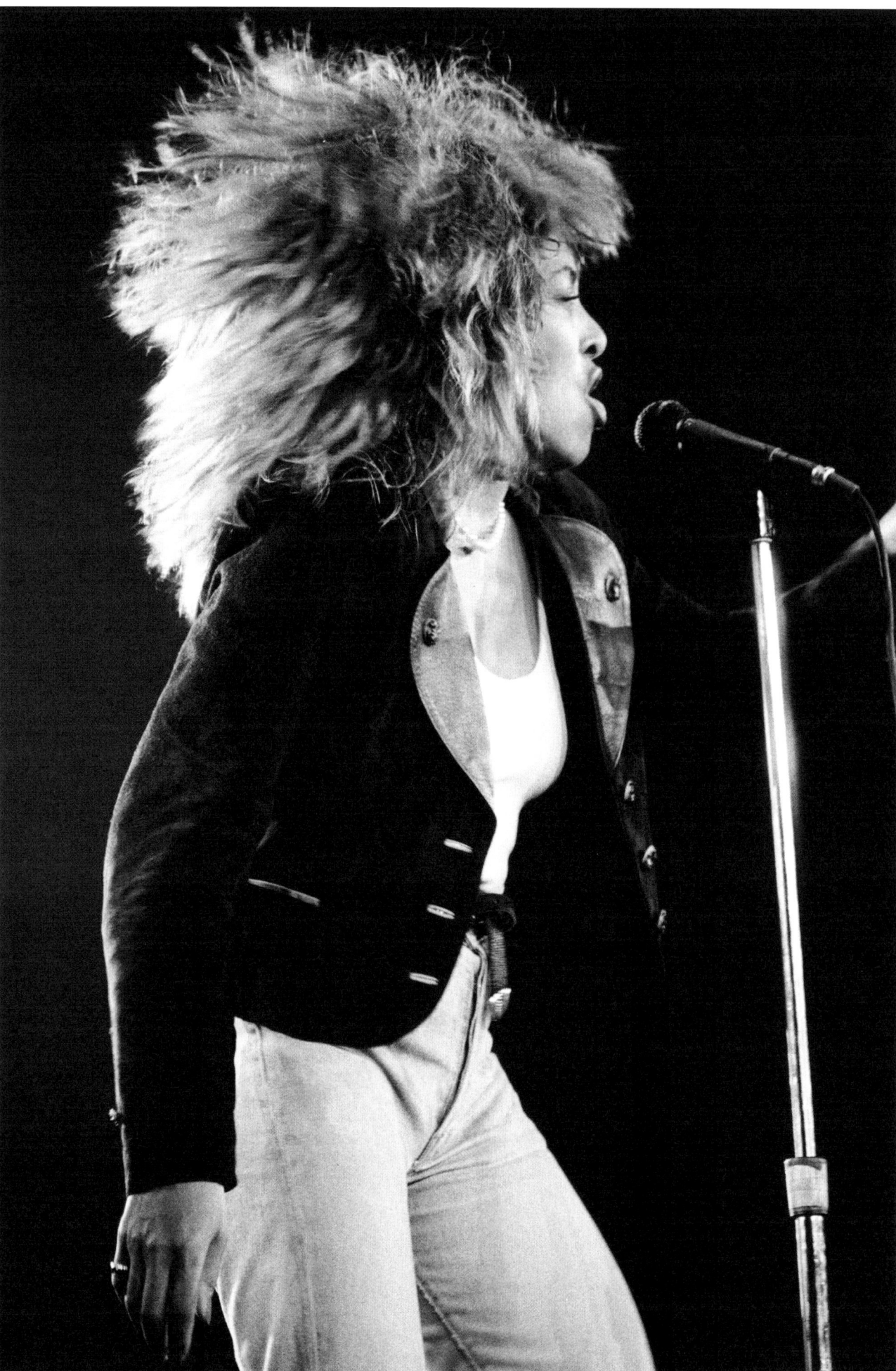

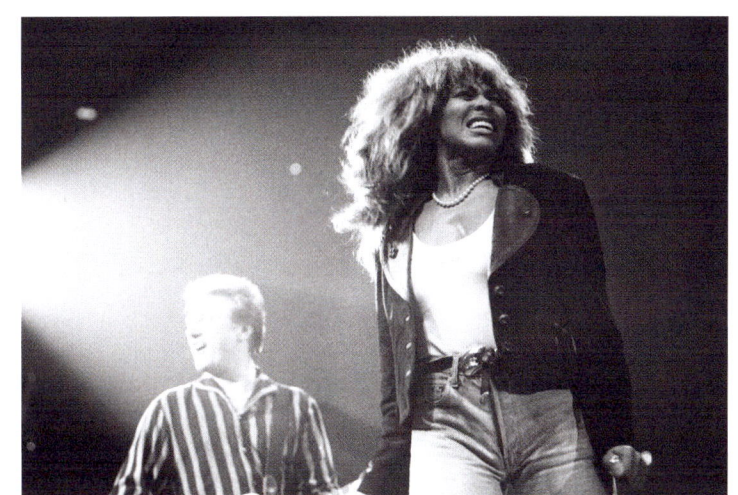

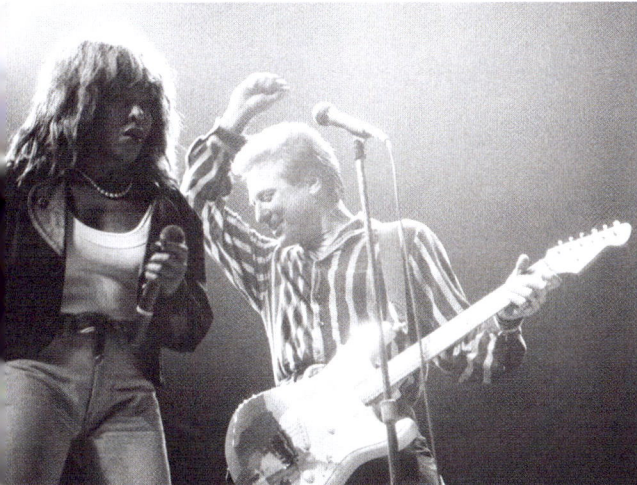

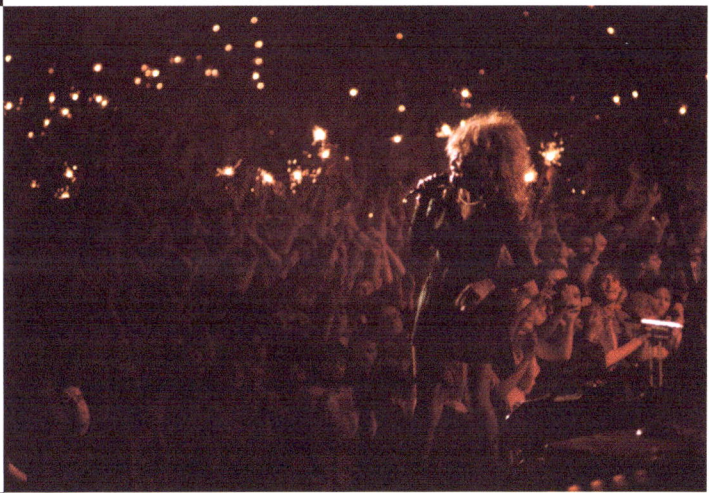

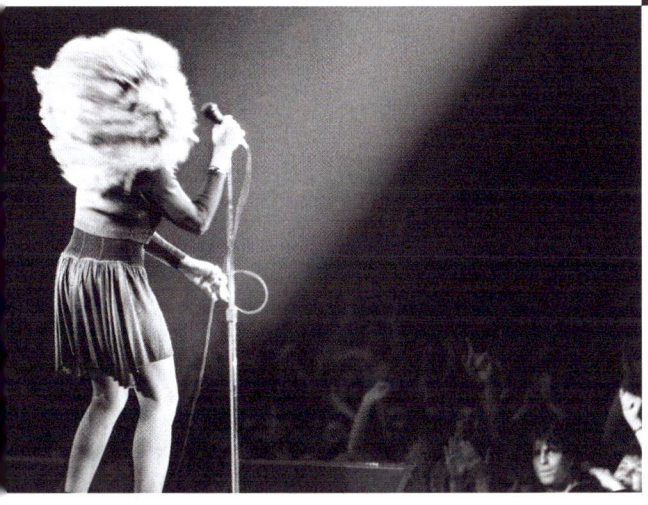

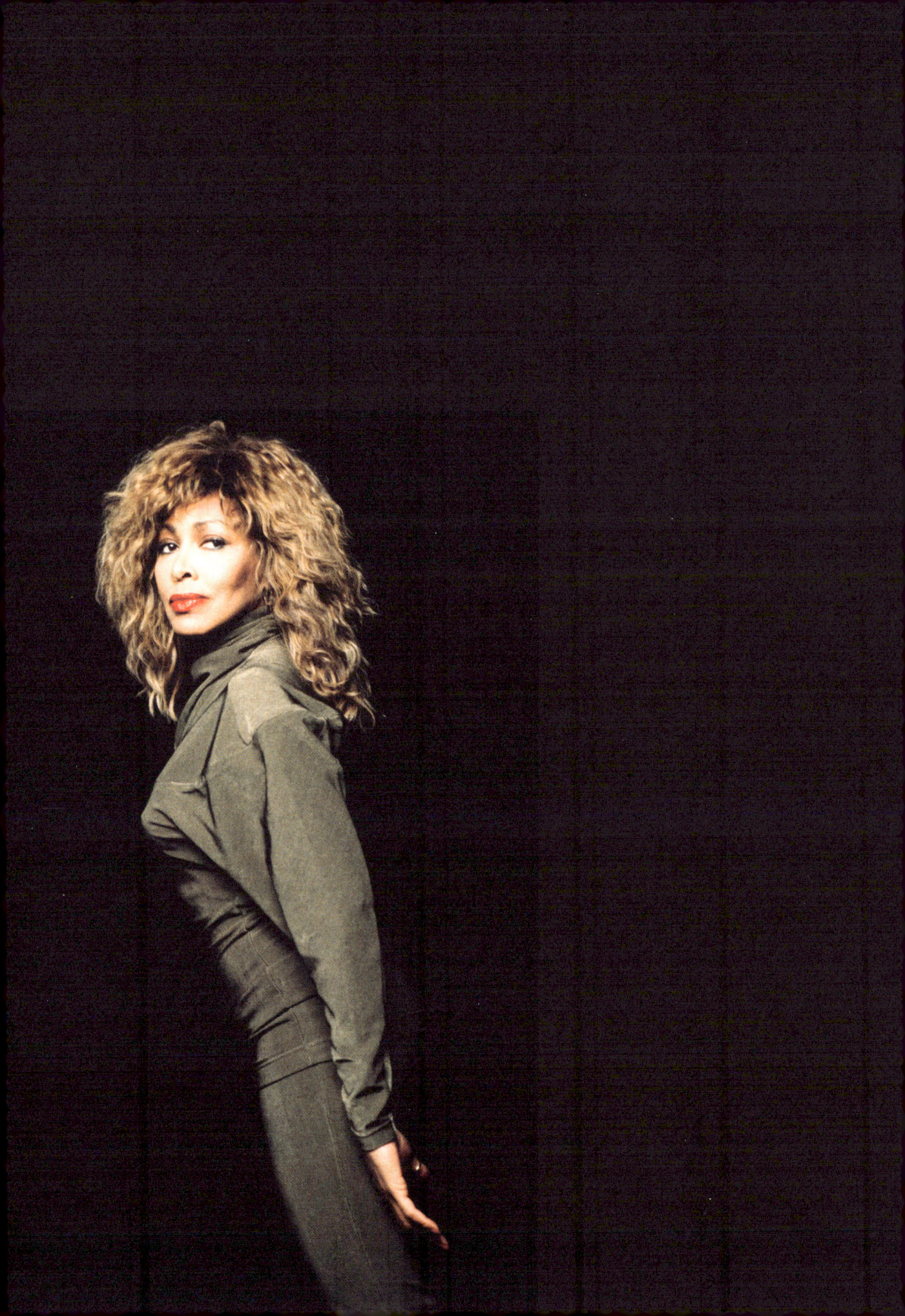

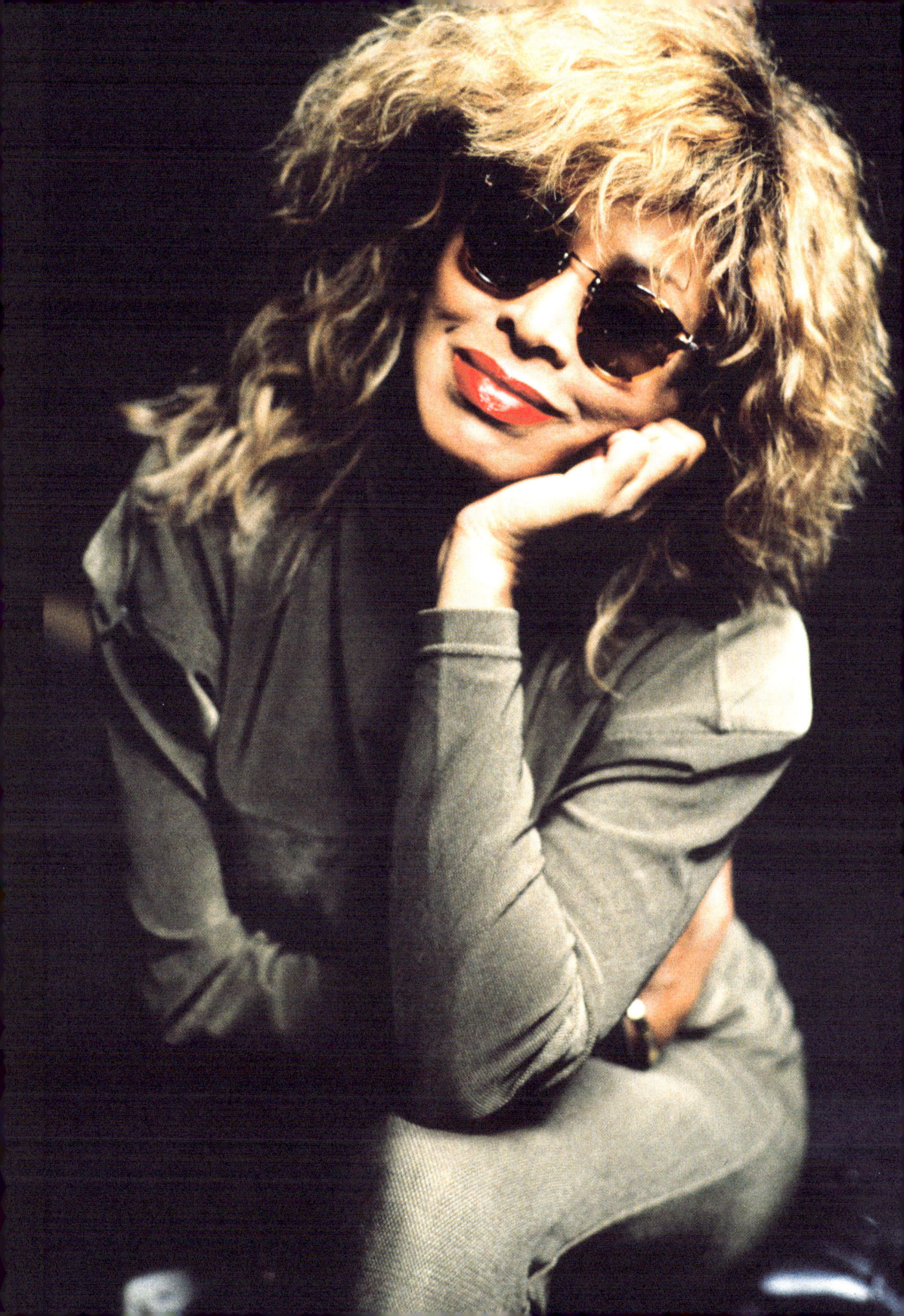

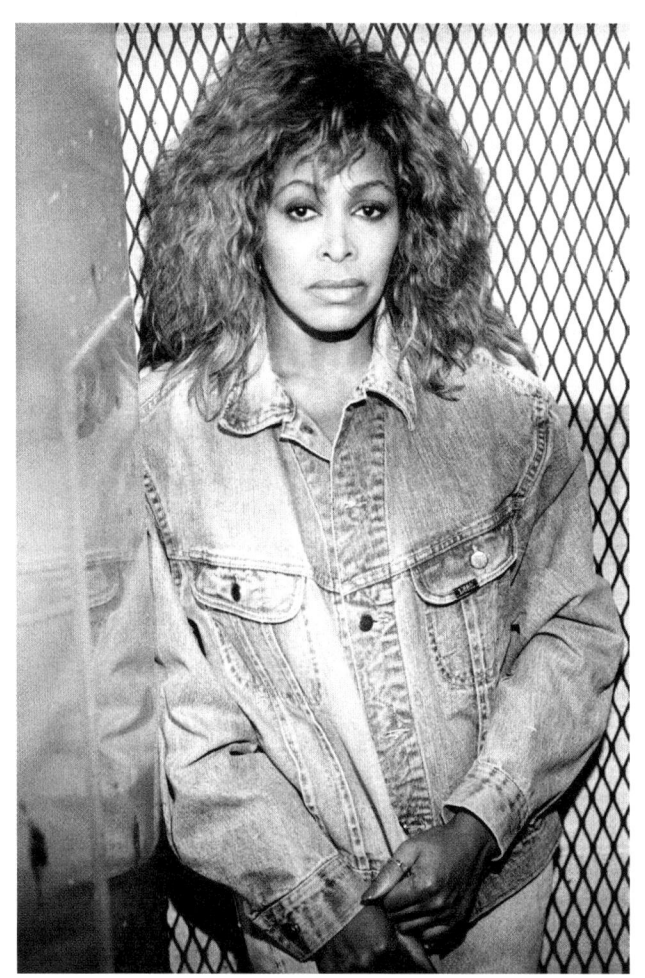

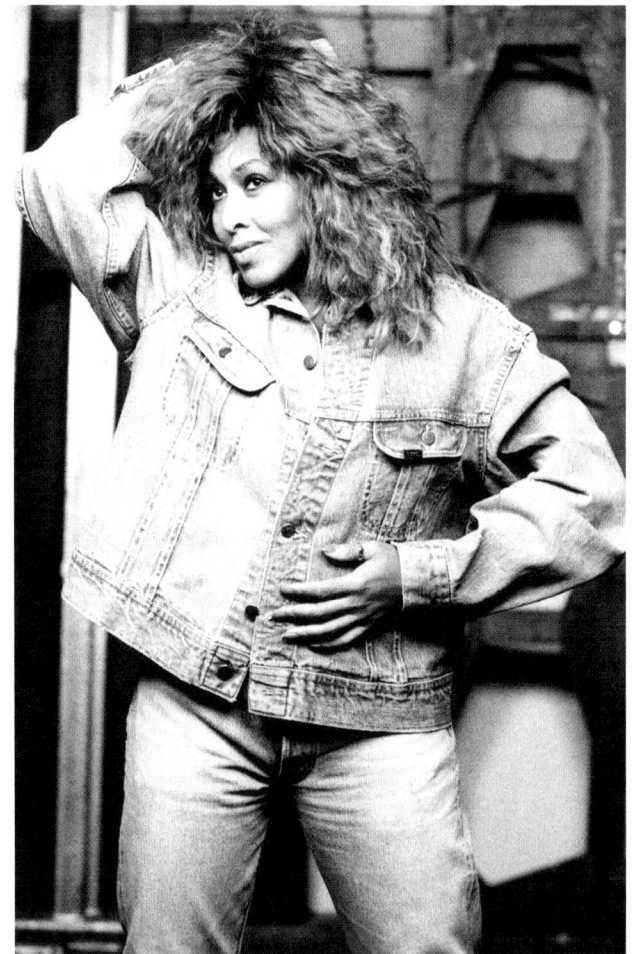

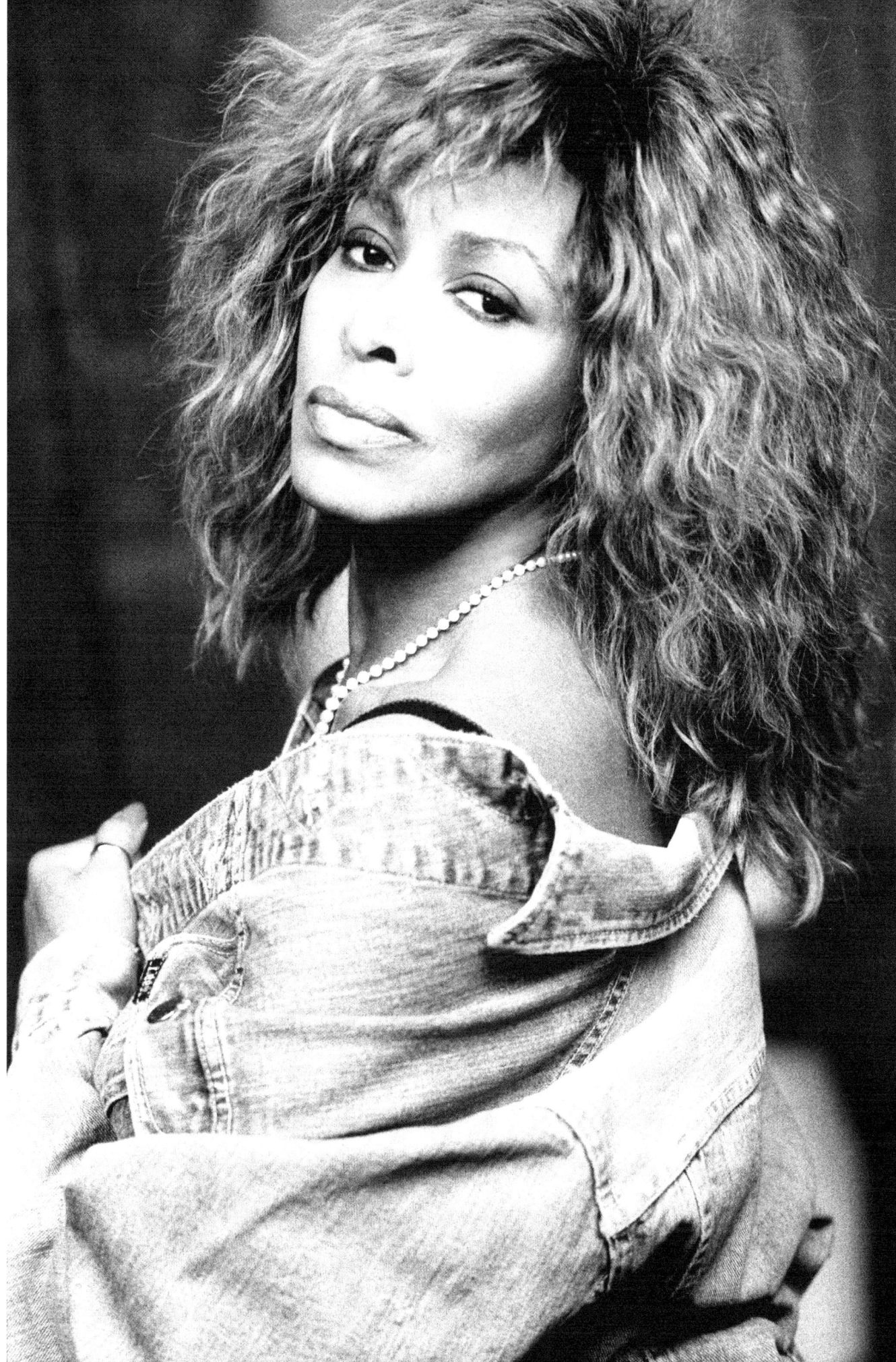

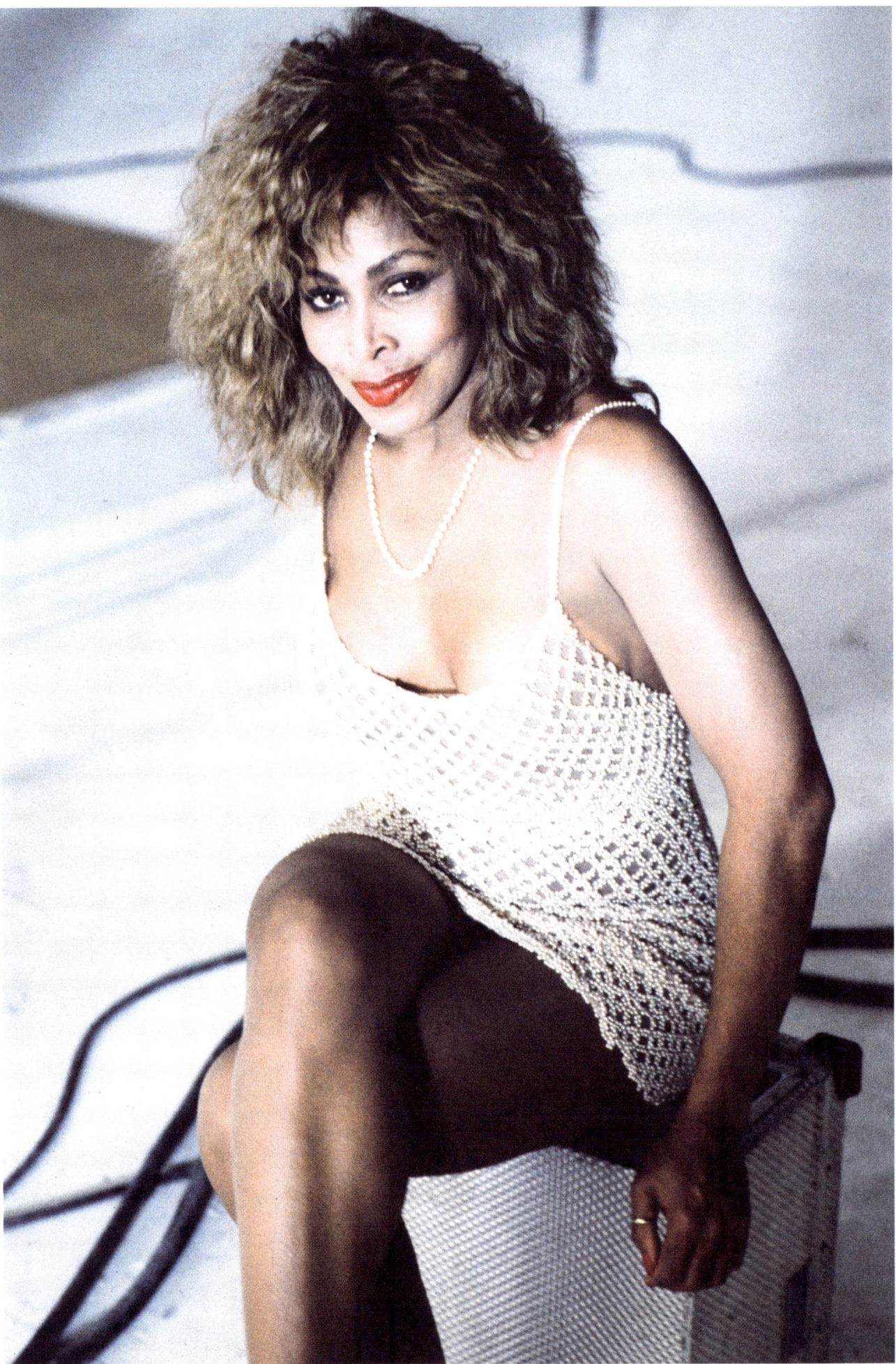

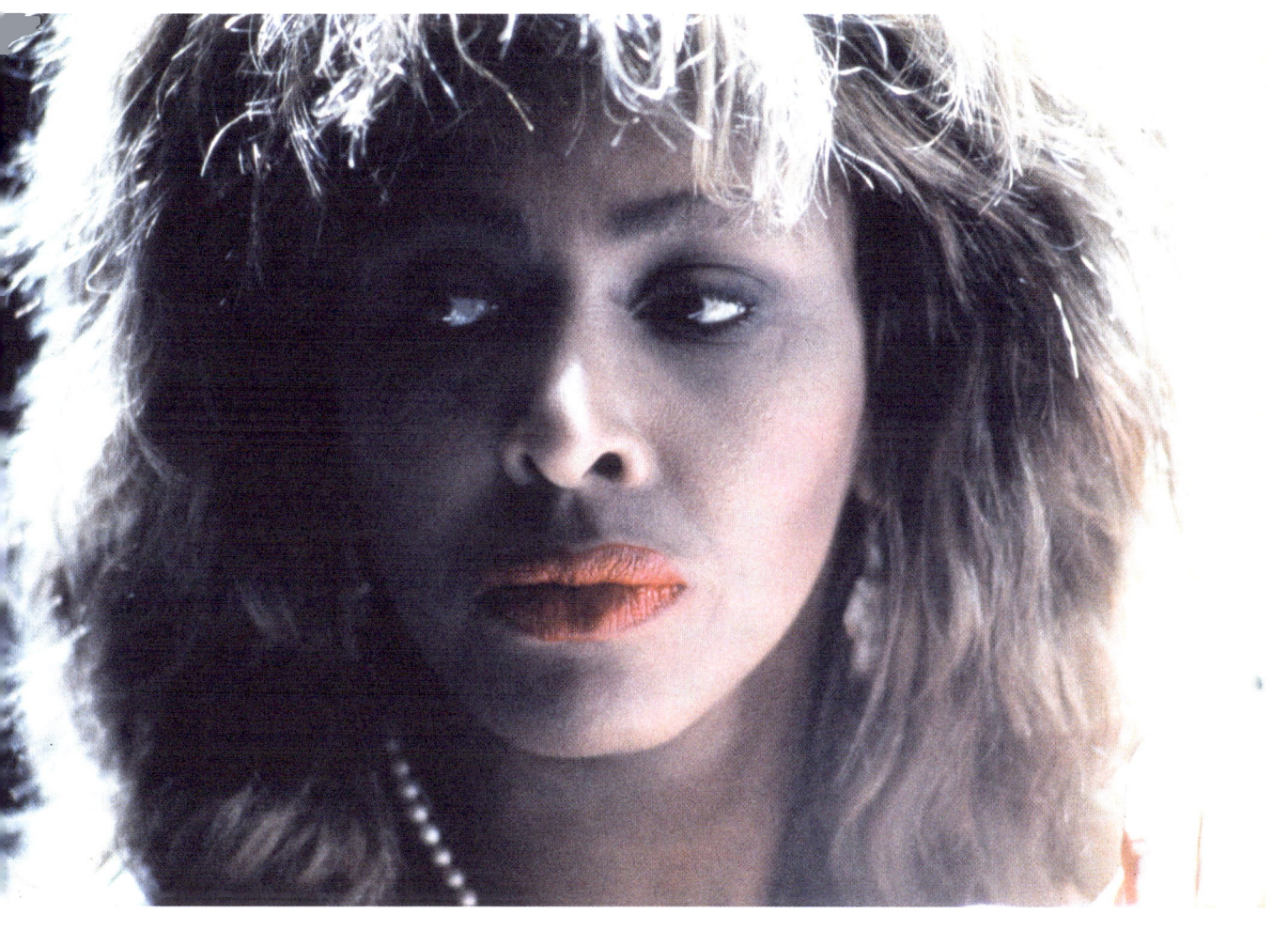

1989

'STEAMY WINDOWS' **video shoot**

The sequence of stills Paul took of Tina during Andy Morahan's video shoot for the third single from her *Foreign Affair* album, are some of his favourites. 'She's pouting and pulling these extraordinary shapes,' Paul says. Filmed at Pinewood Studios, Paul was now adept at finding his moment: 'These shoots would just go on and on, whole days. It was about using the breaks you had, and then capturing what was going on without getting in the way – dodging around and not being seen.' The jumper dress shots came from this session and as trust was built between photographer, subject and manager, more time was allowed: 'It went from two minutes to five!' Paul remembers.

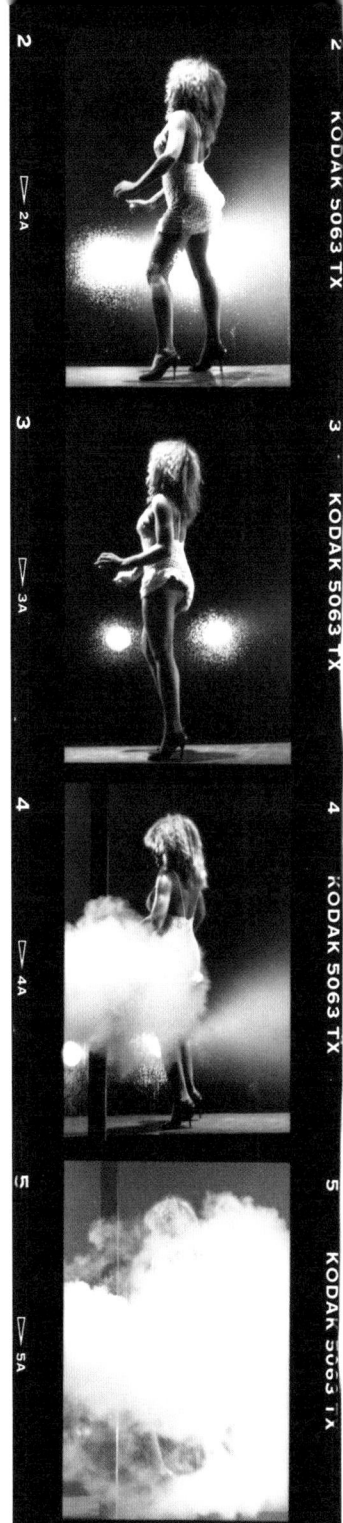
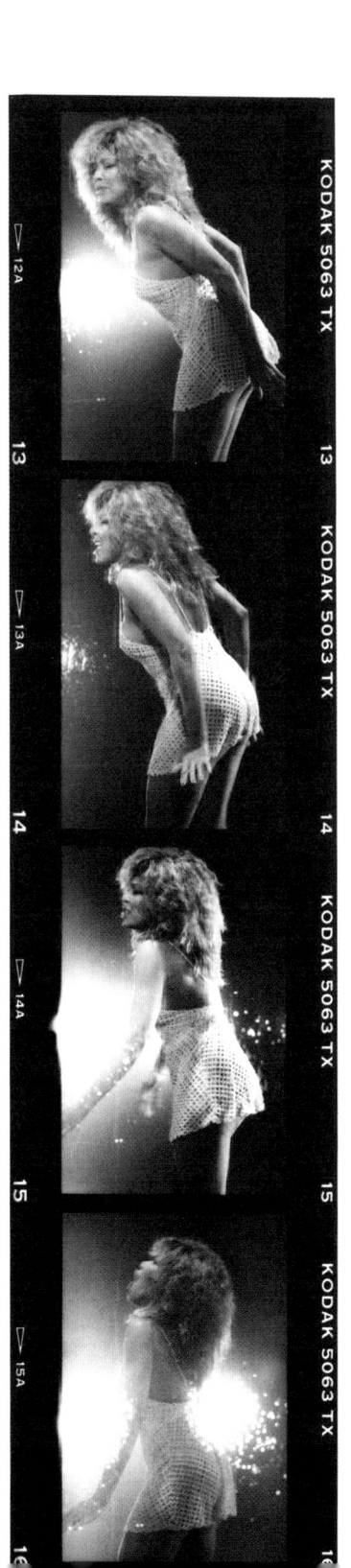

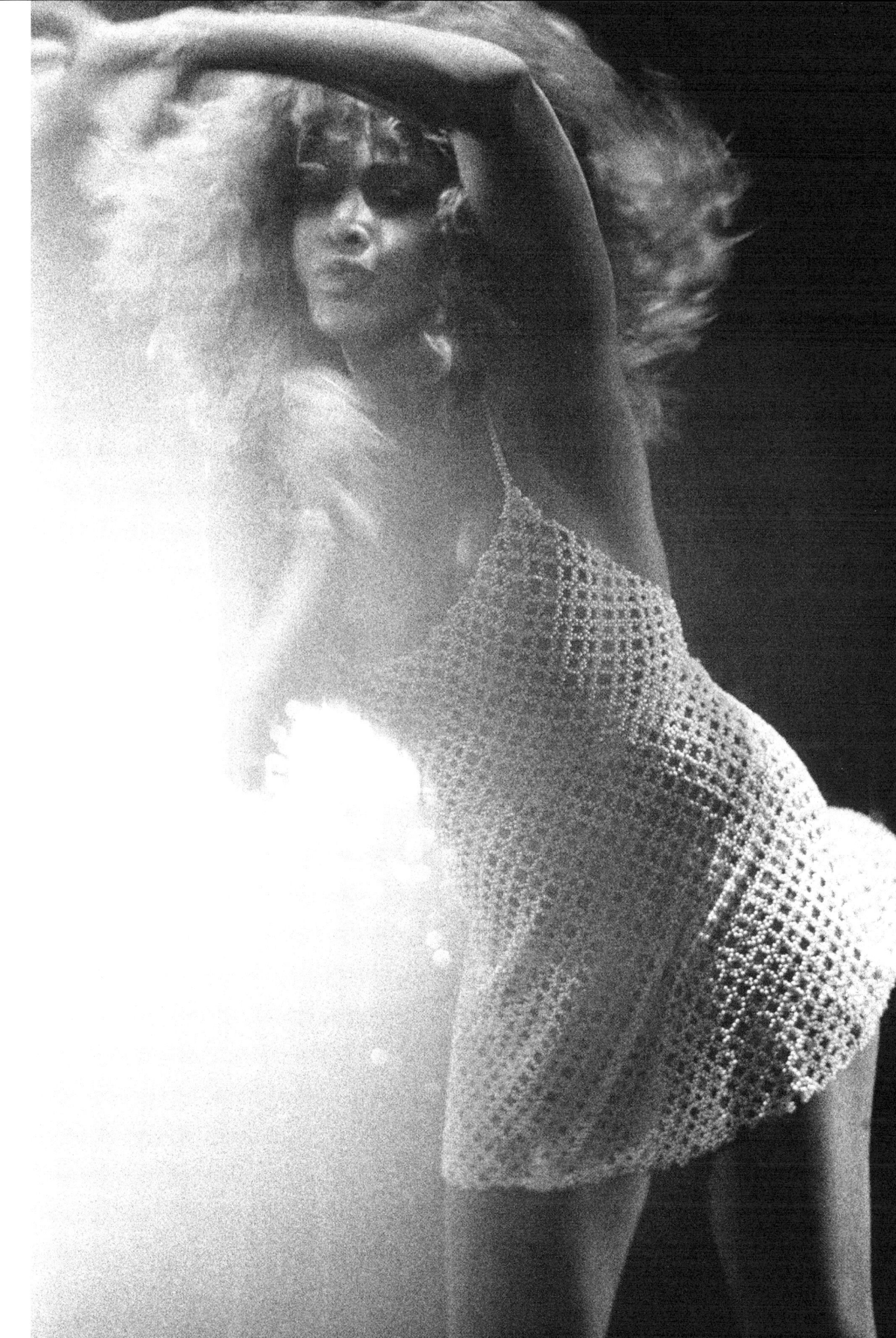

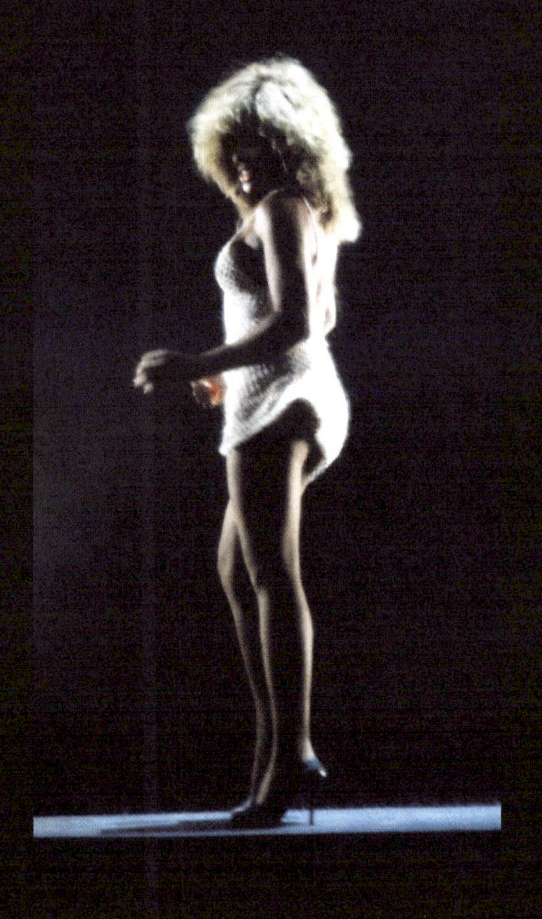

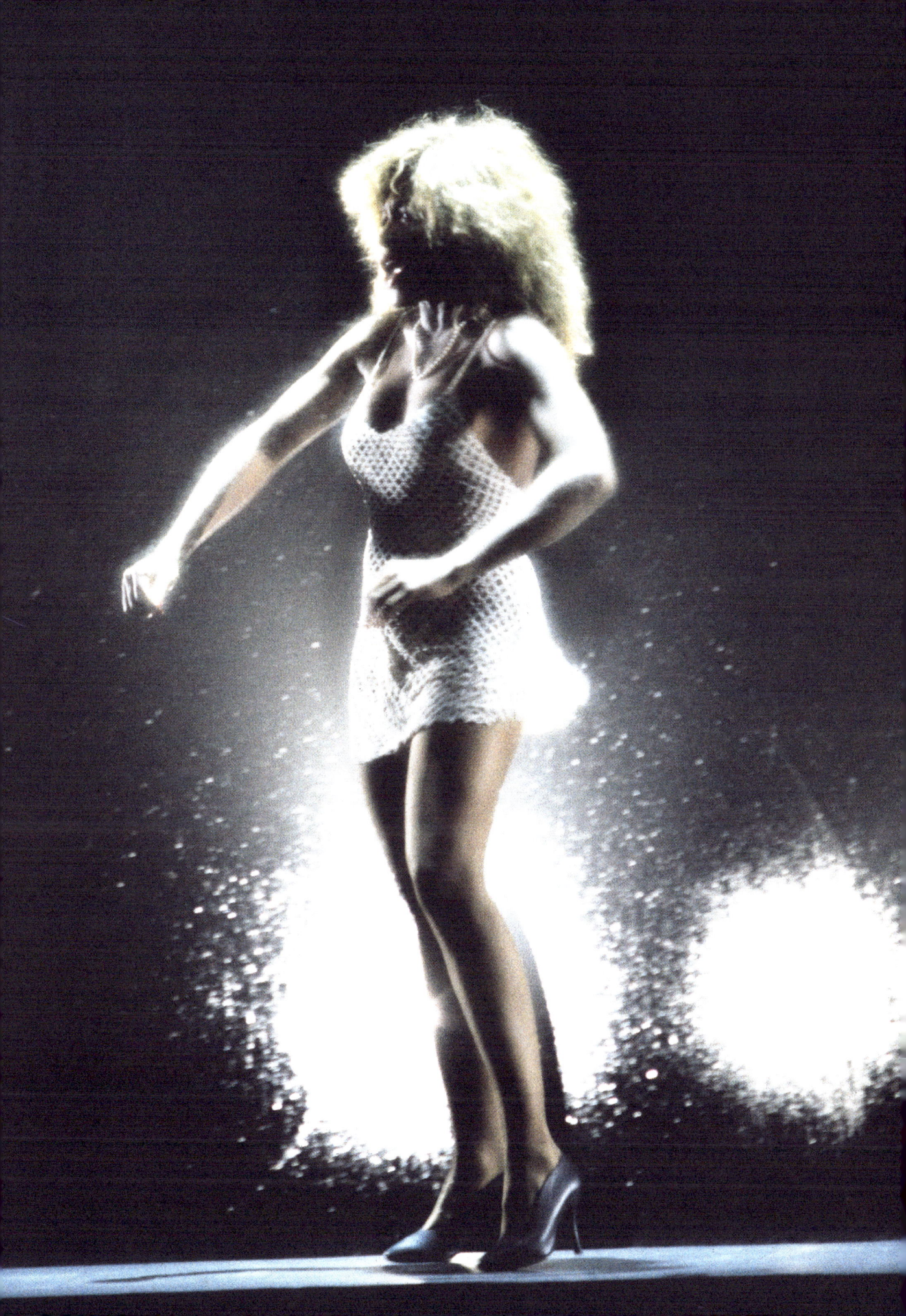

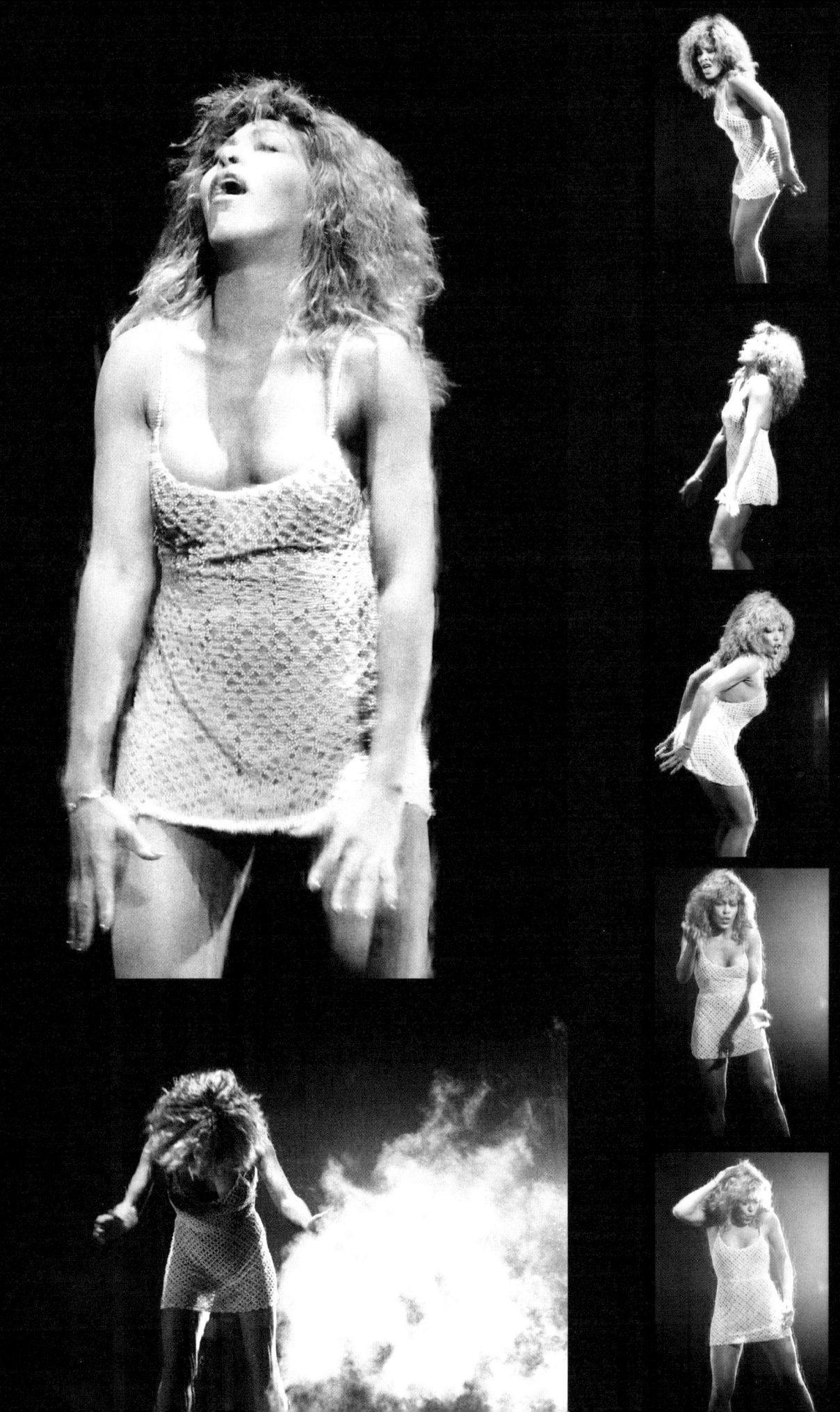

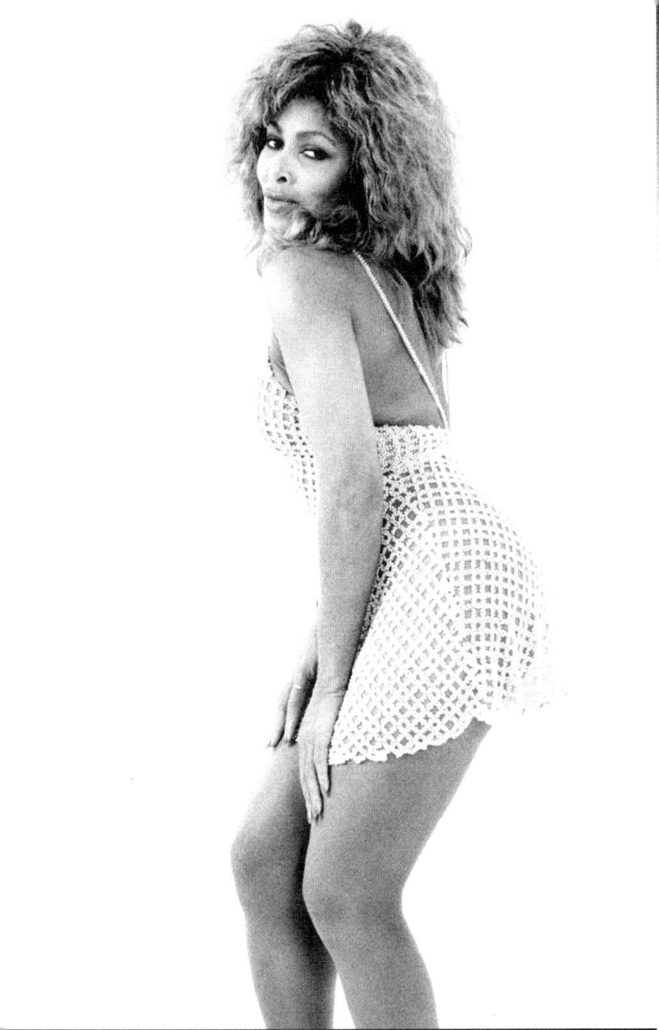

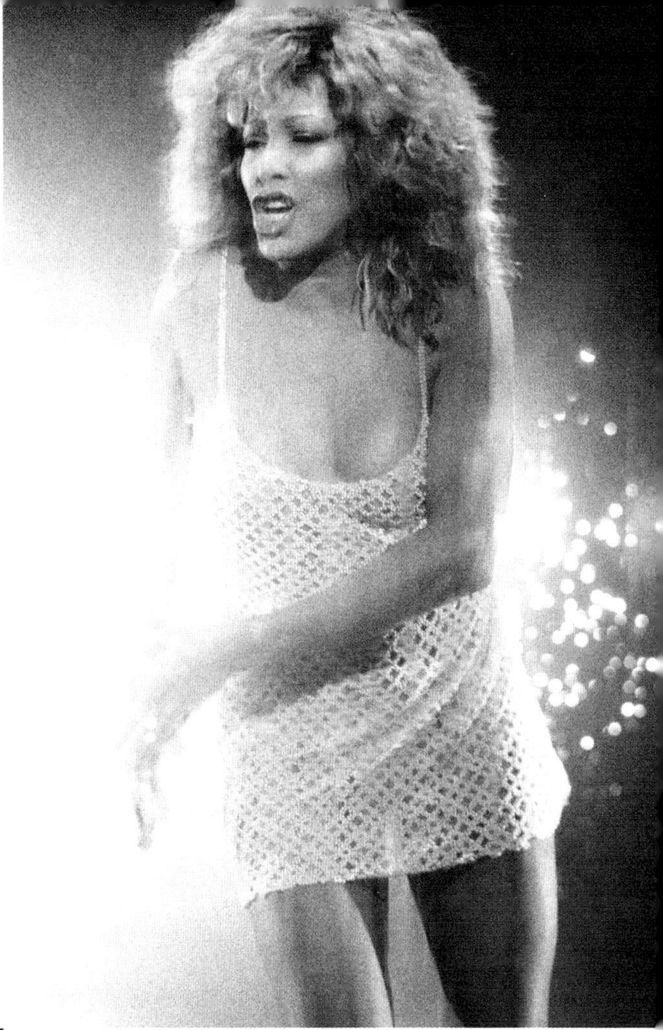

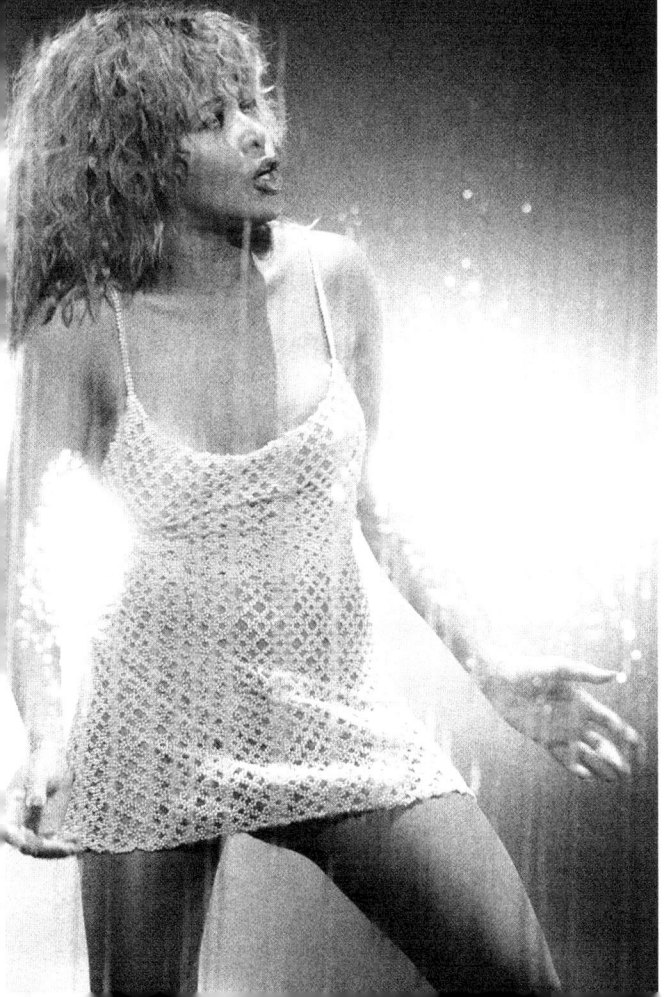
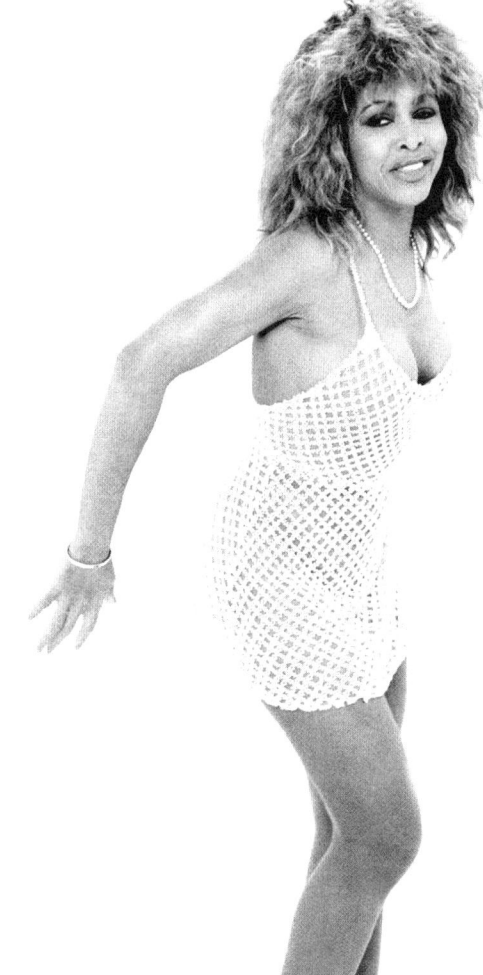

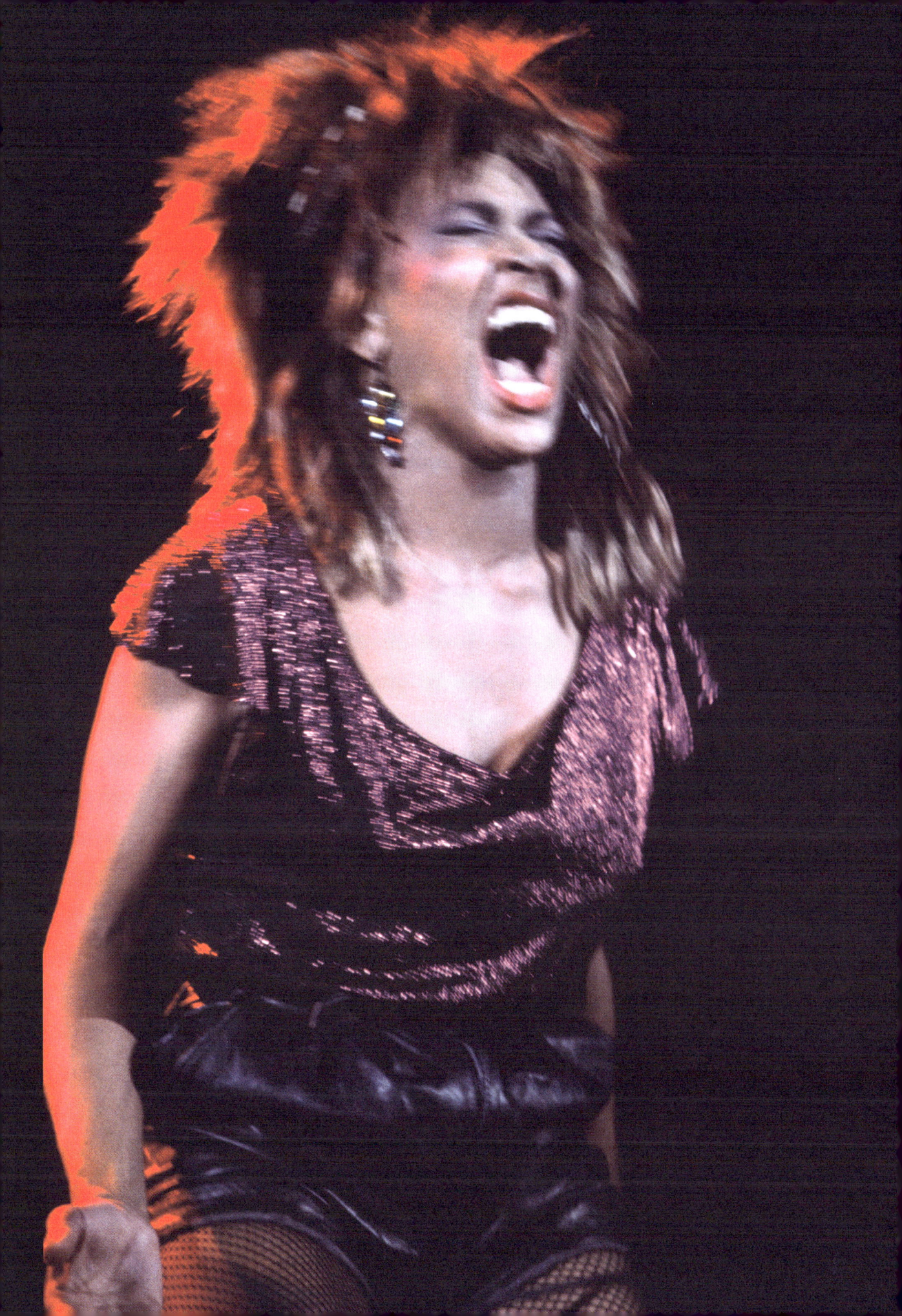

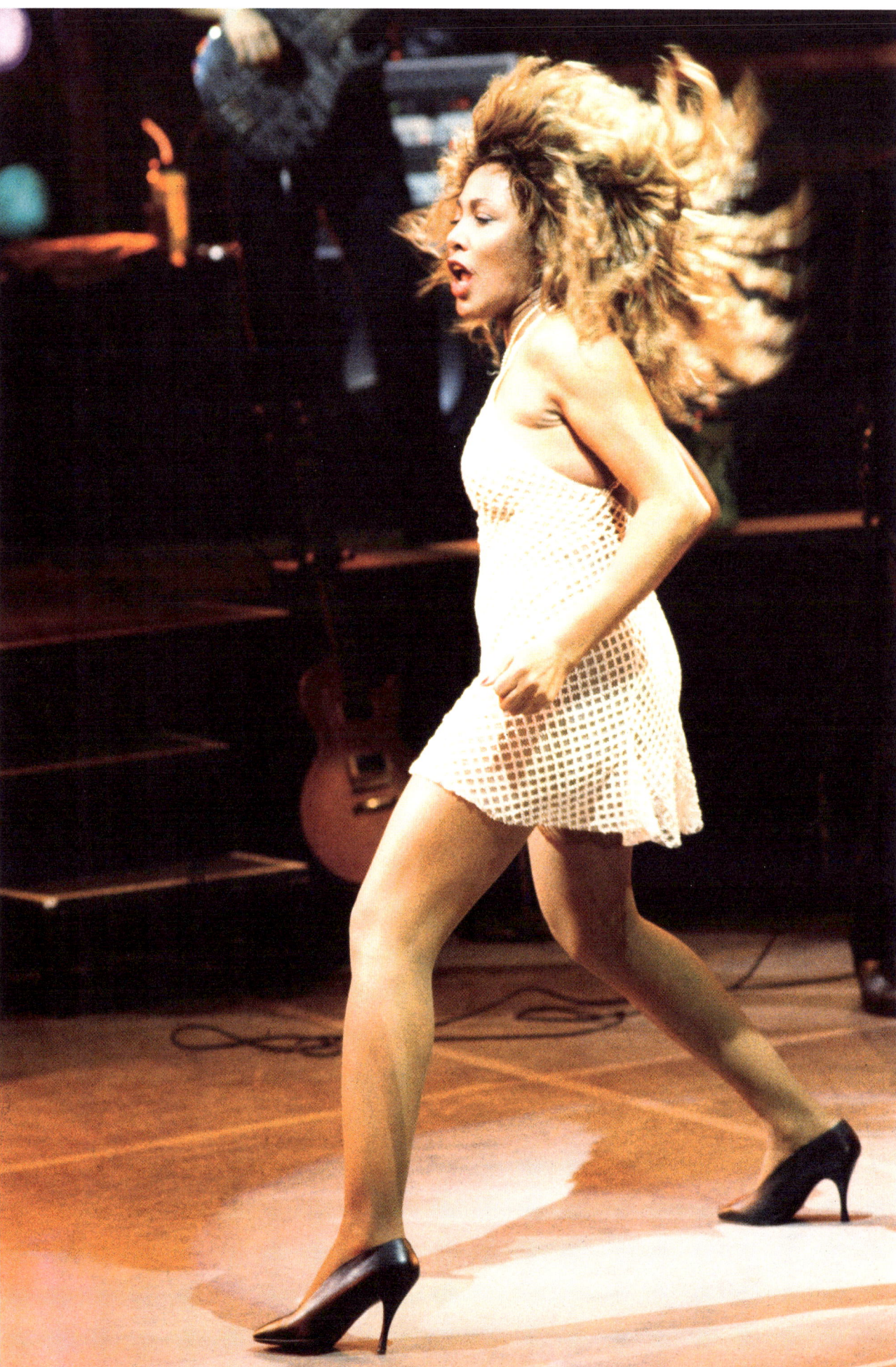

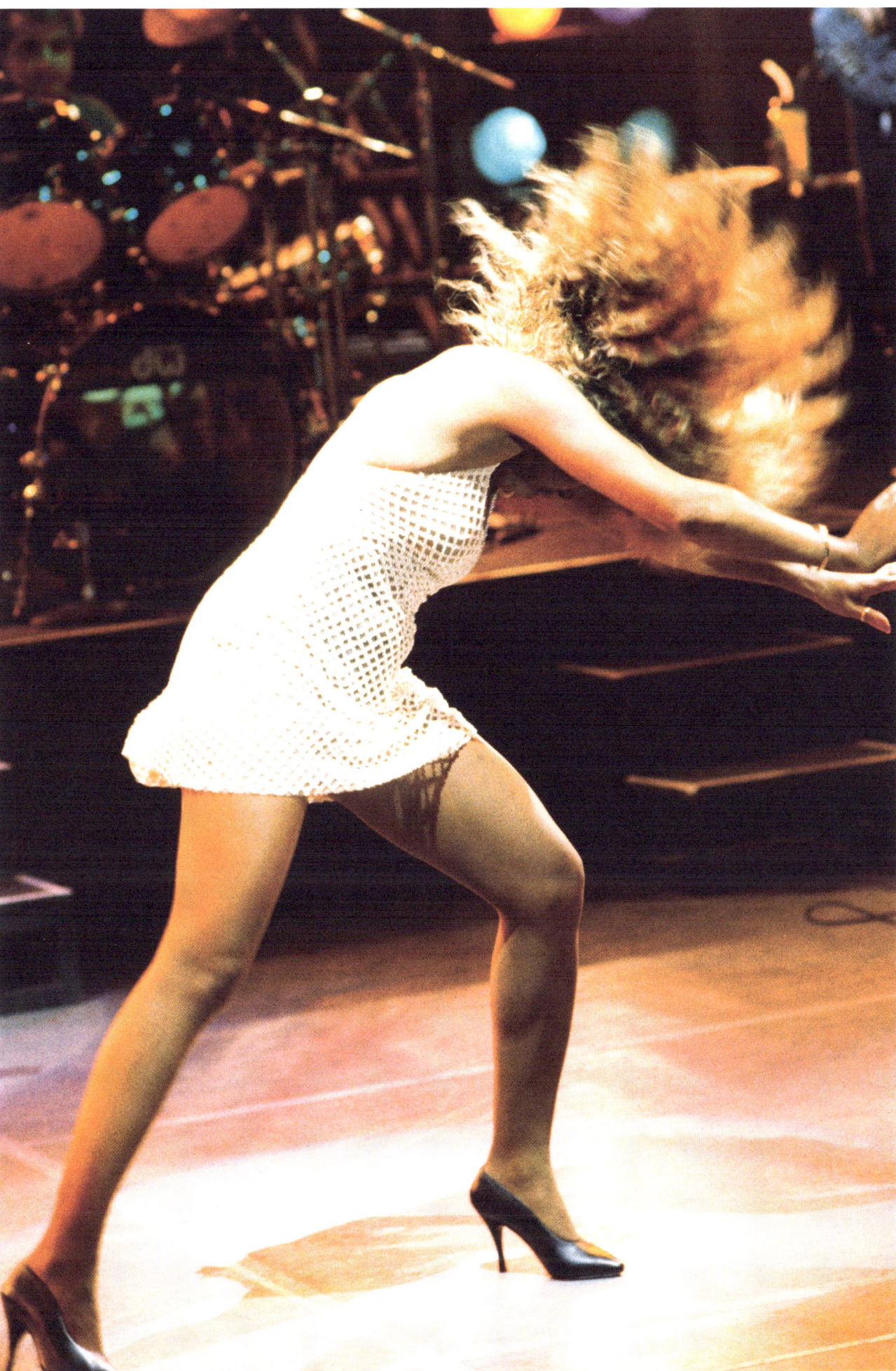

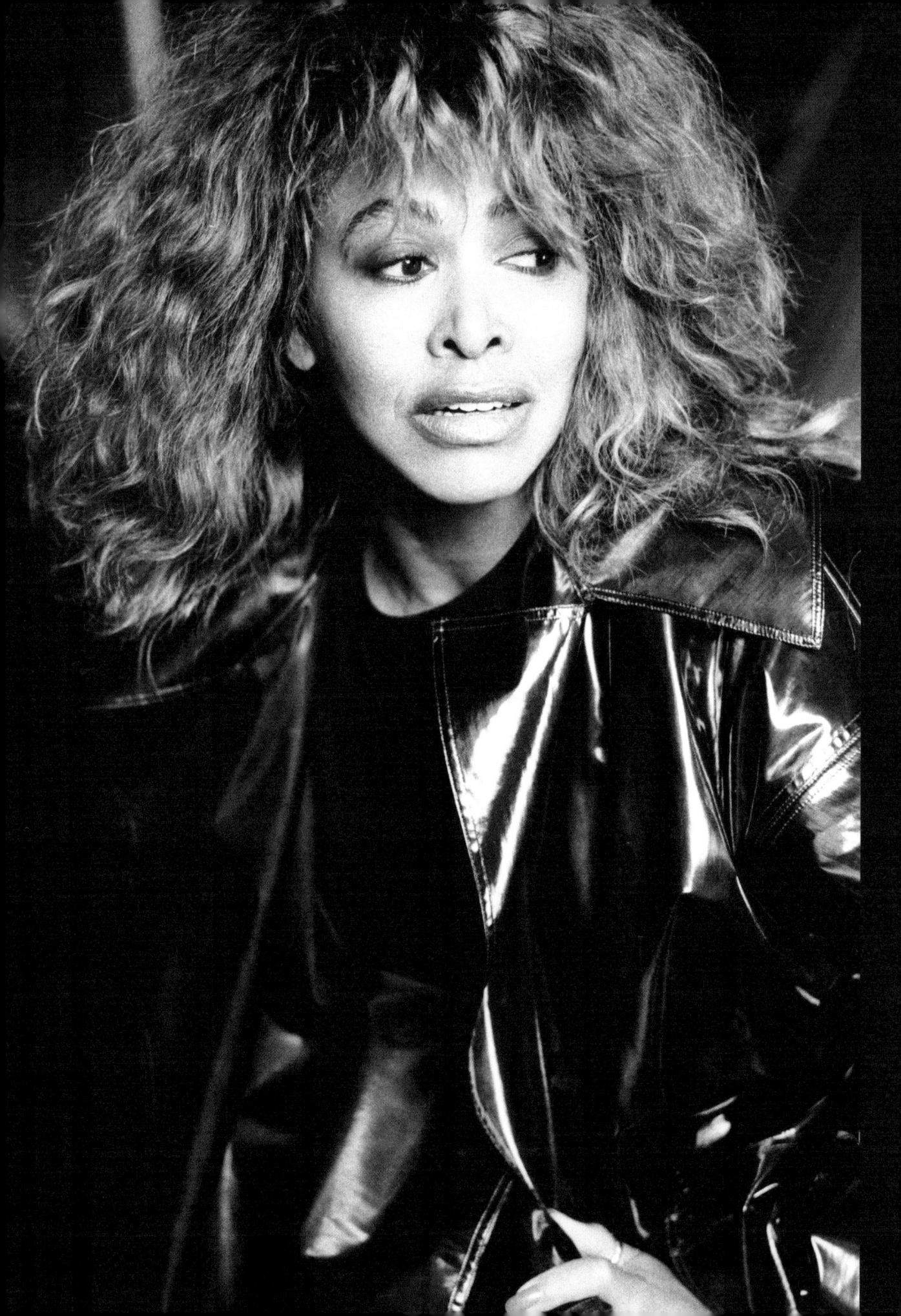

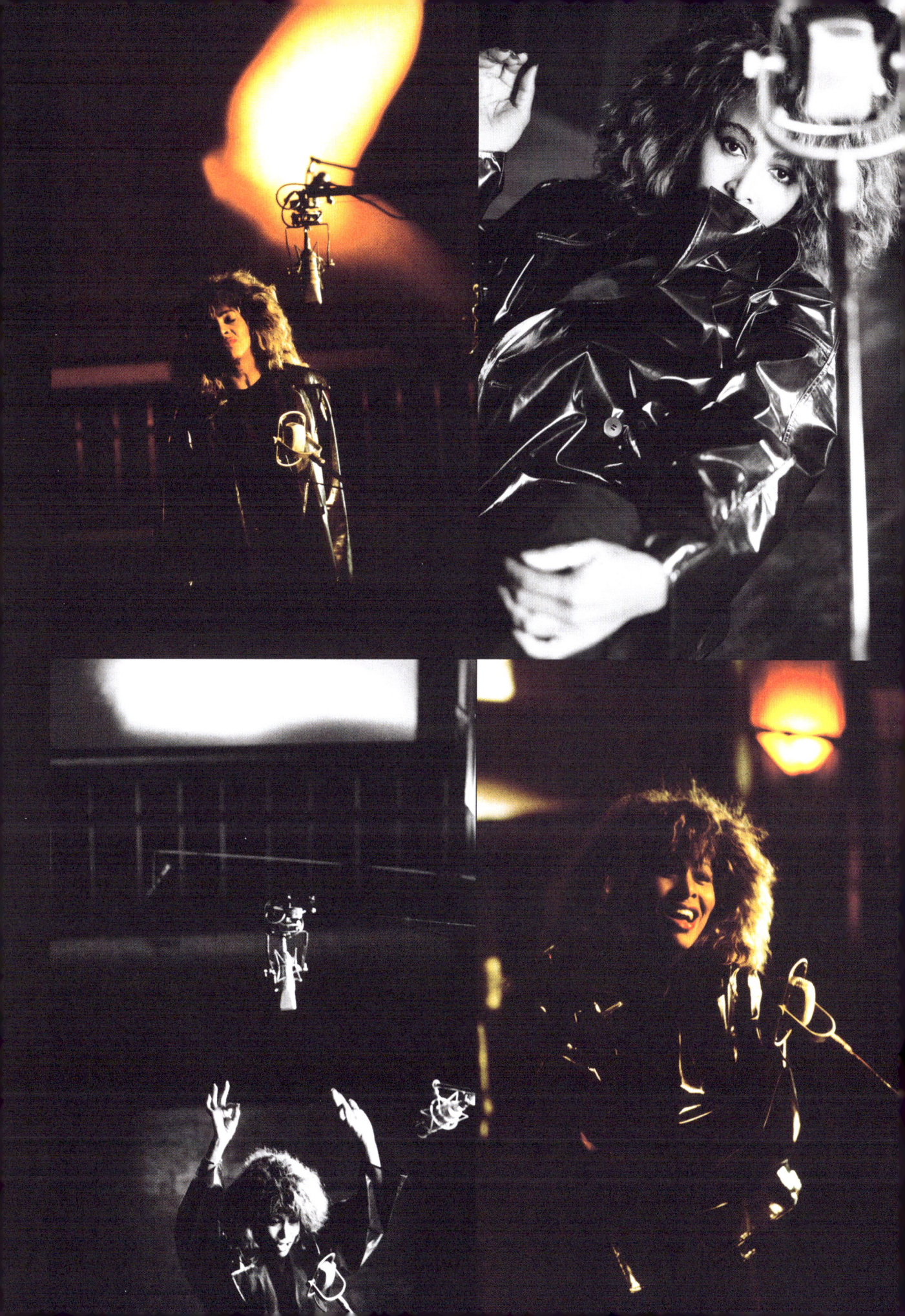

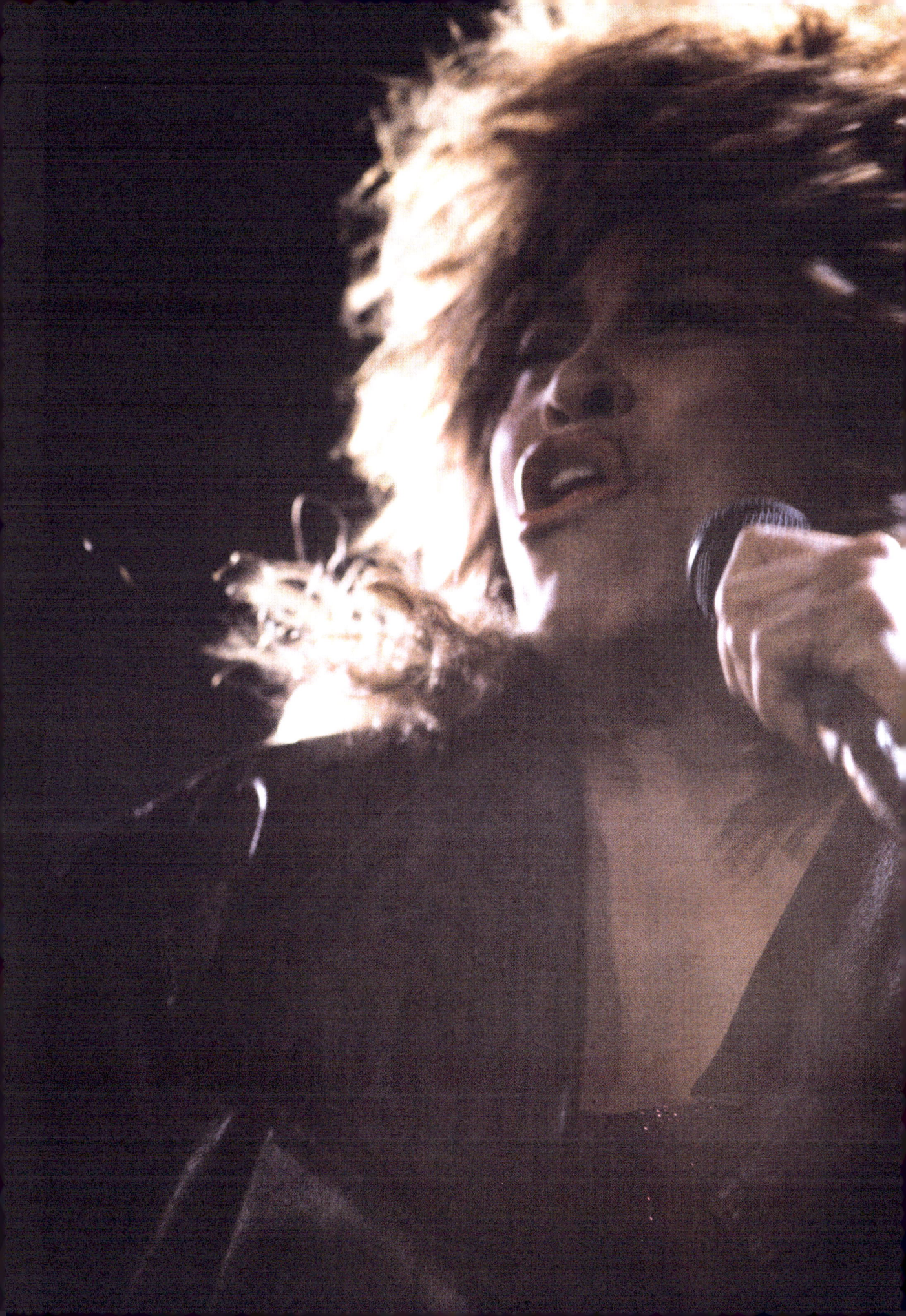

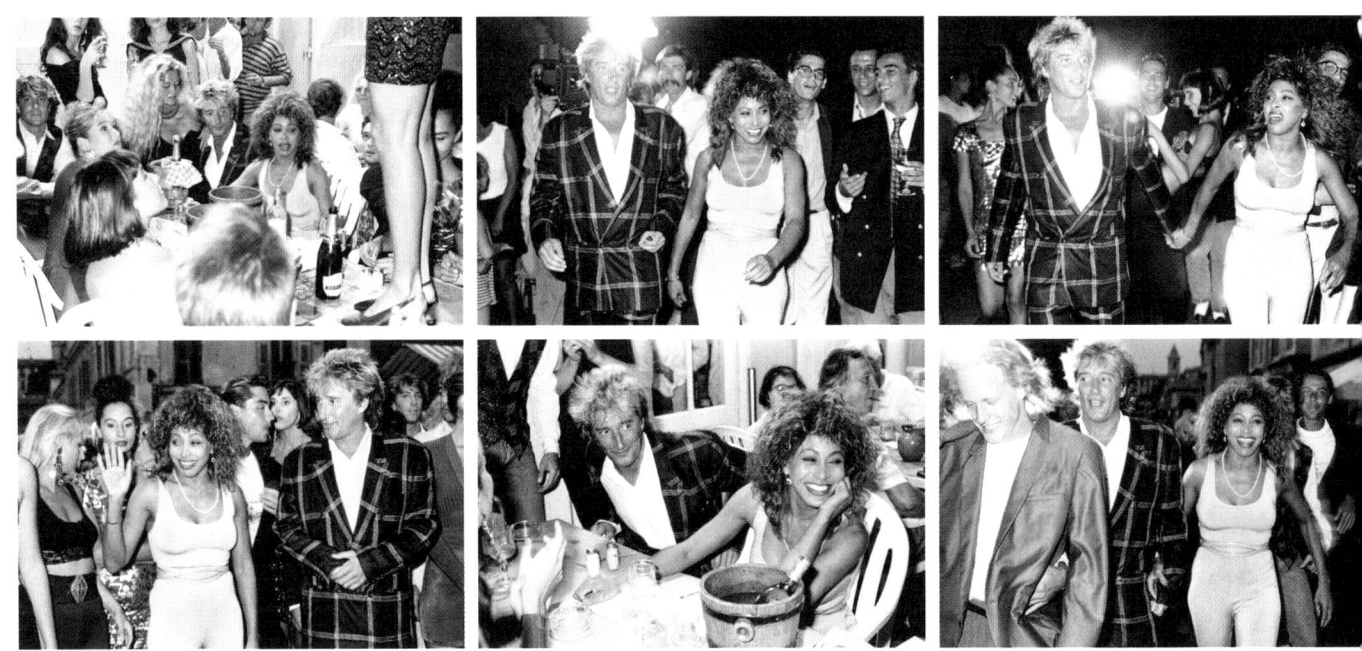

1990

SOUTH OF FRANCE
Pepsi ad

From Joan Crawford in the fifties to the present day, Pepsi has used popular stars for advertising. For this particular campaign, Tina was joined by Rod Stewart, who she'd supported on tour back in 1981. 'Tina had a good rapport with Rod, and I took some lovely shots of them walking around Cannes together,' Paul recalls. Paul had to use his skill and diplomacy to convince Rod to wear a black jacket instead of a white one in the main pictures. 'I explained white wasn't going to work, I could see that clearly through my camera lens. Rod listened and changed his jacket!' Tina and Rod's version of Motown standard 'It Takes Two' from the ad became a huge hit.

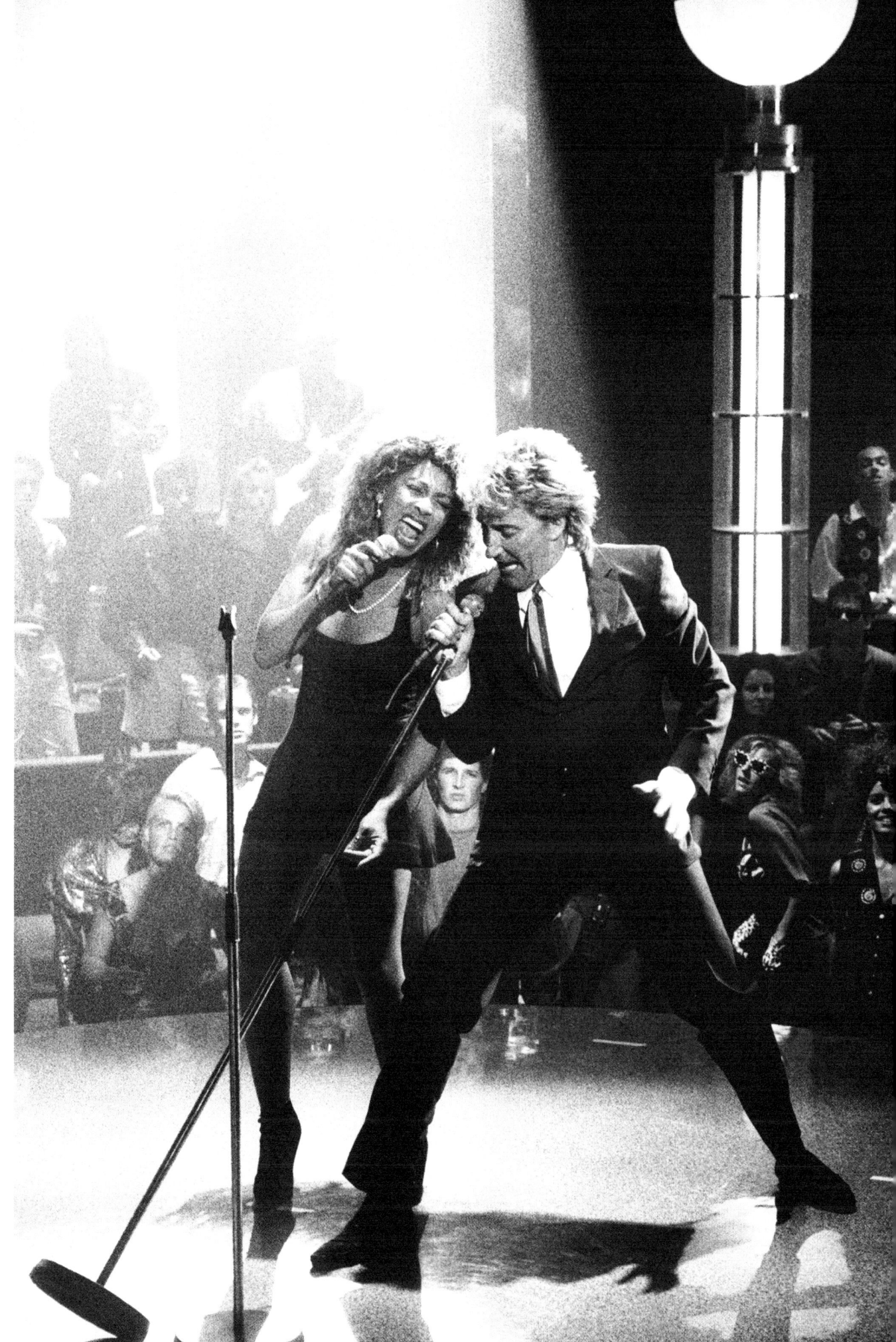

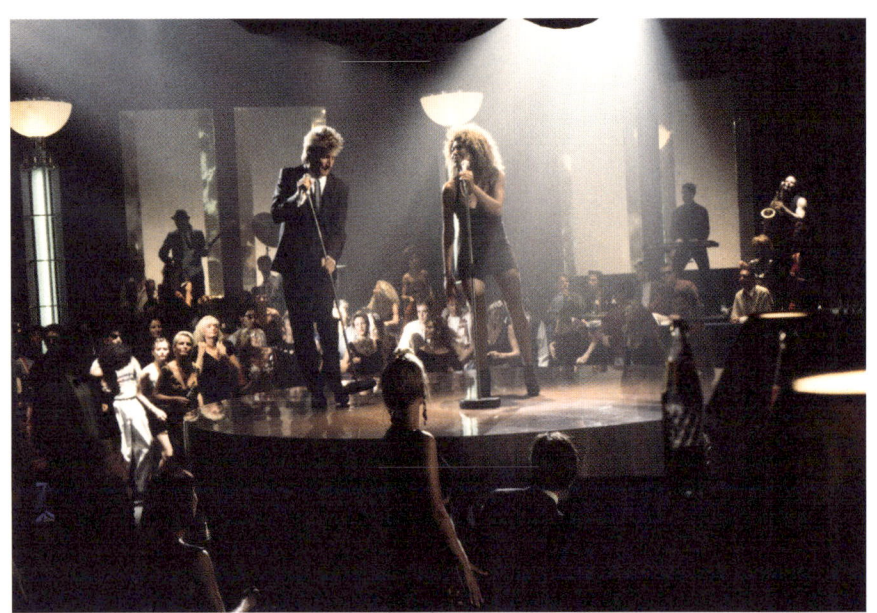

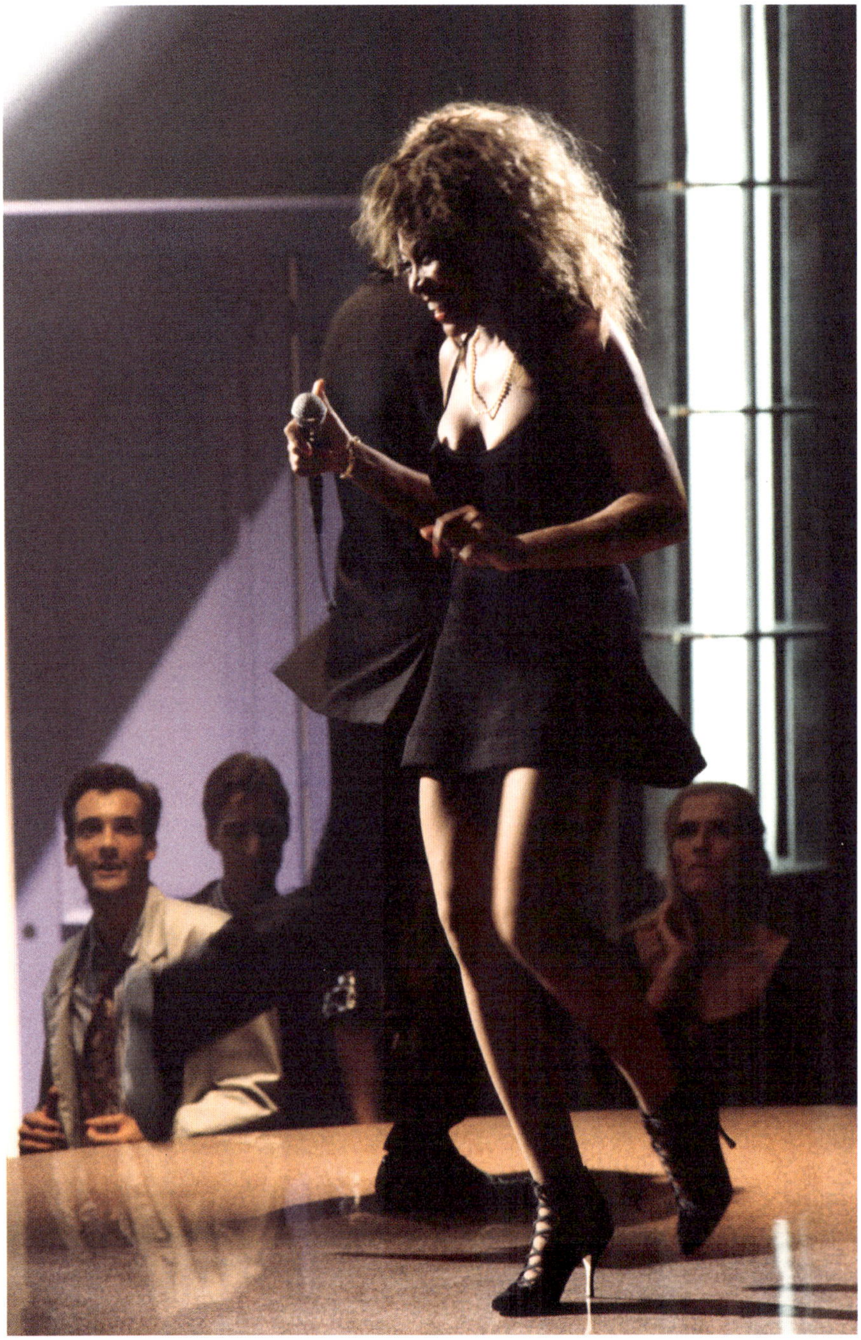

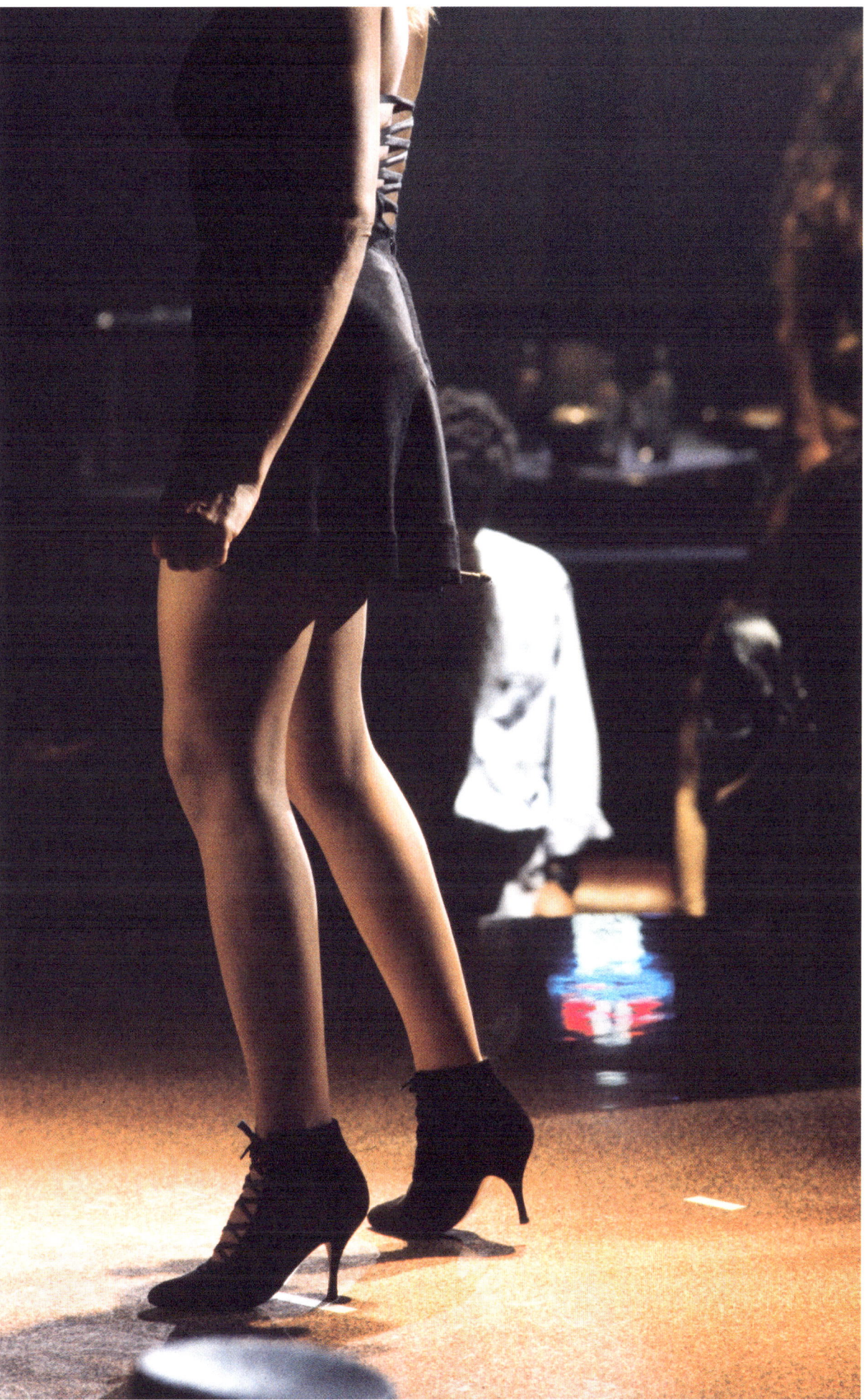

1992

'THE BEST' video for Australia

Tina's manager, Roger Davies, struck a deal in 1990 with the New South Wales Rugby League premiership to use 'The Best', which became one of the most popular promotional campaigns in Australian history. 'Roger loves his rugby, and Australia is his home country, so it was a no-brainer,' Paul says. Two years later, Davies paired Tina with Jimmy Barnes – one of the most successful Antipodean recording artists ever – and guitarist Johnny Diesel for a new version of the song to celebrate that year's Rugby League season. Paul was able to get some great, informal shots of the process, as well as Tina in front of the NSW RL flag, keeping the photos 'on message'.

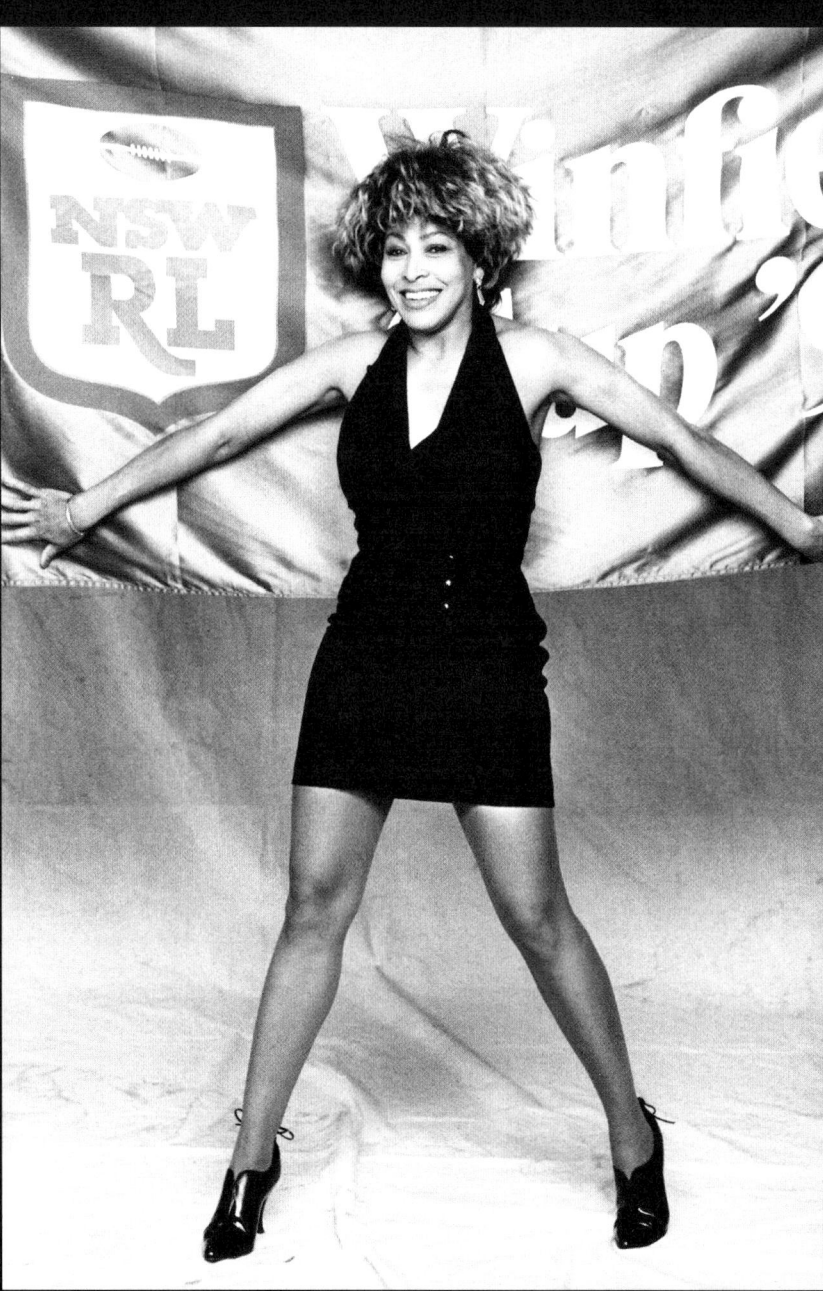

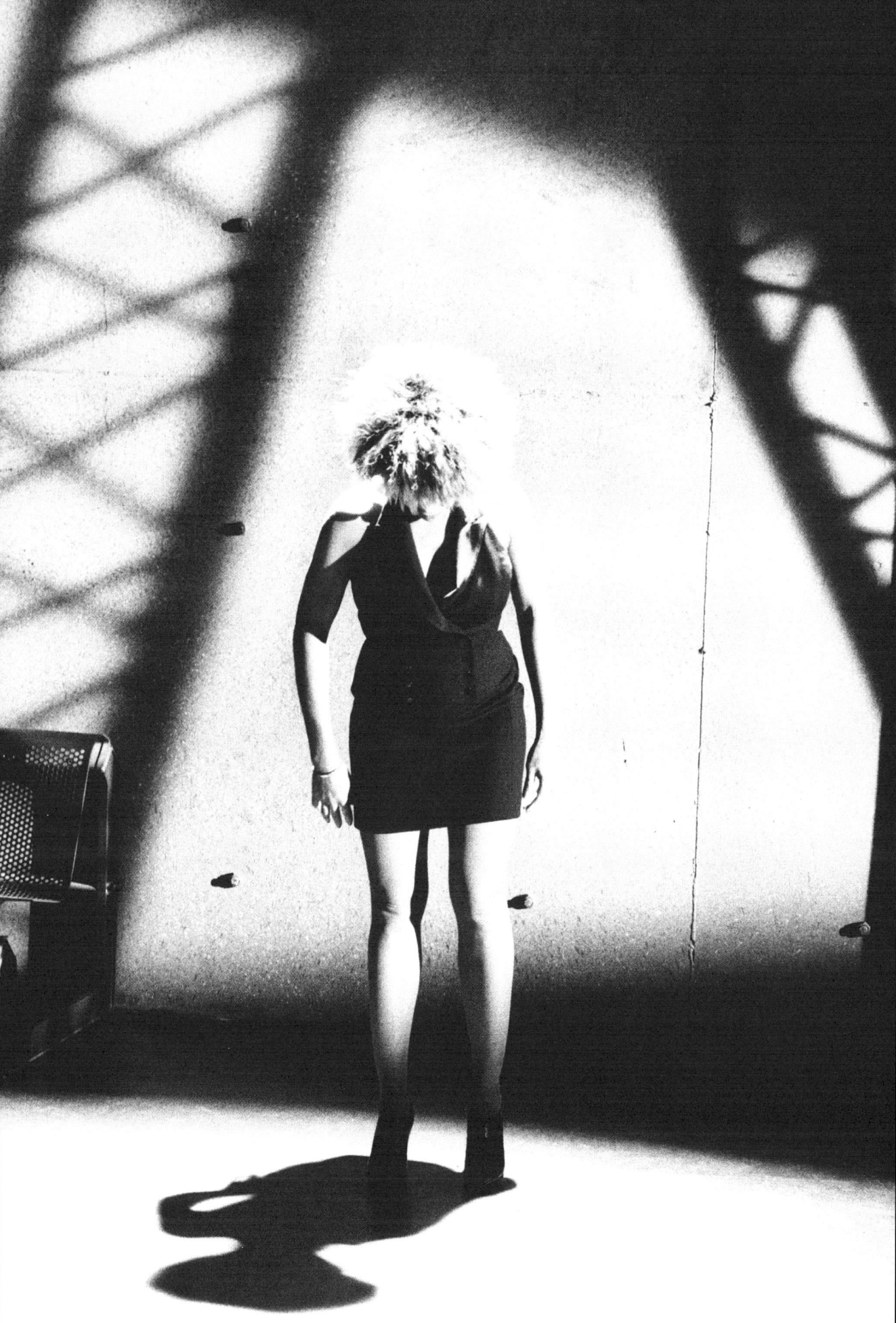

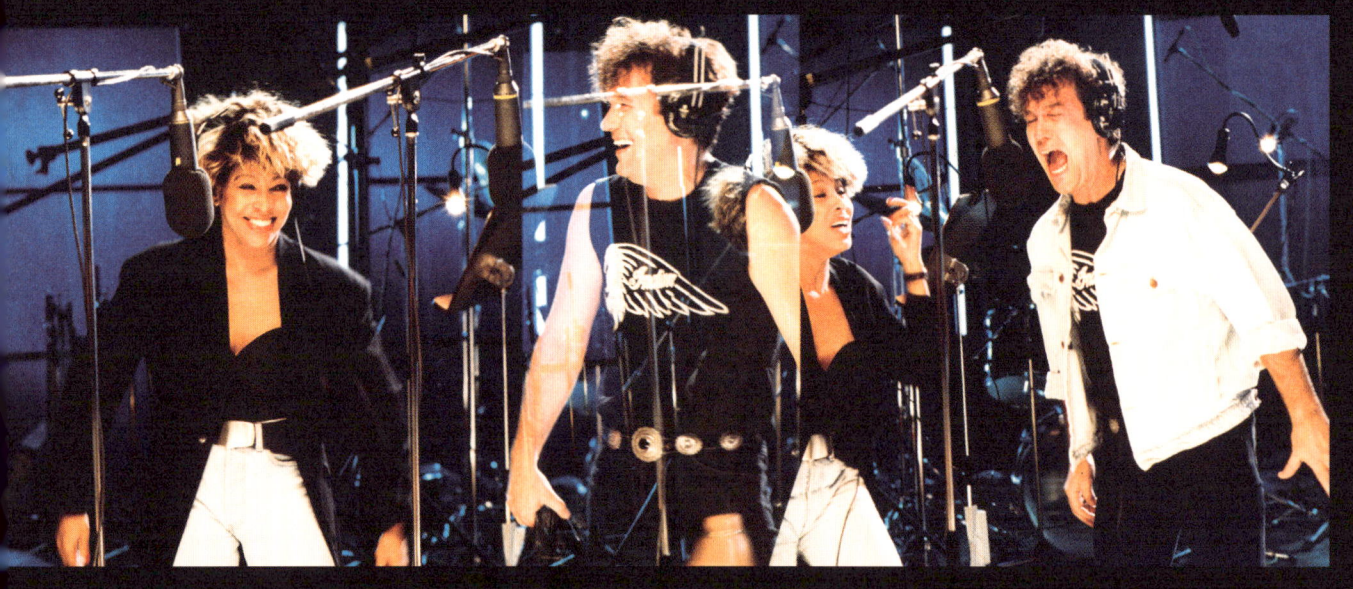

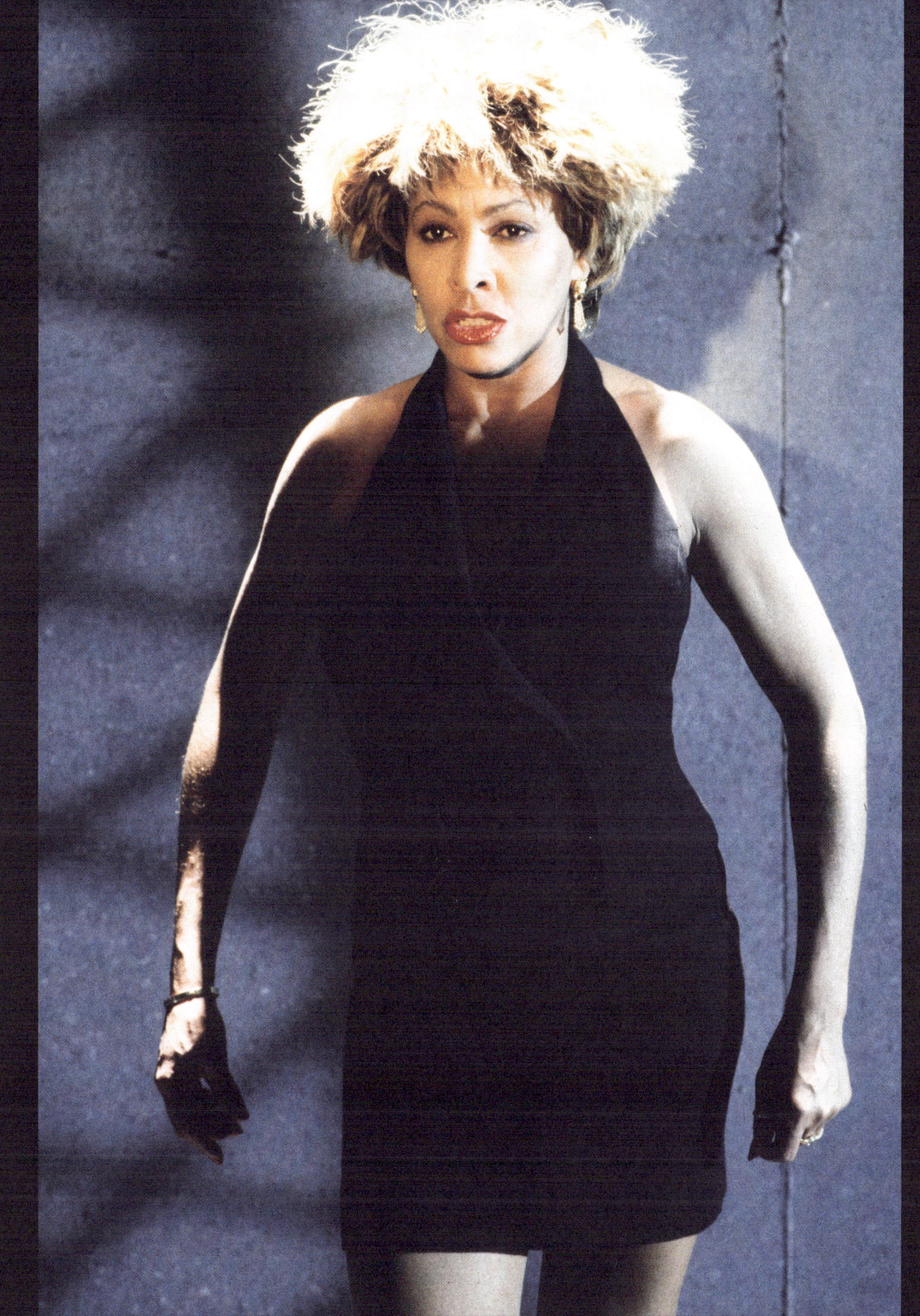

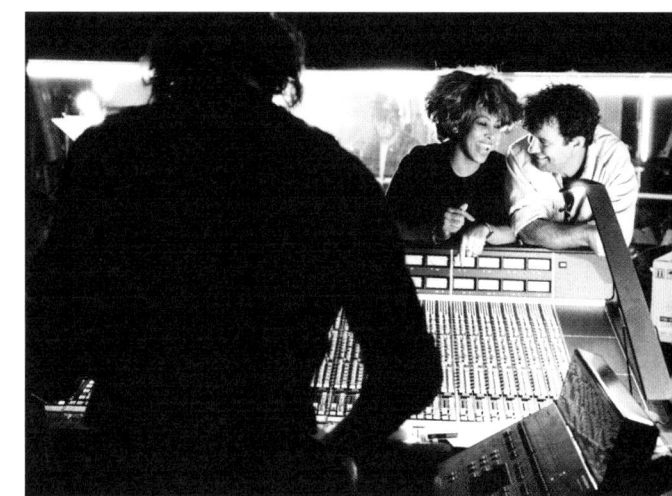

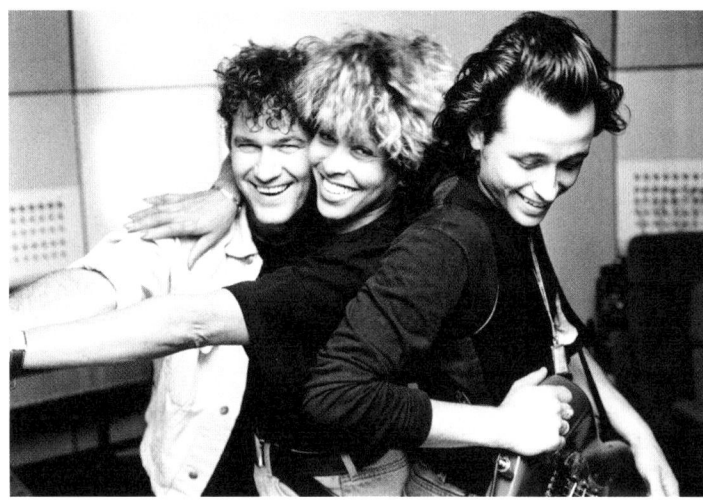

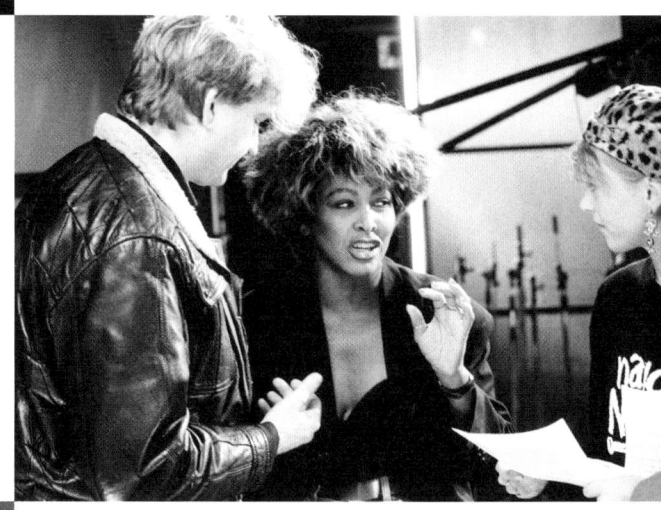

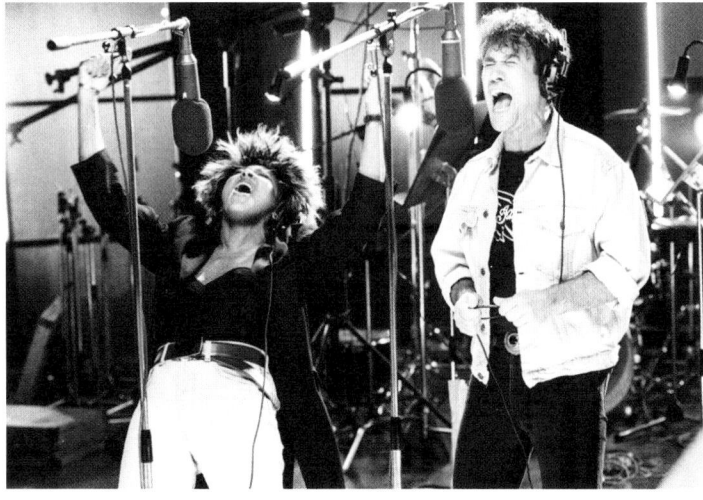

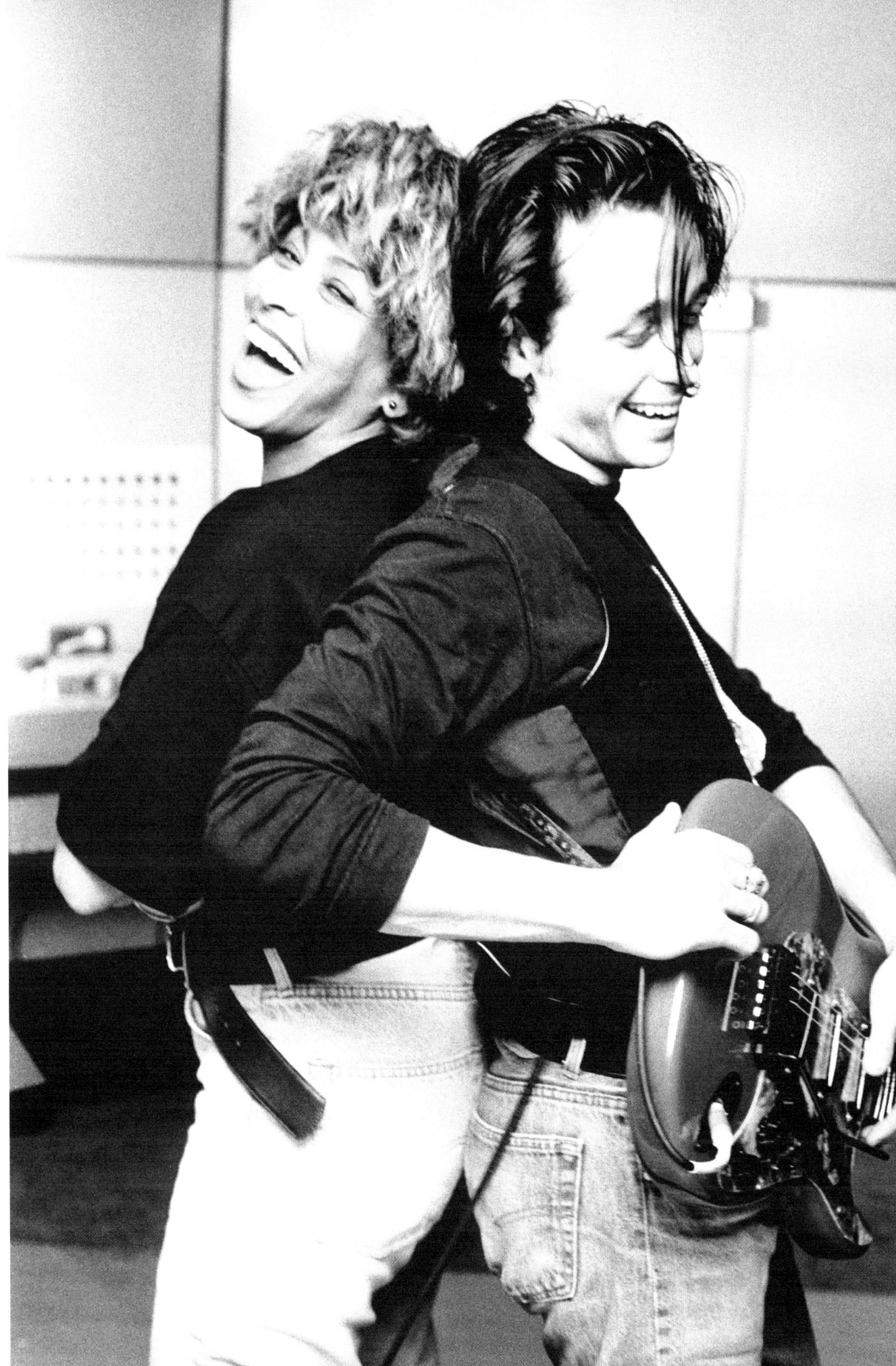

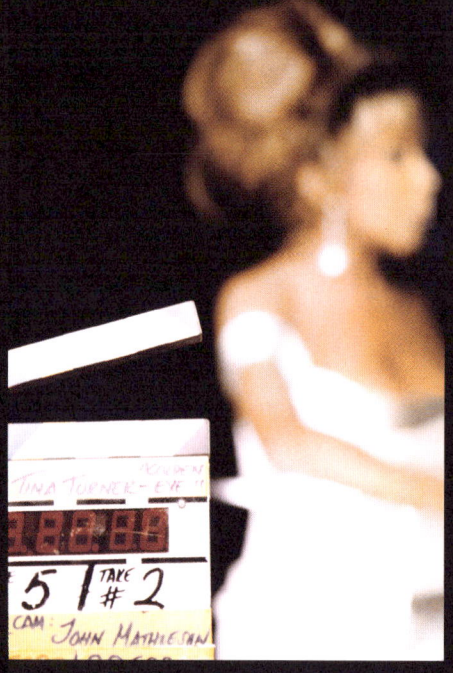

1995

GoldenEye
JAMES BOND MOVIE

To cement her position in pop's firmament, Tina was asked to sing a James Bond theme. *GoldenEye* was the first Bond film of the nineties, starring Pierce Brosnan. The title song was written for Tina by Bono and The Edge of U2. Paul was present at the video shoot, directed by Jake Scott. By now, Paul and Tina had been working together for over a decade. 'Tina would always joke, "Oh, it's you again!" each time she saw me. One of my daughters, Charlotte, would always call her "Tina Tippy-Toes" when she was young because Tina would flick her feet when she was dancing. Tina would ask after her, and she sent Charlotte a signed picture from "Tina Tippy-Toes".'

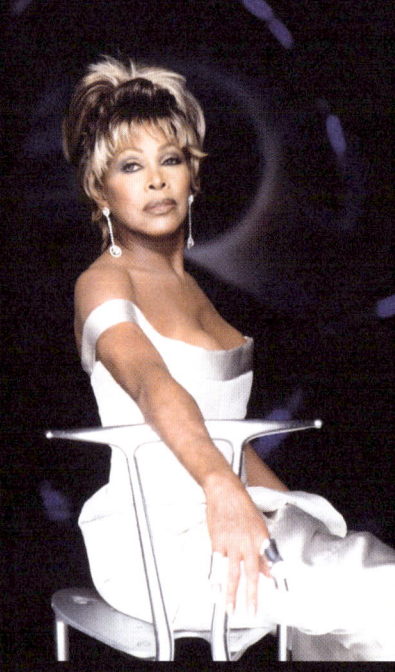

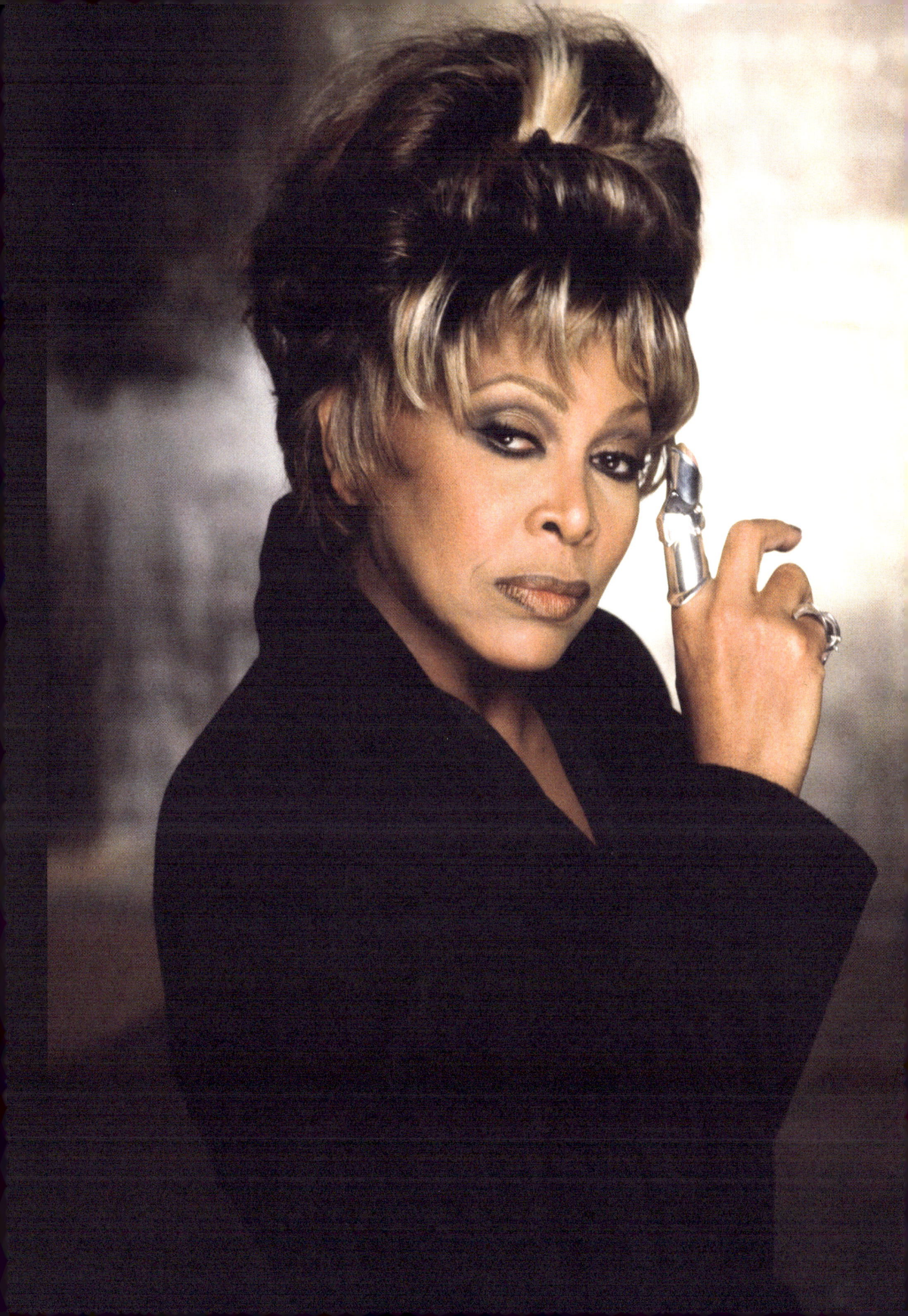

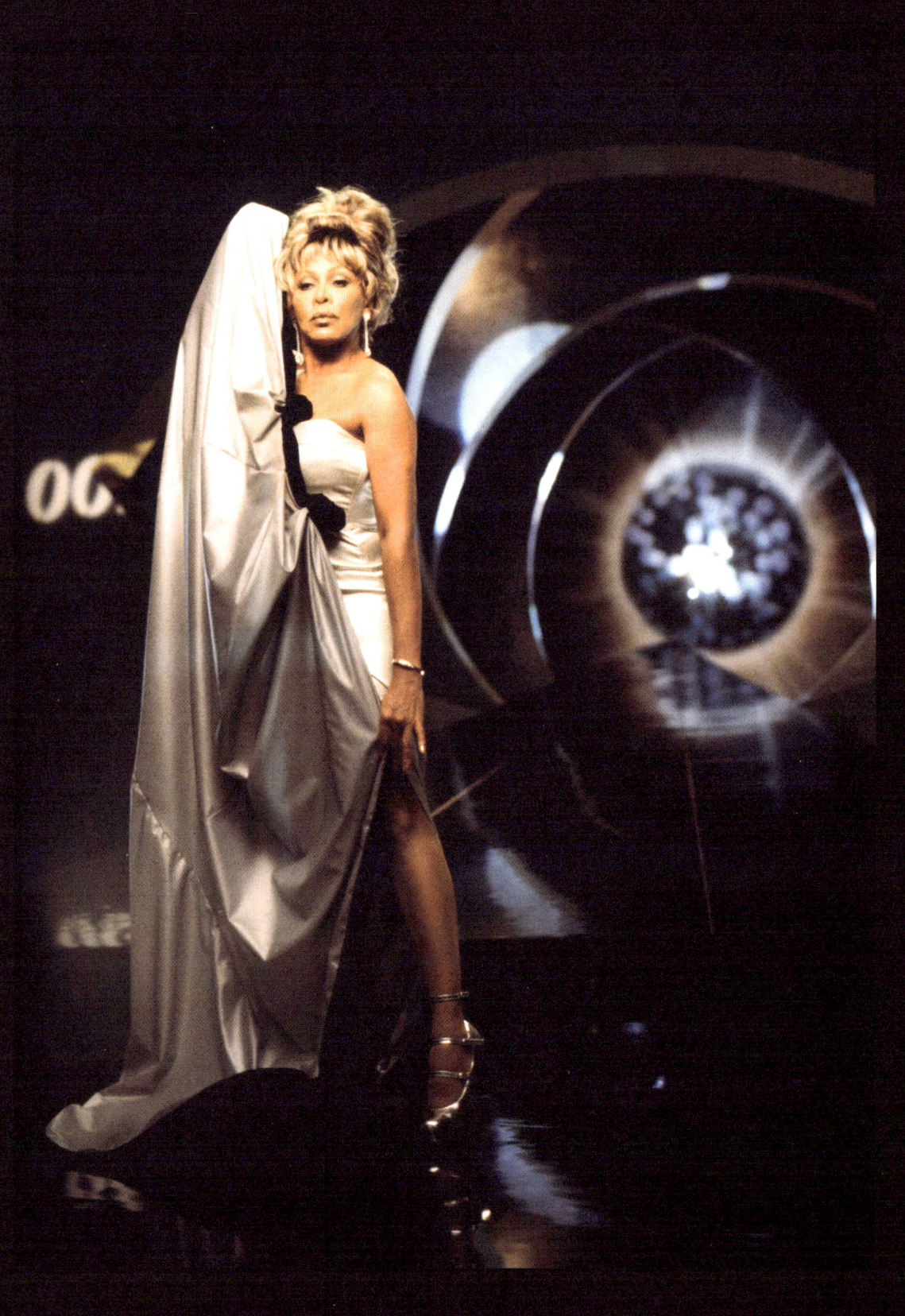

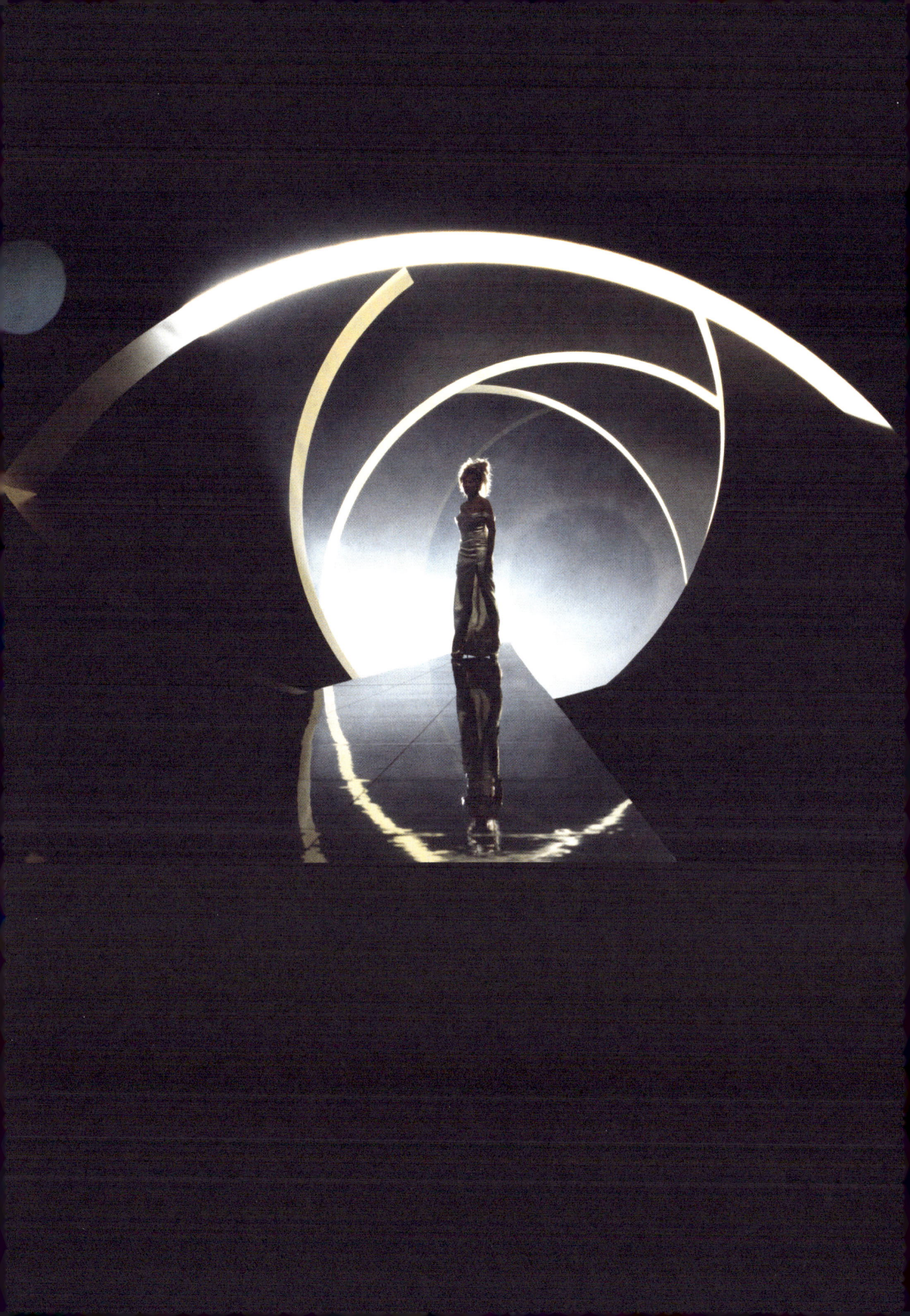

1995

ADVERTISING
FOR UPCOMING TOUR

After years of trying to get her there, Tina finally visited Paul's studio in Fulham, London for a proper three-and-a-half-hour photo shoot ahead of her upcoming Wildest Dreams Tour. 'It was a big deal. She had three outfits with her. She picked up the brolly and started spinning it and then, as you see on the contacts, just started strutting her stuff. The pictures of her in the [fake] fur coat where she's all blurry and smiley have never been used before. We did it as a little extra bit of fun, but it wasn't in-keeping with the rest of the photographs.'

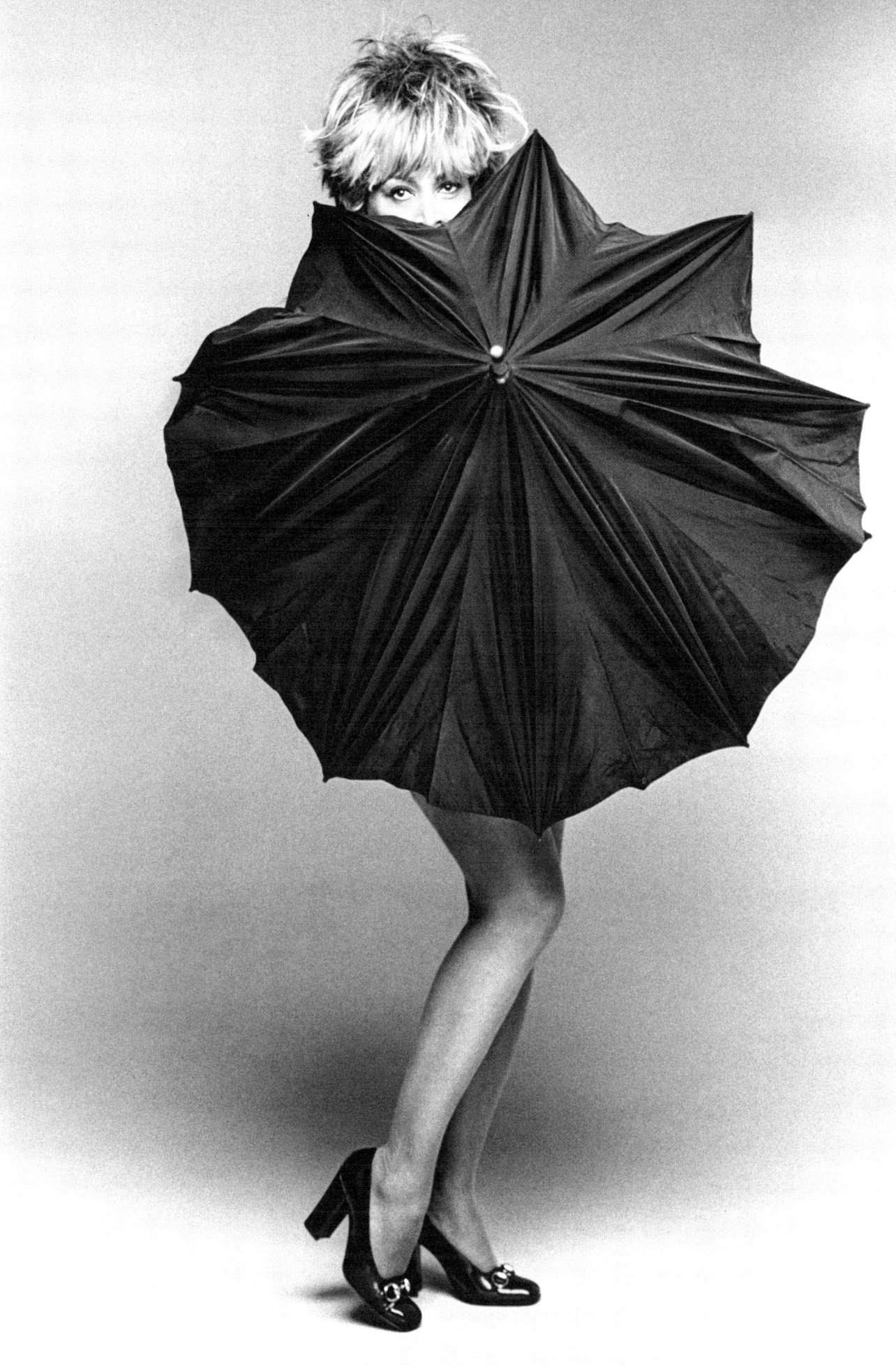

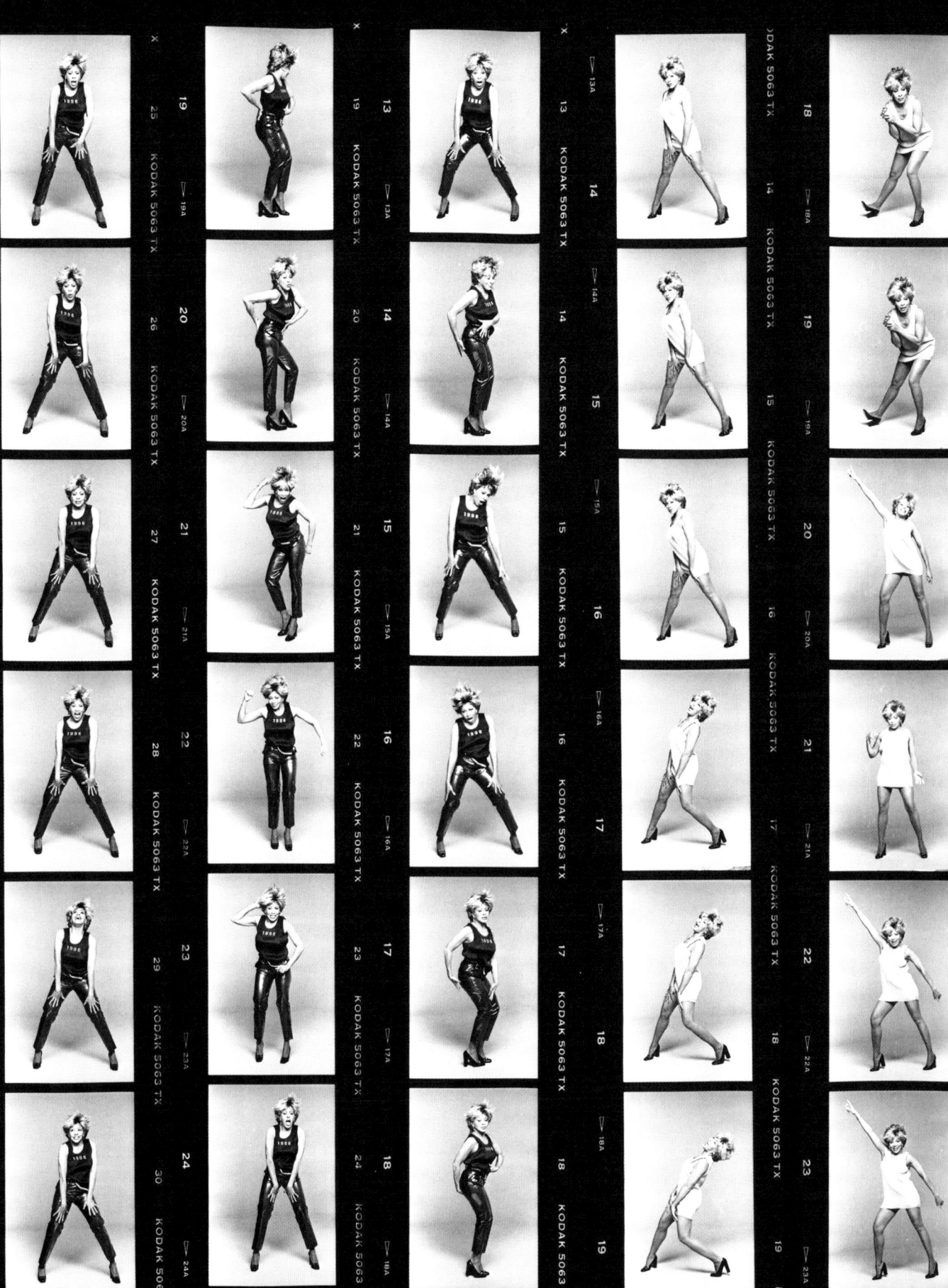

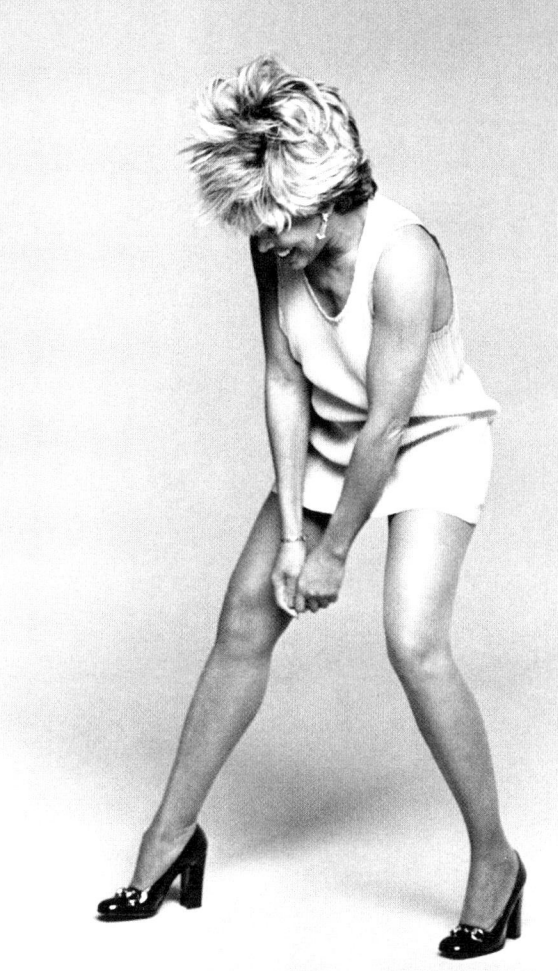

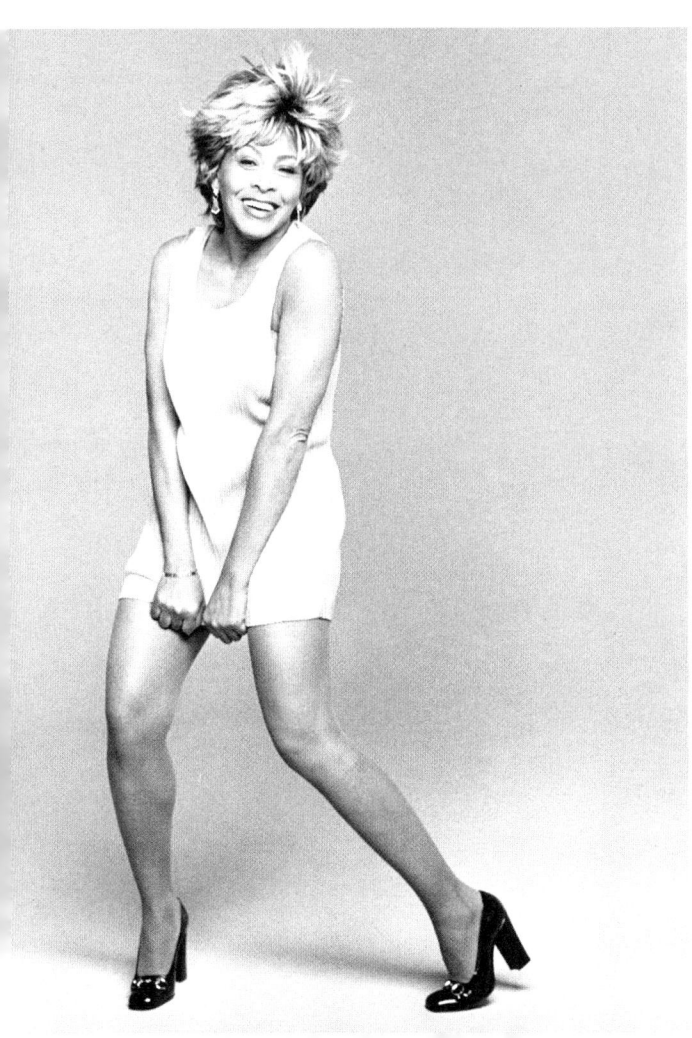

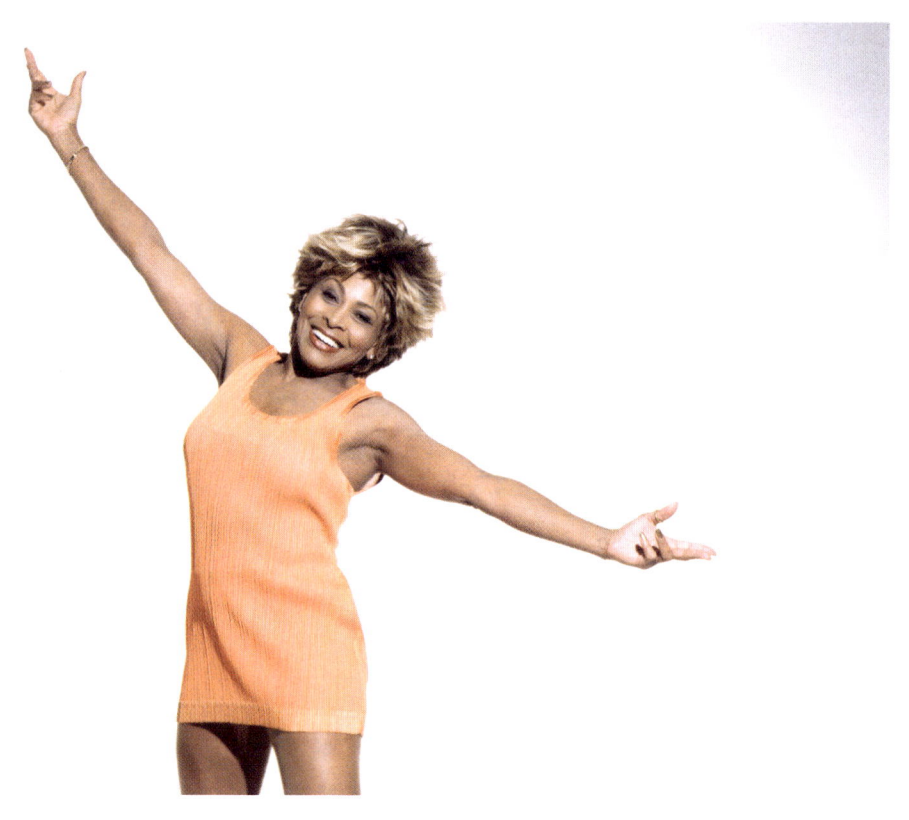

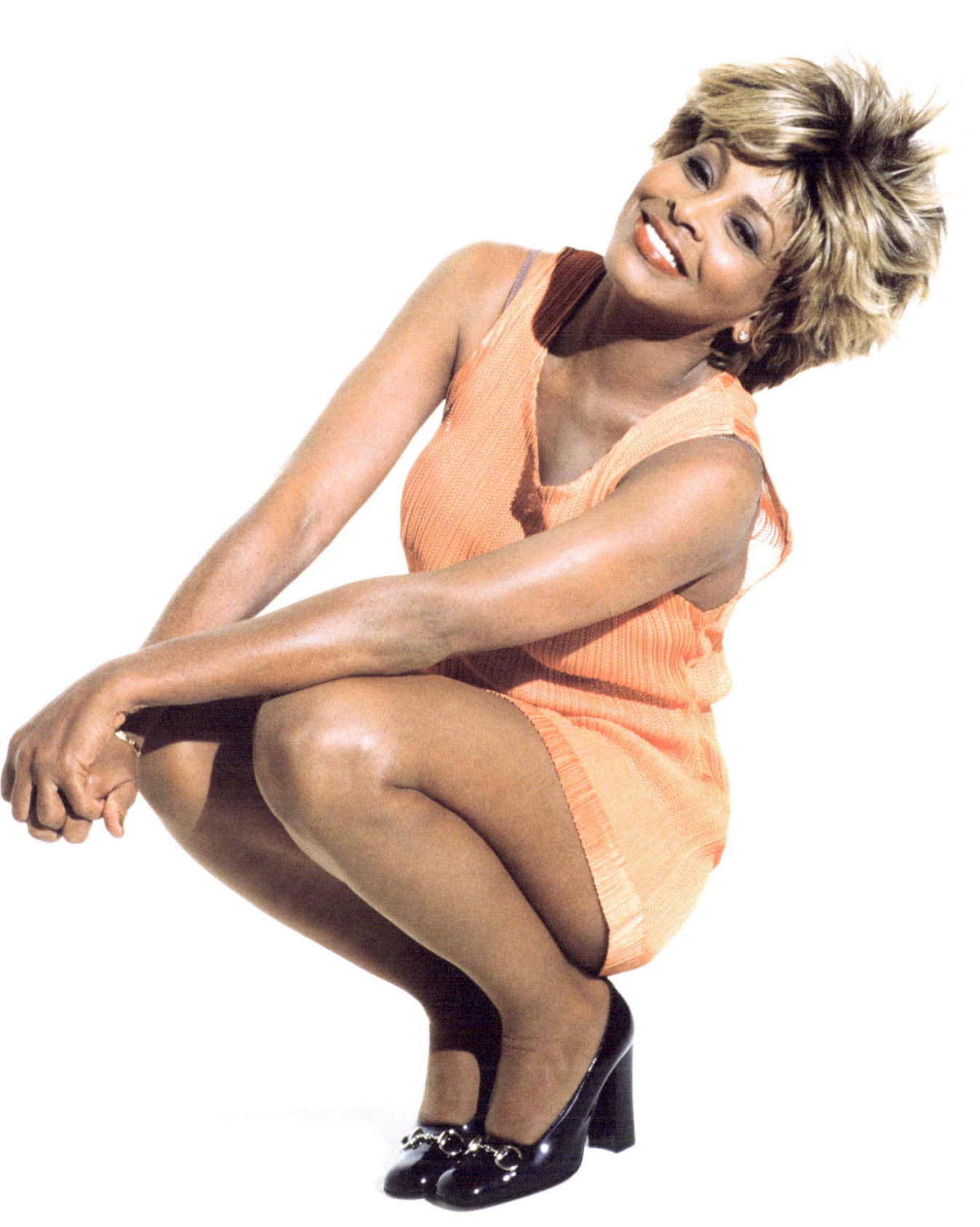

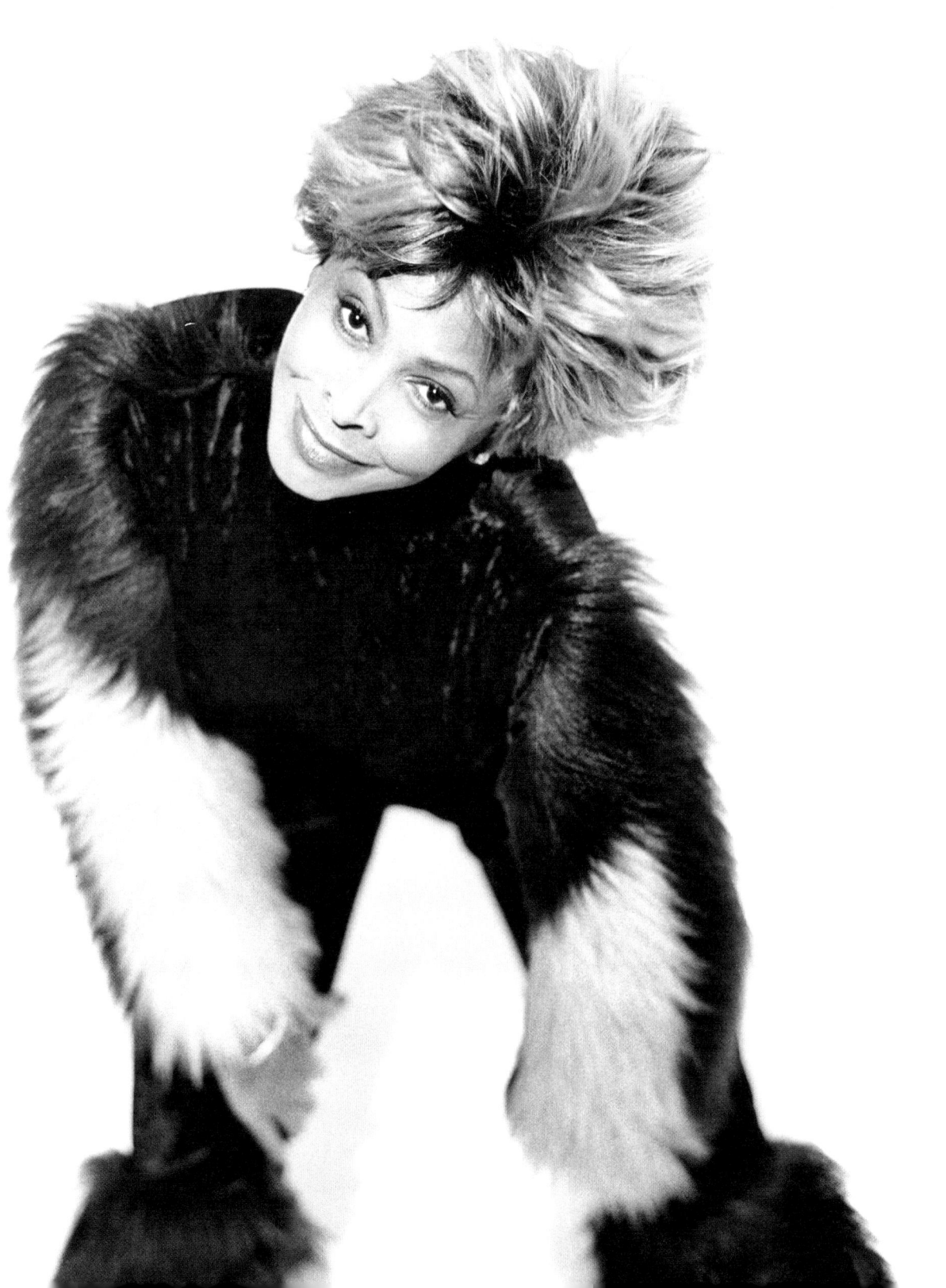

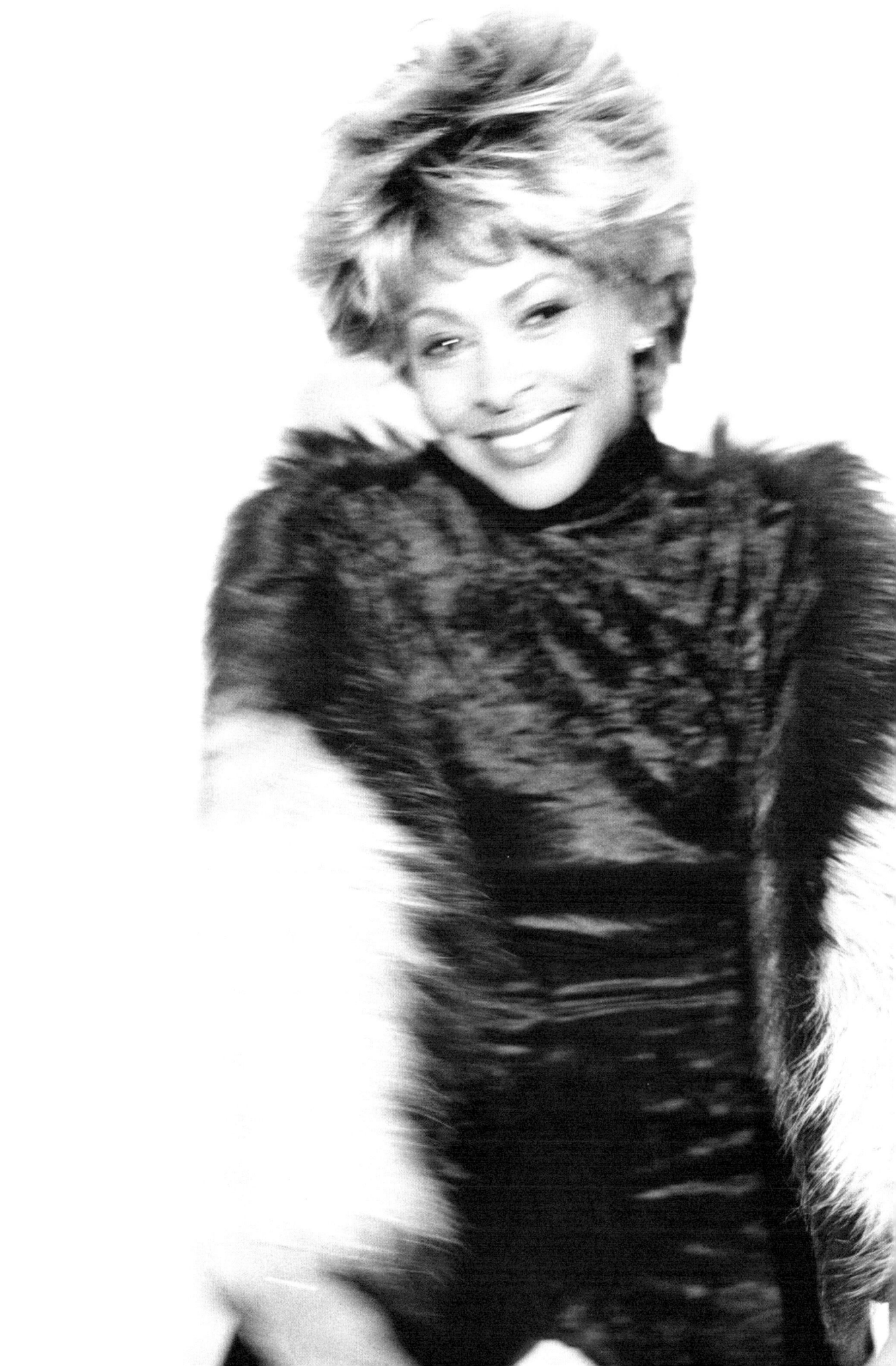

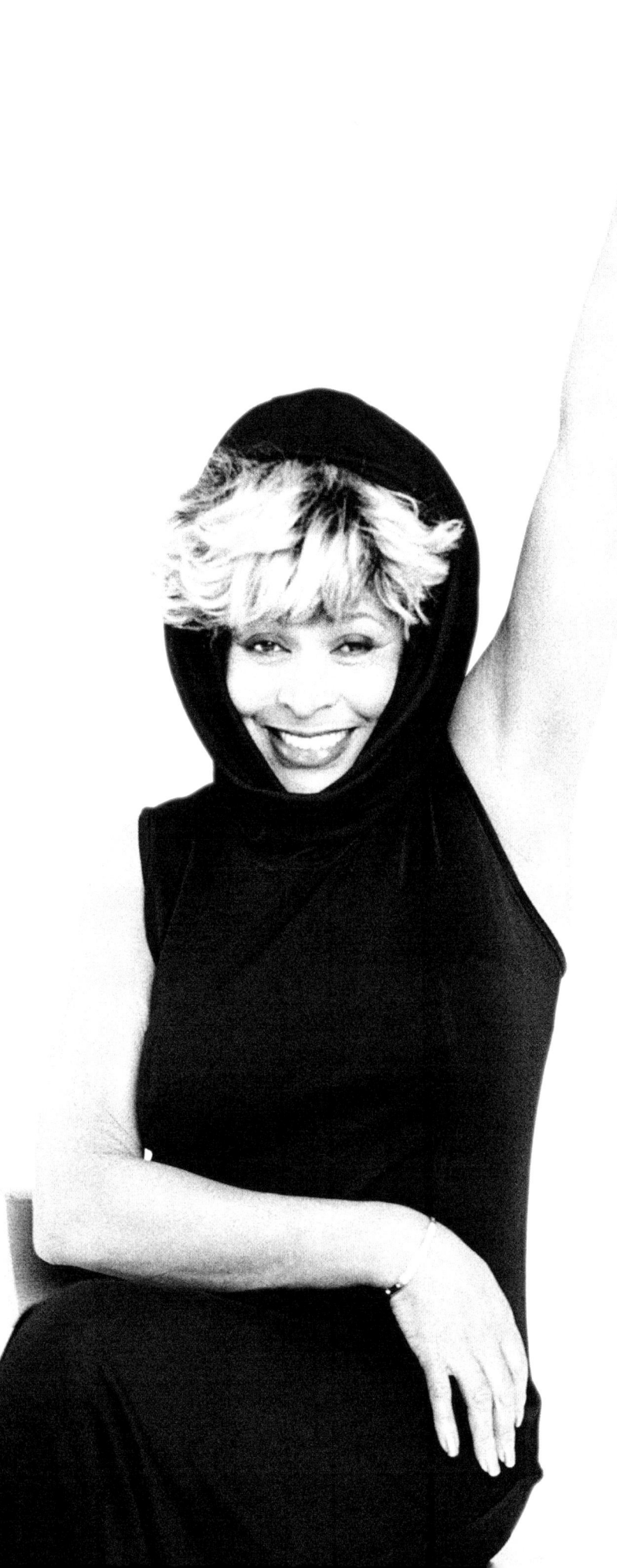

2000
TOUR PROGRAM

To celebrate the new century, The Twenty Four Seven Tour became one of the biggest tours of Tina's career, taking in 95 concerts in the US and 21 open-air shows in Europe. Paul took the photographs for the tour brochure. 'I didn't have enough space in my studio for the whole 12-piece band,' Paul says. 'I took the full range of shots, Tina alone, Tina with band, girls alone, etc. I've always liked the one of her with her dancers and backing singers [L-R Claire Louise Burton, Solange Geniere, Stacy Campbell, Tina, Gloria Reuben and Ivona Brnelic]. Tina was happy and never gave anyone unnecessary grief.'

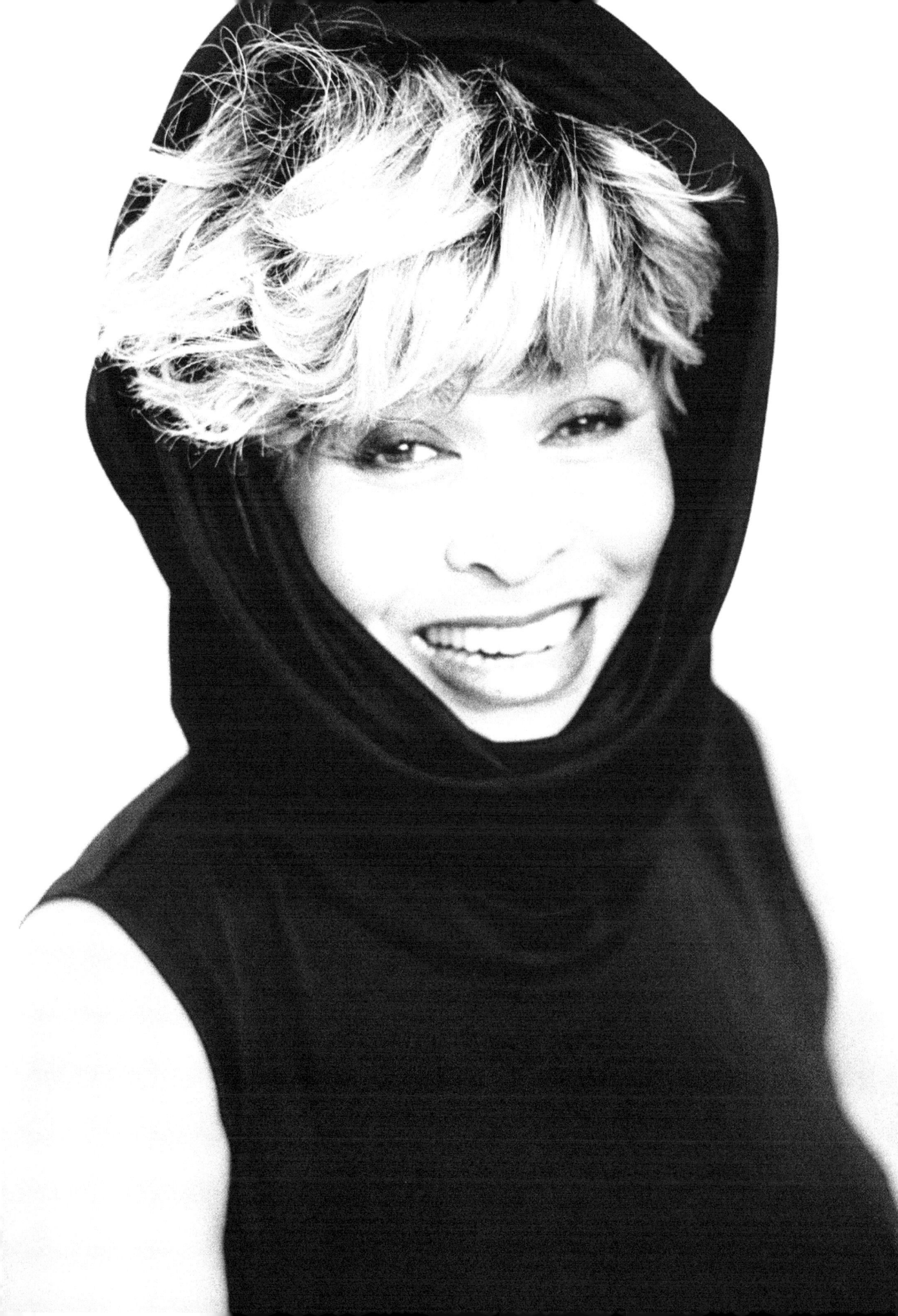

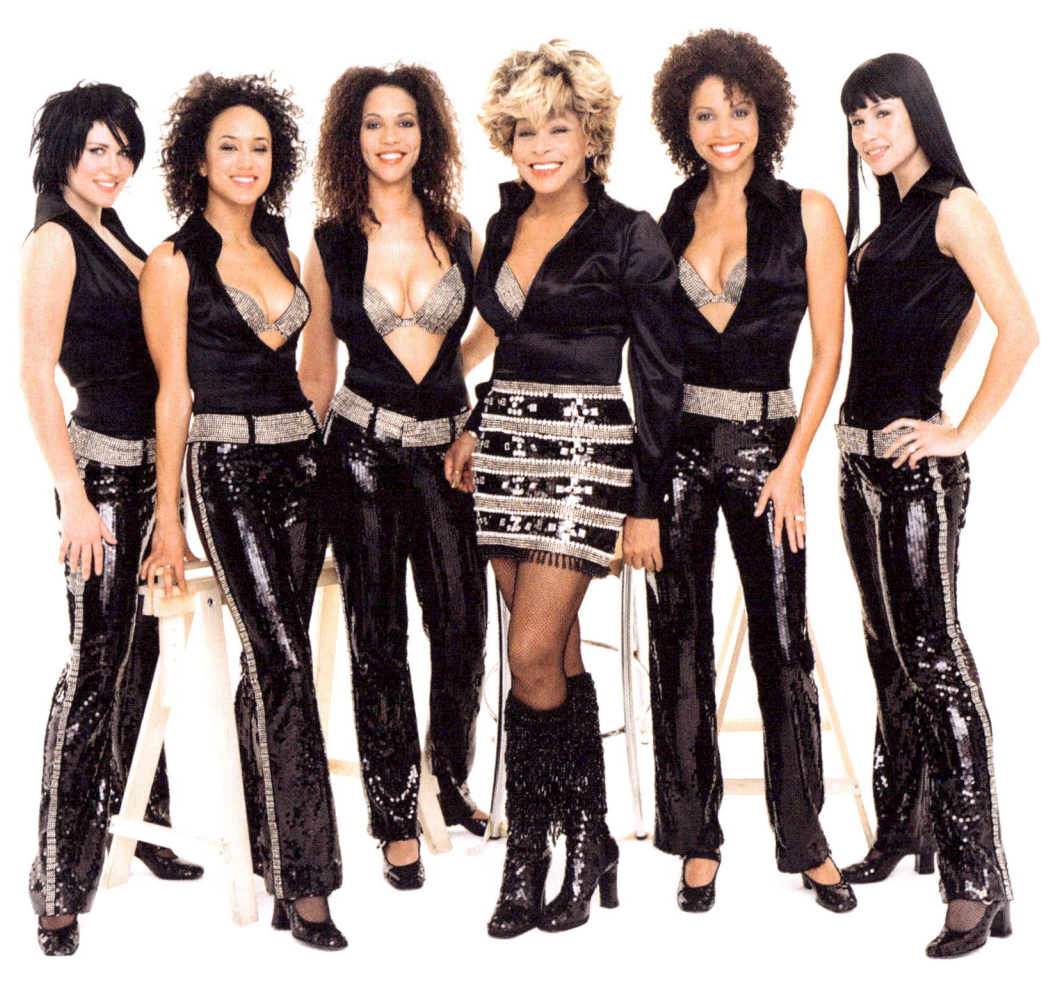

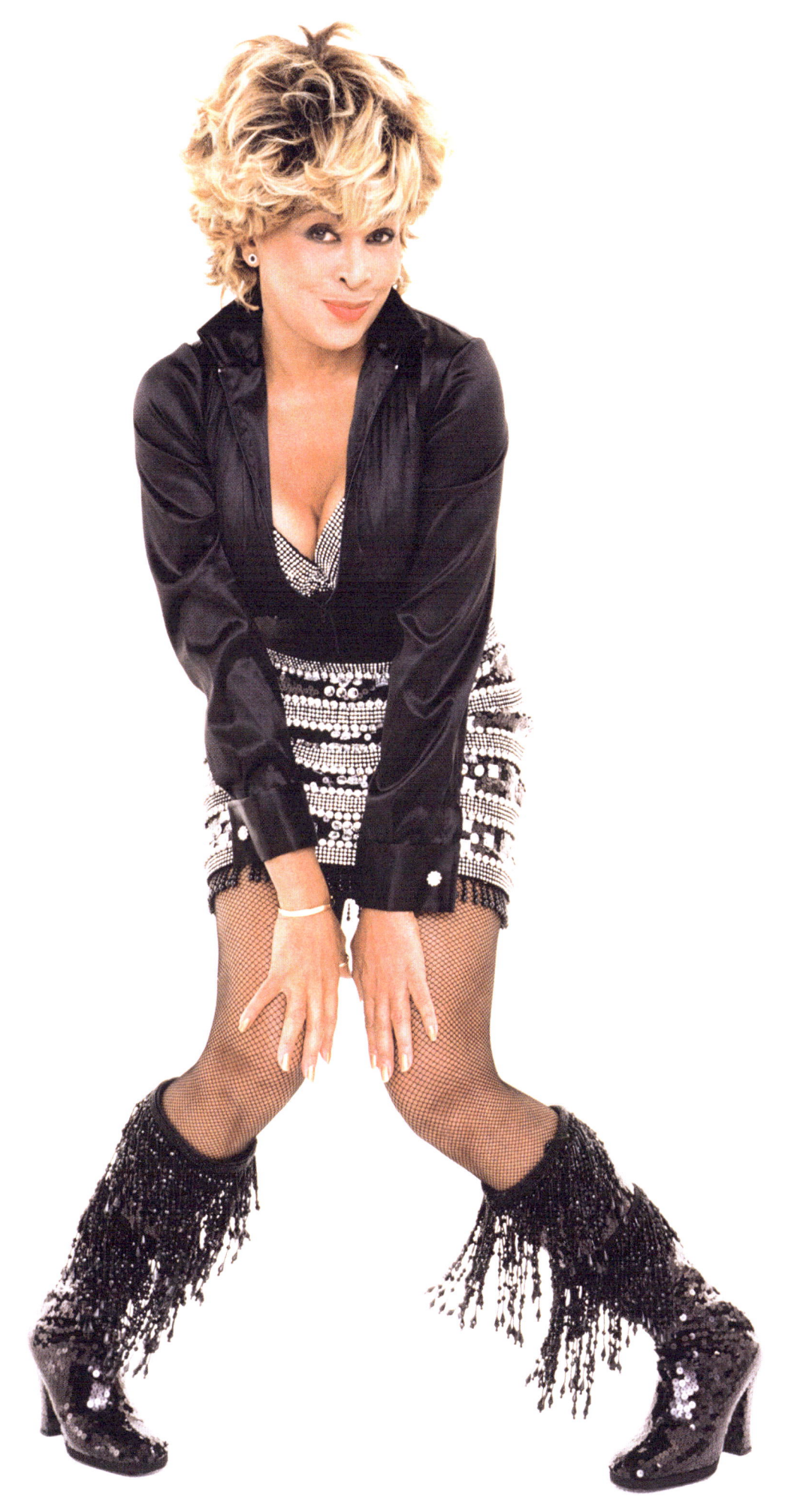

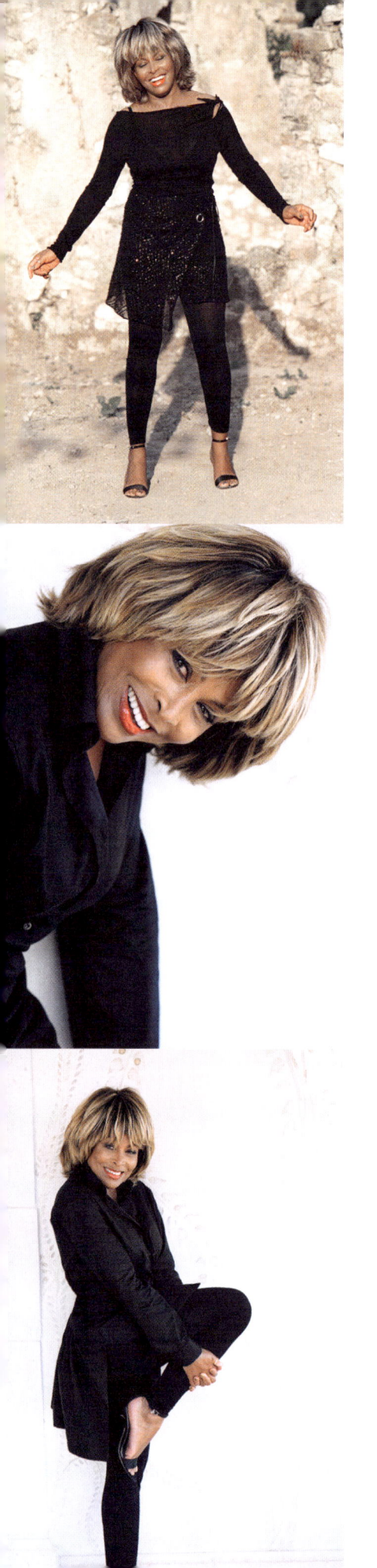

2004
SOUTH OF FRANCE

'This was probably my favourite of all the sessions with Tina – a whole day's shoot at her home in Cannes for an album sleeve. We were in her back garden. She had these high heels on and, as she came down these steps, she just went over, did a forward roll across the lawn and then just got up and carried on as if nothing had happened,' Paul laughs, her professionalism as strong as ever in her mid-sixties. 'Her lifestyle had changed dramatically since our first meeting. But, as a person, I don't think she'd changed at all. She was never, "I'm a superstar. I'm so important", like some. That's why people liked her.'

Inordinately photogenic, Tina worked with many of the biggest names in the photography world – Richard Avedon, Herb Ritts and Peter Lindbergh to name but a few. However, it is clear from these intimate shots and the photographs throughout, that Tina and Paul had a real connection.

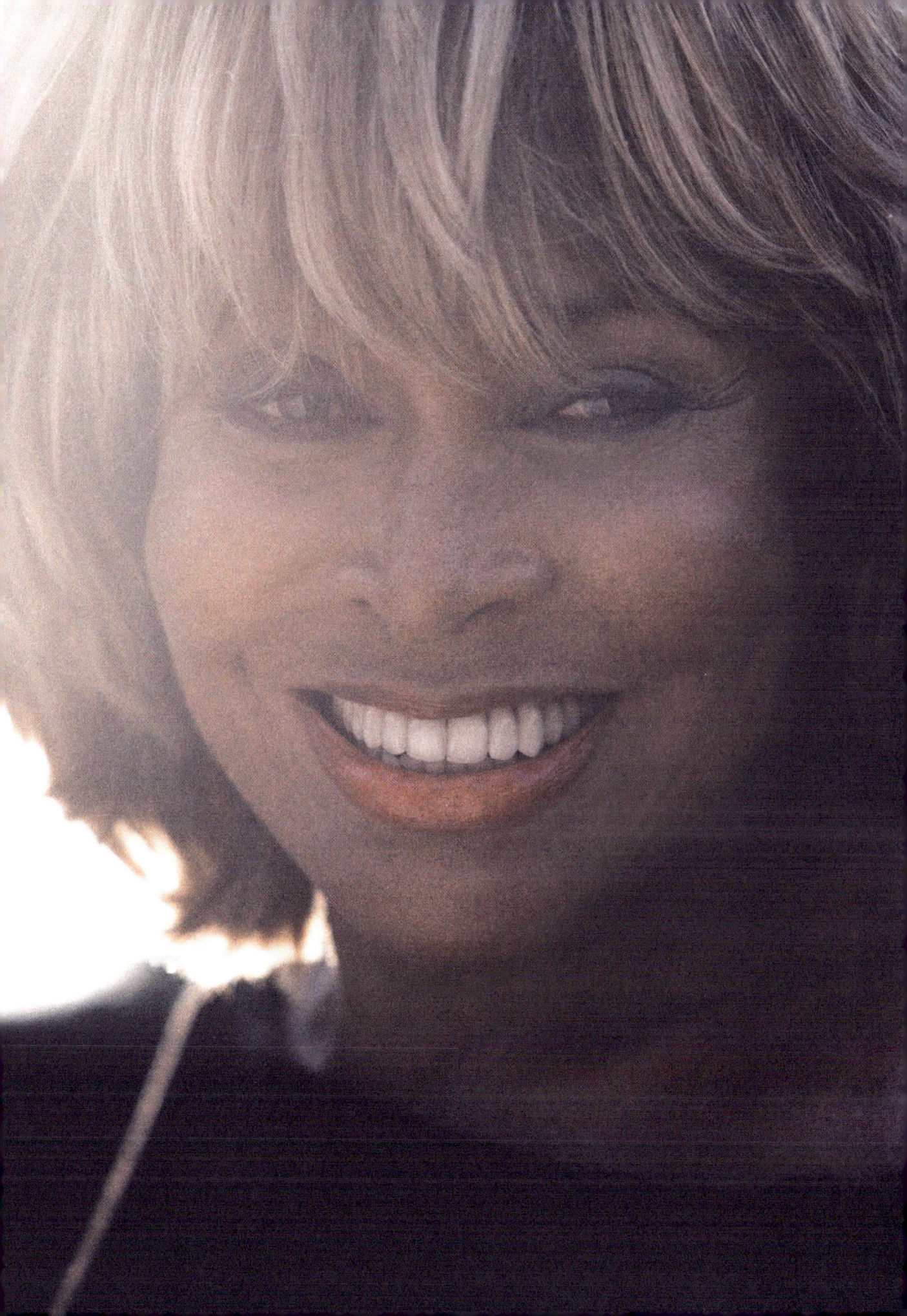

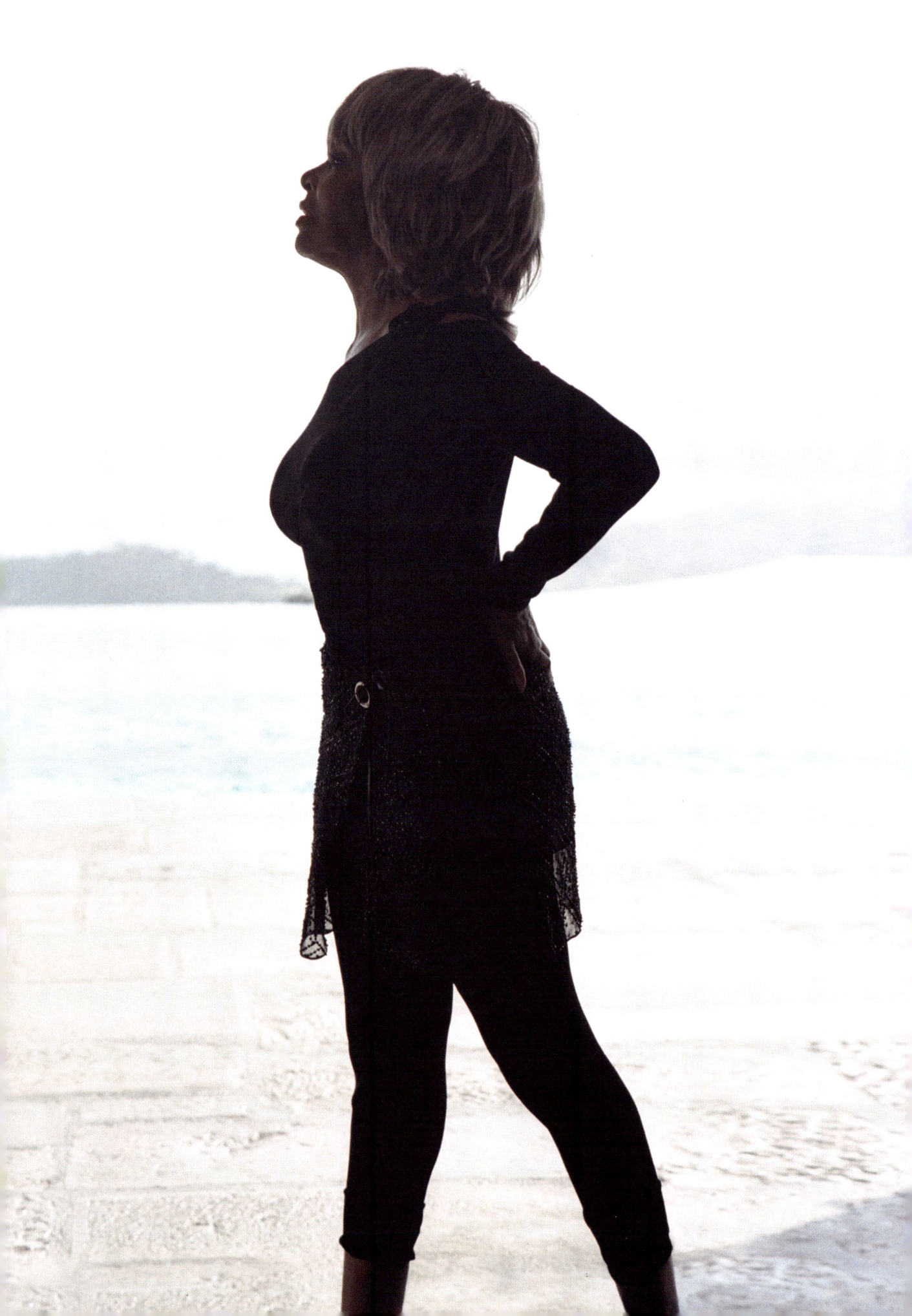